Directory of Grants for Organizations Serving People with Disabilities

Ninth Edition

A Guide to Funding Sources in the
United States for Organizations Serving
People with Disabilities

Research Grant Guides, Inc.
P.O. Box 1214
Loxahatchee, Florida 33470

Richard M. Eckstein
Publisher/Editor

Andrew J. Grant, Ph.D.
Writer/Grant Consultant

Research and Administrative Staff:
Debra Reese
Lorraine Moynihan
Nancy Moore
Claire L. Eckstein
Amy L. Bachmann

Marketing Representative:
Cathy J. Tosner
President
CJ Marketing

Printed in the U.S.A.

ISSN 0777-3282
ISBN 0-945078-10-2

Table of Contents

Preface

The *Directory of Grants for Organizations Serving People with Disabilities* is in it's ninth edition. The *Directory* was formerly known as the *Handicapped Funding Directory*.

The following subjects are some of the areas profiled in the *Directory*: blind, deaf, developmentally disabled, learning disabilities, mental health, mentally disabled, physically disabled, and speech impaired.

Funding sources may change their priorities and expenditure levels. Corporate foundations frequently respond to the general economy and may curtail their grant-making programs until profits reach a satisfactory level. Don't be discouraged if your proposal is not funded on the first try.

To get started, use the *Directory* to research funding agencies supporting your type of organization. Be careful to remember that many foundations award grants only in their own geographic area. Geographic restrictions and grant range are listed when available to our research staff. Next, send a brief letter to the funding agency and request a copy of their most recent grant guidelines, if they publish them. Guidelines issued by the funder should always be followed. Before writing a grant proposal, read the guidelines listed in *The Realist's Guide to Foundation and Corporate Grants* beginning on page 20.

Several elements in a successful grant proposal include:

1) Uniqueness of proposal subject matter

2) A clear, well-written application

3) A realistic budget

4) Qualifications of the Project Director

5) Issues of concern to the proposed sponsor

If the proposal warrants, there should be a table of contents to guide the reviewer. A timetable depicting your proposed progress also may be helpful. Try to present a readable, professional-looking proposal written in clear language that avoids jargon.

Identifying and Setting Trends:
Maximizing Funding Opportunities by Staying on the Cutting Edge
by
Andrew J. Grant, Ph.D.
and Karen Luxton-Gourgey, Ed.D.

The Executive Director of a not-for-profit organization serving people with disabilities waits apprehensively for word about a proposal submitted for foundation funding. The proposal is for a project to launch a new service. The project will fill an important need in the community by providing transportation services to people who cannot drive or easily use public transit facilities. The foundation response arrives and informs the organization that although the idea is worthy, only a few projects can be supported. The foundation regrets that there is insufficient funding to make a grant for the project.

In the office of a similar organization in a city of similar size and demographic composition, another Executive Director opens a letter from the same foundation with the good news that a large grant will be made to enable the organization to train persons with disabilities in the use of public transportation facilities. The need among the client population of that organization is no greater than that of the clients served by the rejected organization. What made the difference?

Both projects focus on the need of persons with disabilities to be able to travel from place to place. The first project approaches the problem by providing new transportation services. The second, seeks to train clients in the use of existing services. The staff of the organization that received funding is aware of the trend among people with disabilities to favor services promoting self sufficiency. They capitalized on that knowledge in their application for grant support. The foundation was impressed that the applicant presented a proposal that reflected current philosophy.

Dr. Grant is President of Grant Services Corp., a consulting firm specializing in grants development, proposal writing and computer networking. The firm is located in Woodbury, New York, and offers consulting services on a national basis. Dr. Grant has had a twenty-year academic career in grants development and research administration. He teaches proposal writing and grants management at Hofstra University.

Andrew Grant holds a Ph.D. in Public Administration from New York University. He also has an M.A. in Education and a Master of Urban Planning, both from NYU. His B.A. is from SUNY Binghamton. Dr. Grant's e-mail address is ajgrant@interramp.com.

Karen Luxton-Gourgey has served as the Director of the Computer Center for Visually Impaired People at Baruch College, City University of New York since 1983. She has brought the Center from a pilot project to its current status as a permanent and respected resource within the City University System. She has written and spoken extensively on disability issues, particularly as they relate to computer training and higher education. She holds a doctorate in Special Education from Teachers College, Columbia University.

In addition, that project will be much more cost effective because it takes greater advantage of existing facilities. The developers of the rejected project, had they been funded, would have been right back where they started when it came time to replace the vehicle to have been purchased with the grant. By that time, the funded training project will have used its grant to enable many people to become mobile through the use of public transit. Thereby, they showed sensitivity to another trend favoring public transportation over reliance on individual motor vehicles.

Understanding Why Organizations Make Grants

Many prominent grant making organizations, be they government agencies or large foundations, see their mission as promoting change. They make project grants with the potential for developing or expanding new approaches to existing problems.[1] Such grants may also serve to identify emerging problems and propose solutions. These agencies and foundations assume the role of investment bankers to provide necessary risk capital for new ideas that promise to advance the state of knowledge or service delivery. They are exceptionally alert to trends that signal progress in the service areas they support. Grant makers working with organizations serving persons with disabilities are especially sensitive to such trends.

Concern with trends is an important characteristic of project grant funding. Federal grant programs originated early in the development of the United States as the result of Constitutional restrictions against direct federal action in the affairs of the states. Strict interpretation of the concept of separation of powers written into the United States Constitution limits the areas into which the central government may, through legislation, determine policies effecting the states. The Constitution limits direct federal government action to areas of defense, currency, patents and copyrights, postal service, interstate commerce and conflicts, federal courts and foreign treaties.[2] These are known as the "enumerated" powers because they are specified in the Constitution. All other areas, or residual powers, are reserved to the states.[3]

Yet, today we have federal Departments of Education, Health and Human Services, Transportation, Housing and Urban Development, Agriculture and Labor, among others, whose activities could certainly be interpreted as violations of the provisions of the Constitution. As a practical matter, narrow enforcement of separation of powers would not have permitted the country to expand. In order to grow, the young government of the United States needed a mechanism to create consistent policy in critical areas all across the country. Judicial interpretation has provided maximum flexibility in how the Constitution responds to the need for change. Grants were invented to take advantage of this flexibility and provide a system of incentives through which the federal government could influence state policies indirectly.

---

[1] Grants for operating funds or grants to provide service programs differ in purpose from those described here. Not-for-profit organizations seeking such support must take care in identifying sponsors who will be receptive to their proposals. The *Directory of Operating Grants*, also published by Research Grant Guides, provides information on this type of grant maker. In this article, we address the subject of proposal writing for projects designed to implement new methods or approaches to providing services to persons with disabilities.

[2] *US Constitution*; Article I, Section 8.

[3] *US Constitution*; Amendment X.

Agriculture and economic development are good examples. An early need was to improve farming methods so fewer farmers could produce more food for greater numbers. This would get people off the farms and make them available for industry, commerce and westward expansion. Separation of powers, however, prevented the federal government from imposing modern agricultural methods on the states. In order to meet the need for more up-to-date farming techniques and still remain in compliance with the Constitution, Congress created the land grant concept in 1862 with the first Morrill Act. This early grant program transferred federal lands to the states. The program required that each grantee build a school teaching modern agricultural and mechanical methods on part of that land. Thus, the federal government achieved its purpose without violating the letter of the Constitution by providing an incentive for voluntary action.

That was the beginning of the complicated system of grants in use today. The system evolved, substituting money for land. It has survived several judicial challenges and continues its role as an agent of change. Private foundations and corporate giving programs are based on the same incentive concept. They offer monetary grants to promote their own policy agendas.

With this background, it is easy to see why project grant programs are on the forefront of professional trends. It is their mission to seek out projects that have the potential to change the nature of service delivery. They are not intended to provide basic operating funds for not-for-profit organizations. Grant seekers who understand and make use of this concept are more likely to receive funding than those applicants whose proposals reflect an attitude of conducting business as usual.

Promoting Change or Reacting to Circumstances

Generally people resist change. Organizations are especially reluctant to move away from practices and methods of doing business that represent stability and comfort. When external conditions change, however, resistance can have unfortunate consequences. It exemplifies a propensity in the American character toward being reactive. As a culture, we tend to react to change rather than anticipate and plan for it. Recent American economic history offers more than a few dramatic examples.

The American automobile industry provides a valuable lesson, as does the experience of the I.B.M. Corporation. In both cases, huge corporations came close to disaster because they failed to respond to external changes in consumer preferences and industry trends. The major American automobile manufacturers produced cars according to their own vision of what the consumer wanted. Through the sixties and the early seventies, almost all American cars were large and inefficient in fuel consumption. The industry scoffed at the thought of foreign competition from smaller, less wasteful cars. The oil crisis of the seventies sent waves of car buyers to foreign competitors, both for fuel efficiency and the general perception that the American manufacturers could not compete in quality.

By the time the industry recognized the need for change, the damage had been done. In addition, the manufacturers' unresponsiveness to fuel and safety concerns prompted government regulation in these areas. The industry today is much more sensitive to consumer needs, competitive pressures and federal mandates.

I.B.M. learned a similar lesson about industry trends. The company was successful in its mainframe business and failed to anticipate the shift to networked micro, or personal, computers in corporate environments. It continued to promote large mainframe computers despite the shrinking demand for that type of machine. Its slow response allowed competitors to win market share in the growing personal computer business. It found, as did the automobile manufacturers, that major corporations had lost some of their power to dictate product preferences. Circumstances and consumer demand became the controlling forces in these examples. The same dynamics have been taking place in the sector of our economy that provides services to people with disabilities.

Until the decade of the seventies, there were few government regulations mandating services for people with disabilities and protecting them from discrimination. There were few associations championing rights for persons with disabilities largely because the isolation created by disabling conditions worked against the formation of such associations. During the seventies, however, a few leaders adopted the techniques of organization and lobbying learned from the Civil Rights movement of the sixties.

Slowly at first, and then with greater momentum, people with disabilities organized into groups and demanded legislation to protect them from discrimination and provide for services to enable them to participate equally in activities taken for granted by most people without disabilities. Legislation, combined with litigation, created a system of services and regulatory requirements designed to promote equal participation.

This emerging political consciousness among people with disabilities created a dilemma for private agencies that were providers of disability services. These organizations had relied heavily on two related ideas for their fund-raising. One was the charity model, whereby people with disabilities are portrayed as needing the help of the stronger, more fortunate community. The other can be termed the medical model, in which people with disabilities are portrayed as being desperately ill and in need of cure. These themes which played on the compassion and the guilt of individuals, corporations and foundations brought in money and in some circumstances still do. But the underlying premises were and are directly contrary to those which now predominate within the disability community. Moreover, they fly in the face of what is the current law of the land.

Organizations were thus caught in the tension between the ideas that had been major drivers of fund-raising, and the demands for equality and full participation on the part of their constituents. Organizations of people with disabilities, and parents of children with disabilities, have formed and become a major force. Organizations whose leaders understand the changes in philosophy will be in the forefront of grant seekers and service providers establishing the trends and providing the models for others to follow.

From Ideas to Practice

An idea can come from anywhere. There's the case of a foundation executive who observed his preschool child watching television. He noticed how absorbed the child was when watching TV and became concerned about the lack of programming that could provide educational stimulation. He discussed the idea of an educational TV program for children with the director of a New York antipoverty program, who liked the idea and felt it had potential for diminishing some of the problems of inner city children. The director's wife worked for an educational TV station. She put together a grant proposal that sought funds for a study on the subject of what children watched on TV. The foundation executive helped get the funding for the study through his organization. The study found that children responded to the 30 and 60 second format of TV commercials. The foundation then funded a much larger grant to help develop a program that used strategies borrowed from TV commercials to teach educational basics to preschoolers, especially targeted to the inner city. This story describes the origin of *Sesame Street* through the efforts of Joan Ganz Cooney.[4] She started not only a trend, but an entire industry.

Many successful grant proposals start just that way. Someone has an idea and persists until funding is secured to see if the idea will work. Let's go back to the hypothetical example at the beginning of this article and examine a set of circumstances that could have led to development of the successful proposal.

A community not-for-profit organization provides recreation activities for people with disabilities. The Executive Director calls in the recreational specialist and suggests that the organization could enhance its services if it had a van to transport its clients to various community sites, rather than concentrate activities on the premises of the organization.

The recreational specialist begins work on the proposal, but knows that the clients have expressed a preference for learning to become more independent. Why not develop a program that trains the clients to use the town bus and taxi system? The recreational specialist presents the idea, but meets with resistance. The Executive Director wants a van. The recreational director counters by indicating that the sponsor most likely to fund a van, the Federal Transit Administration (FTA), has requirements to open services of the van to the entire community. That would mean establishing a route and offering service to persons not affiliated with the organization. FTA, furthermore, funds only the van purchase. What about staff to drive it, fuel and insurance?

The training program, on the other hand, presents none of these problems, and it is consistent with feelings about increased independence expressed by the clients. It would also serve as a model, bringing recognition to the organization. The Executive Director agrees to abandon the proposal for a van and submit the training project to a major foundation for consideration.

That scenario could occur in any number of organizations. It is typical of the dynamics of service delivery. A sensitive staff member or administrator in tune with the needs of clients wants to try out something new. Most organizations don't have funds in their budgets to experiment with new ideas or approaches. But as we noted above, that's exactly the role filled by many grant makers.

Emerging Trends

Increasingly, the language within rehabilitation agencies and other provider organizations is less about clients and more about consumers. "Independent Living" is a major component in rehabilitation law which governs much of the federal money available for disability services. Independence, i.e. movement away from "client" status, is a goal worth funding, at least in principle. The Technology-related Assistance for Individuals

---

[4] Craig W. Smith and Eric W. Skjei, *Getting Grants*, Harper, 1980, pp 36-41.

with Disabilities Act, (the Tech Act) includes provisions requiring that approaches to assistive technology be "consumer-responsive." Assistive technology includes devices that help people with disabilities communicate, travel and function in general, for example - computers with voice synthesizers so people who are blind can hear the words on the screen. Anyone who has reviewed federal disability-related grants knows that criteria now include consumer involvement at all stages of the project, from design, to implementation, to evaluation.

Within the disability community itself, the issue is less one of consumerism than of social justice. Assistive technology, access to buildings, access to transportation, and access to information are not just to be provided with the consumer in mind. They are to be provided as a matter of right. The "consumer" is not merely to be the one responded to, he/she is to be the one in control, the primary decision-maker. After all, it is his/her life that is under discussion. The person with a disability is not a client who has been upgraded to a consumer, but a citizen who is demanding access to the same basic building blocks of life in society that are available relatively automatically to those without disabilities.

The Americans with Disabilities Act (ADA) goes part way in supporting this notion. In essence, it states that people with disabilities shall have access to employment, transportation, public accommodation and governmental services, as long as it is "readily achievable" by, or does not constitute "undue hardship" for the entity concerned, the employer, the transportation provider, etc. Further, government has made this more murky as an issue, since it provides no money for the implementation of ADA. The law and philosophy have evolved. However, the funding sources have not moved in the same direction, or at the same rate of speed. Where does this leave the agency or university program looking to fund an innovative project related to people with disabilities?

Alternative Strategies for Funding

Given the complex relationship between funding and philosophy, grant seekers will, as mentioned above, sometimes find themselves caught in the tension between the needs and values of those they serve, and expectations and constraints imposed by a potential funding source. If an organization seeking funds finds itself in this or a similar dilemma, a partial solution may be to consider a mechanism other than a simple grant for funding the work.

Let's return once again to the example at the beginning of this article. The successful agency, whose project sought to train people with disabilities in the use of existing transportation services, wins on more than one level. Not only did the particular foundation in question see the value of the idea and fund it, but the grantee has other options for continuing funding, i.e. transportation facilities themselves.

Transit properties across the country are scrambling to respond to ADA's mandates, not only with capital improvements moving toward access, but also with dollars for enhanced customer service, and travel training. They are often eager to form partnerships with qualified disability-related organizations as a help in fulfilling its legal mandates. In the example, the agency providing the training will inevitably have contact with representatives of the town's bus and taxi systems. As the training for consumers is being executed, it may occur to both agency and transit provider that taxi drivers and bus drivers could also benefit from training in how to be most helpful to passengers with disabilities. The agency knows the needs of its consumers; the transit provider knows the constraints under which its drivers must work. They may elect to collaborate for their mutual benefit. The initiative will probably come from the agency, but the funding may well come from the transit provider. ADA, with all of its limitations, has forced the creation of new markets for providers of disability services.

Organizations need to consider a different view of themselves, not just as recipients of grants or awards, but as marketers and contractors of knowledge, skill and experience. The service provider with innovative ideas and the ability to implement them, may find one of the best possible niches to be that of helping a mainstream entity get up to speed in meeting its ADA requirements. Thus, while there may be relatively less money available through traditional "grant" channels, grant seekers may be able to accomplish the same goals in a broader-based and more long-lasting way through some form of partnership.

Occasionally, a nonprofit may find that one of its activities, previously seen as minor, might become a significant producer of cash. A program at a college whose mission was to train people who are visually impaired in the use of computers had a small facility to produce Braille. The facility was used to support students within the college by preparing tests and other important documents in Braille. From time to time, the program received requests to produce Braille conference agendas, meeting notices, etc., from outside agencies. A major arts facility approached program staff regarding ideas for making its concerts and other performances more accessible to patrons with visual impairments, and both an idea and a partnership were born. The center produced concert programs in Braille and large print for the arts facility, which, as a result, sought and obtained major funding to endow the effort for the long haul. Of course, things reached a point where the arts organization chose to take the project as an in-house responsibility. The center and its Braille production staff supported this initiative, and acted as training consultants as the new system was being implemented.

An important emerging need, then, is the requirement for very specific accommodations to meet the needs of people with specific disabilities within the context of the larger community. Those nonprofit organizations that can develop flexible approaches to offering their services in the manner and at the location where they are needed are likely to find themselves in demand. As the above example demonstrates, however, flexibility is crucial. A partnership may begin in one form, e.g. the nonprofit center produces the Braille and change to another, the center acts as a consultant to help the arts organization implement their own in-house Braille production facility.

Similar collaborations can and do occur in services for children. An agency serving a particular disability group seeks funding to begin a nursery school program. It finds the money hard to come by. It may have a better chance if it joins forces with a "mainstream" nursery school within the same geographic area and enhances the existing program to include the children for whom it has concern. Such an approach capitalizes on the currently popular educational strategy of "inclusion," in which students with disabilities of all ages, and regardless of severity, are placed in regular educational settings.

Funding Concerns vs. Programmatic Values

Marketing one's services or partnering with another organization for mutual benefit are both potentially fruitful strategies for funding. There is a danger in these and similar approaches, however, in that the mission can become controlled and even subverted by requirements of the funding source. For the agency in the above example, a shift was required in a basic long-held value, that of serving their constituents in a segregated setting.

Many organizations have in recent years confronted such dilemmas. One organization that serves a particular disability group had run a recreational group program for older adults practically since its inception. Many of the participants had been coming to this agency all of their lives for a variety of services and had learned to depend on it for much of their social, recreational and educational stimulus. By the early 90's, overall funding for the agency was down, and the group recreational program had no means by which to sustain itself. Funding was available from the city's Office on Aging to set up a program where former participants in this program could receive volunteers in their homes to help them with various activities.

This is, in fact, what happened. For the participants, the original program was essentially a group experience at a familiar agency outside the home. These were precisely the elements that needed to change because of the constraints imposed by the available funding source. In the minds of the participants, however, the program, on which they had come to depend, was lost. These were senior citizens for whom such change was felt as a major displacement.

Change Needed to Keep Up with Emerging Trends is Necessary and Inevitable

Providers of disability-related services are now required to look beyond traditional funding sources. The "investment bankers" are in different places and have varying specific and sometimes contradictory strings attached to the funding they are willing to give. An organization must balance its need for funding with its philosophy and the needs of its consumers. Where these needs diverge, serious consequences can result.

The grant seeker now needs new levels of flexibility in order to take advantage of changing funding opportunities. Also needed, however, is a strong sense of the organization's mission. Are there qualities, principles, or even program components which cannot change if the mission is to remain intact? Or, is it appropriate for the organization to modify the mission consistent with trends in practice and funding? The organization that can speak with one consistent voice to its funders and its constituents alike is itself a model of the new equity that has and will continue to emerge.

How to Communicate An Understanding of Trends in the Proposal

Having a great idea is only the beginning. Successful proposals must convey the applicant's thorough understanding of current professional trends. The needs assessment must contain several elements based on research and professional awareness of current practice and emerging trends. The proposal should raise and answer the following questions.

Is this really a new idea? Proposal reviewers, in general, are familiar with issues related to professional practice in the areas their agencies or foundations support. If their personal background is limited, they have access to consultants with the expertise required to evaluate proposals from professionals in the field. There's nothing more deadly to the success of a proposal than suggesting something is a new idea when, in fact, the idea has been in use elsewhere for some time. Or worse, the idea has been tested and demonstrated a failure.

Proposal writers must be expert in their professional literature and be able to discuss other approaches in relation to the idea they wish to try out. Research is critical. It includes review of journals, research studies, press reports and consultation with other professionals.

The proposal should discuss the new idea in terms of current professional philosophy and indicate how it represents progress. It should include a discussion of alternative strategies and describe why they are or aren't feasible. It should also, where possible, describe how other organizations deal with the problem.

Presentation of the literature review is also important. A formal proposal would include citations and, possibly, a bibliography. A letter proposal would make references to research and other professional documents in the body of the narrative. An additional fact sheet could be included as an attachment. It's worth keeping in mind that, regardless of the importance of the literature, this is a proposal, not a research paper. References to research documents should not distract the reader from the flow of the proposal. They should be presented in a manner appropriate to the type of proposal in which they're included.

Why is this idea likely to improve practice? The proposal writer must indicate clearly why the new idea is timely and likely to work. Professional expertise again is the key. The proposal should document how the new approach was developed. To what needs is it responding? What changes will result from implementing this idea? How will it change service delivery to clients? What next steps might be taken if the new idea works in practice as anticipated?

Even if the idea works, will it work elsewhere? Even if the new idea or approach proves successful, will it be able to serve as a model for other organizations? The proposal should describe the characteristics of the applicant organization and show how they are similar or different from other organizations. The proposal writer could contact other professionals and document their enthusiasm for the idea and their willingness to try it out if it is successful as a pilot project.

These are the basics of proposal structure for presenting ideas that promise to change the way organizations deliver services. These ideas must reflect awareness of rapid changes in consumer preferences and professional practice. Organizations must be cautious not to make dramatic changes just for the sake of winning grants. Change should be the result of the natural evolution of the organization and the needs of the people it serves, tempered with careful consideration of the possible consequences. When these elements are all present, the potential for securing funding is at its highest.

Getting the Most from Federal Funding Information Sources

by
Andrew J. Grant, Ph.D.
and Frank G. Bowe, Ph.D.

Identifying appropriate funding sources is time-consuming and labor intensive. Funding source research is a process of elimination that usually starts with hundreds of prospects, but may yield only a handful of potential candidates. Many research tools, including print media and electronic data bases, are available to speed this process. These products are useful because their publishers conduct the preliminary research necessary to narrow the search. Directories such as this one have already done the work of eliminating sources unrelated to the general topic of the grant proposal.

It is a mistake, however, to assume that all the research has been completed. As noted in the opening paragraph, only the preliminary steps in this lengthy process have been performed. The grant seeker still has a long distance to travel before ending the search for the most appropriate sources. The purpose of this article is to describe the complete search process for federal sources and point out the information items that will help determine how suitable any specific funding source may be.

Understanding the Environment

Prior to undertaking a search for federal funding sources, it's a good idea to review how federal agencies are organized, especially for anyone conducting his or her first search. An almanac contains such information, but the *United States Government Manual* is a better, more comprehensive choice. The *U.S. Government Manual*, available at library reference counters or for purchase through the U.S. Government Printing Office (GPO), provides agency-by-agency descriptions of all federal departments, agencies and many sub-agency level offices. It also contains general information on the federal system itself, branches of government and federal regional structure. The *Manual* also includes organization charts for cabinet level departments and some other agencies.

The address for the GPO is U.S. Government Printing Office, Washington, DC 20402. In addition, the GPO has bookstores open to the public located in the federal office buildings of major U.S. cities. Check your local phone directory federal agency blue pages to determine if there is a GPO bookstore in your area.

Browsing through the *Manual* will provide an overview of how different parts of the government relate to each other. It's useful to begin this way to get a sense of the magnitude and complexity of the bureaucracy and to locate the agencies of greatest relevance to the funding search. Closer examination of the descriptions of such agencies will offer a delineation of their missions and activities. There may even be a summary of their grant programs, albeit in general terms.

The *U.S. Government Manual* is an inexpensive book containing a vast amount of valuable information. It should be on the shelf of every grant seeker and of anyone wishing a handy reference to government organization. After reviewing agencies of interest in the *Manual*, the funding search can begin in earnest with the *Catalog of Federal Domestic Assistance*.

The Sears Catalog of Grant Programs

The starting point of any search for federal grant funds is the *Catalog of Federal Domestic Assistance*, or the *CFDA* for short. The *Catalog* is published by the Office of Management and Budget (OMB) in loose-leaf format, arriving pre-punched and ready to be placed in a binder. OMB collects the information for the catalog entries from all federal agencies that have assistance programs (loans, scholarships and technical assistance as well as grants) and compiles these into the *CFDA*. It is approximately 99% accurate and comprehensive. OMB must rely on each individual agency to submit descriptions of its grant programs. In rare instances, an entry may be too late for inclusion or may contain inaccuracies. Any such items will be corrected in the updates to the *CFDA*.

Like the *U.S. Government Manual*, the *CFDA* will be found in the reference section of most libraries. It's also available from the GPO as a subscription, considered such because it is updated several times during the year.

The individual entries are grouped by Department or Agency. Each is assigned a five digit identification number arranged as follows — xx.xxx. The two digits to the left of the decimal identify the agency; the three digits to the right identify the specific program within that agency. The *CFDA* number 84.023, for example, belongs to the program entitled *Special Education - Innovation and Development (Research and Demonstration Projects In Education for the Disabled)* within the Department of Education (see page 141). The *CFDA* number is important. Not only does it locate the program within the *Catalog*, it must be entered on the face sheet of the standard federal application form for most agencies. Many agencies include the *CFDA* number in the tracking number assigned to pending proposals.

The *CFDA* includes an excellent set of instructions and several indices. The indices allow the user to search for grant programs by subject matter, agency, deadline date, eligibility criteria and others. It can take hours to structure a search, locate the entries that meet the criteria and sift through them, eliminating all but the most appropriate. This is the work performed by the editors and publishers of subject-specific directories and by computer searching a funding source data base.

The federal source descriptions contained in this *Directory* are duplicated from the most recent edition of the *Catalog of Federal Domestic Assistance*. It's advisable to become familiar with the *CFDA* to gain an appreciation of the larger base from which this set of sources is derived and to extend the search if necessary. Each entry contains a wealth of information about the program. Before deciding if the source offers potential for submitting an application, the grant seeker should become proficient at interpreting the material presented in a *CFDA* entry. The following sections discuss how to approach the *CFDA* without missing important information.

Maximizing CFDA Information

Program Name and CFDA Number - Although it may seem obvious, it's critical that the precise name and number of the program be noted while the search is in progress. Many programs have similar sounding titles. Searches may require several trips to the library and multiple sessions with reference materials. When time is limited, it's frustrating to have to sift through the documents, trying to remember a program whose name and number weren't noted correctly or were not on the list at all. In addition, as noted above, the application form will require entry of the exact program title and number.

Program Type - Program type is perhaps the most critical element to consider when using *CFDA* entries. In most cases, not-for-profit organizations will be looking for **project grants**. Project grants are awarded on the basis of competition. The grantor (sponsor) and grantee (recipient) have a direct relationship. Funds do not flow through an intermediary, such as a state agency.

In contrast, **formula grants** are made to states. They are based on a formula written into the legislation authorizing the grant program. States reallocate funds to the agencies under their jurisdiction if those agencies meet the criteria of the formula. When conducting a search, the grant seeker may find many prospects whose goals, objectives and other requirements are consistent with the subject of the grant proposal. Even if everything else about the sponsor looks perfect, funds will not be accessible if the grant type is formula. The federal sponsor will not accept applications from organizations other than jurisdictions or agencies of state governments. These programs also are known as entitlements.

In some cases, however, it is possible for not-for-profits to obtain funding through formula grants. State agencies may have the option of contracting out services with federal funds. States may also use some of their formula grant funds, if permitted by the federal program regulations, to sponsor competitions within the state. Most federal information sources will not contain details about any of these options. Such information is available only by researching procedures within the individual states. Professional networks, informal contacts, state agency newsletters and liaison with federal program administrators are a numbers of means through which grant seekers can discover if they may qualify for participation in formula programs. The need for this type of informal research emphasizes the importance of maintaining an active professional network.

Eligibility - Most *CFDA* entries list two types of eligibility requirements. Criteria for each, applicant and beneficiary, are different. Proposed projects must meet both eligibility requirements. Applicant eligibility refers to the grantee organization. Such eligibility may be narrow and specific or it may be quite broad.

For example, the eligibility criteria may include a category for *...other nonprofit educational organizations or ...other nonprofit health organizations*. This type of catch-all classification opens the competition to any nonprofit organization falling under the general service delivery area description. Although many different types of organizations meet this threshold eligibility, those in the specified categories will be most competitive.

Grant seekers must be careful to consider the beneficiary eligibility as well as the applicant eligibility requirements. The proposed project must provide service to the categories of people designated in this section. The application will be ineligible if either requirement is not met. To be considered for funding, organizations must document that they serve the constituency or constituencies specified by the eligibility standards.

Grant programs are intended for nonprofit organizations. For-profit firms, however, can compete for federal funds in the form of contracts. I will discuss information sources relevant to contracting in a section to follow.

Application Process - Despite all the valuable information in the *CFDA*, it is not published frequently enough to report due dates accurately. Some agencies utilize a schedule of standard deadlines year after year for recurring programs. In most cases, however, the *CFDA* indicates that deadlines are *as announced*, or it directs the reader to contact the regional or headquarters office.

In order to keep up with announcements of regulatory changes, program availability and due dates, grant seekers should review another government publication, the *Federal Register*. The *Register* is published each business day. It is a digest of the daily affairs of the Executive Branch, that is, all federal agencies and sub-agencies. *Federal Register* announcements have the weight of law and report a wide range of administrative issues, as well as grant program matters.

The most efficient and timely manner of keeping up with grant program announcements and other regulatory matters is to subscribe to the *Register*. Many smaller agencies, however, cannot devote the time and money required to review their own copy daily. An alternative is to subscribe to privately published newsletters and grant alert programs. Such services are tailored to many fields, including education, health, housing, transportation and any other functional areas in which professionals need to keep current.

Private publications, however, have many drawbacks if used as the single source of information. Time is lost waiting for the current issue to arrive. The grant seeker must rely on the editors to report news in an accurate and comprehensive manner. Some grant programs related to but outside the specific interest area represented by the publication may be missed.

Only government publications have the authority of law. If, for example, there is an error in the *Federal Register*, the agency may extend the deadline. No such protection exists for grant seekers who rely on erroneous information published in private newsletters. These services, especially if they are electronic bulletin boards, may be no less expensive than the *Register*. They are most useful as secondary back-up sources.

Information Contacts - Each *CFDA* entry includes a section listing the headquarters or regional office to make contact with for more information. The same information is included in *Federal Register* announcements of grant regulations and/or deadlines. A conversation with a federal official can confirm that a competitive cycle is coming up, or may yield the unhappy news that the due date has just passed. Again, regular *Federal Register* readers never need to miss a deadline because of lack of information.

Federal officials will also advise about applicant eligibility for organizations not sure if they meet the requirements. A conversation with an agency administrator will not yield any information not elsewhere available, but it may help the potential applicant interpret regulatory language and clarify areas that are unclear. Applicants can also write or call to request a copy of the application kit. Such packets usually include an application form, a copy of the *Federal Register* announcement of due date, a copy of the most recent regulations, telephone numbers and addresses of program officials and specific instructions for preparing and submitting proposals. Some may include such additional information as a copy of the statute authorizing the program, advice on informal priorities of the agency for the competition, examples of previously funded programs and the anticipated range of grants as well as the total amount available.

Some agencies maintain mailing lists from which they send application packets whenever a competition is announced. In recent years, however, the federal government has been cutting costs by eliminating such mailings and instead, publishing complete information in the *Federal Register*, including the application form.

Other Guidance - The *CFDA* includes several other sections describing "...program objectives, uses and restrictions, criteria for selecting proposals, and examples of funded projects." In addition, it provides information on program administration and financial issues. All this information provides a profile of the grant program.

This profile should be used as a starting point to obtaining information as detailed as possible for each funding prospect. Applicants should structure their research process by first reading all that is available about the program, including the complete regulations, authorizing statute and pertinent legislative history, and any secondary materials published by or about the agency, including press clippings about the program.

The regulatory material appears in the *Federal Register* when programs are initially authorized or re-authorized by statute. In interim years, regulations are published in the *Code of Federal Regulations* (*CFR*). The *CFR* will be found in most reference libraries and some large public libraries. It is a set of many volumes, which may be purchased individually and inexpensively. Organizations involved in programs operated under federal regulations are prudent to have the current volumes of applicable *CFR* sections on hand.

After research and reading have provided as much depth as possible, a call and perhaps a visit to the agency can furnish valuable insight into proposal design and focus. At least one federal agency, The National Endowment for the Humanities, will review a preliminary draft of the proposal, if submitted six weeks prior to the deadline.

Helpful guidance will also be obtained by reviewing successful proposals from previous competitions. Some agencies provide access to these as a courtesy. It's also often possible to get copies of a successful application from a previous funding cycle, using the Freedom of Information Act (FOIA). Many agencies also provide, upon request, copies of reviewer comments on your own proposal, with the reviewer names deleted.

A strong professional network may also help to get good proposals from colleagues. Federal funding is extremely competitive. The surest way to narrow the odds is to prepare by studying all the information obtainable about a sponsor and its programs.

Not All Funding Comes In Grants

Grant programs comprise most of the funding of interest to nonprofit organizations. There are frequent occasions when these organizations are eligible to compete with profit making firms for contract funding. Contracts differ from grants. When agencies need narrowly defined, specific services, they may issue requests for contract proposals (RFP) inviting bids from qualified providers or vendors.

The proposal responding to the RFP includes a description of the vendor and its capacity for performing the work specified in the RFP. It also includes a cost proposal or budget. Grant announcements are broader. They invite the applicant to design a program responding to a particular issue or need.

The United States Department of Commerce publishes the *Commerce Business Daily*. This publication lists all the RFPs available for the day of publication. State and local agencies publish such notices in newspapers of general circulation.

A Word About State Programs

Many projects and services are funded by state government agencies. States do not maintain information sources as comprehensive as those described above for the federal government. They vary in the way they disseminate information about the availability of grant funds.

Among the methods are targeted mailings, information meetings, newsletters and requests for applications (RFAs). Keep in mind our earlier caution about relying on private publications. Only official government communications have the weight of law. Maintaining a strong professional network is especially important for nonprofit administrators within their own state. In some cases it means the difference between receiving timely notice or missing deadlines.

A Note on Trends

Some changes have taken place over the past twenty years in the way federal agencies fund new ideas for projects for organizations serving people with disabilities. In the early days of such support, the bulk of the research was investigator initiated. The federal agencies relied upon the research community to know what the "cutting edge" was and what was interesting scientifically. Applicants proposed project content, and federal agency administrators played a more passive role.

Today, the roles have changed dramatically. Federal agencies tend to dictate what is to be funded. There is very little field-initiated work anymore, except in few specialized agencies. Agency administrators defer to field reviewers, who have the decision making power over who and what gets funded. Again, the message is that maintaining a strong and active professional network in order to know current thinking is the most effective way to increase the way to win a grant.

The Realist's Guide to Foundation and Corporate Grants
by
Andrew J. Grant, Ph.D.

Seeking grant support is often frustrating. It can seem that rejection is the most frequent reward for hard work on behalf of the most compelling causes. It is the rare grant seeker who cannot recite some long list of proposals that were rejected despite their engaging content and structural perfection.

A great deal has already been written about proposal writing and how to succeed in winning grants. There is no shortage of books, articles and training courses offering advice to applicants on how to persuade funders to support their causes. Yet, despite every effort to follow such advice, most proposals are rejected.

This essay also contains some advice. In addition, however, it endeavors to add a realistic perspective to the literature on grant seeking by discussing the nature of grants and the role played by personal contacts. It is designed to help the applicant approach the task with a broader understanding of how things actually work in the world of grant programs.

What are Grants?

Although this is a very basic question, many applicants do not possess an accurate answer. Grants are not gifts or charity. The relationship between grantor and grantee is an exchange relationship. It is important to understand that the funder gets something back for the support he or she provides. The exchange varies with the type of grant making organization.

The role of many government grants in our federal system is to serve as an incentive to induce state and local jurisdictions to behave in ways consistent with the national policy agenda. Linking the twenty-one year minimum drinking age to federal highway funds is one recent example. Such grants and the restrictions attached to them are intended to stimulate state activity where none had been contemplated.

Foundations also make grants on the basis of a policy agenda. Foundation priorities and interests may be determined by charter or by the action of the board of directors. Their grants are designed to promote interests of importance to the foundation. The return to the foundation is seeing its agenda set into motion through the work of nonprofit organizations. A foundation with an interest in equal access for people with disabilities, for example, advances its own mission when it underwrites the construction of facilities that include special aids to individuals with disabilities.

Unlike foundations, corporations exist to make money, not give it away. Corporate contributions, therefore, are said to be based on the concept of enlightened self-interest. The corporate grant usually is made with the company's business agenda in mind. Much corporate giving is restricted to locations where the company operates. It receives a benefit when its employees and customers identify it with the positive work its funds helped to make possible. Corporate support of local arts groups serves as a good example.

Knowing What to Exchange

Keeping the concept of the exchange relationship prominent is essential to gaining the opportunity to participate in grant programs. The applicant must offer the funder something of value. The value, of course, is determined by the funder's interest. Failure to take this concept into account results in the rejection of many otherwise worthy projects.

Proposal writing starts with research. In order to approach the funder from the perspective of its interests, the applicant must devote much effort to learning everything possible about the foundation or corporation.

The most important categories of information regarding foundations include the following:

1. Priorities and interests
2. Geographic preferences
3. Size of assets
4. Range of and average grant sizes
5. Applicant type preferences
6. Project type preferences
7. Name and telephone number of contact person
8. List of recent grantees
9. List of projects recently funded
10. Composition of board of trustees

Information about corporations also includes the categories listed above. In addition to these, a potential applicant would want to know the following:

1. Corporate foundation or direct giving program
2. Major subsidiaries
3. Operating locations
4. Corporate officers
5. Major products or services

Unfortunately, this information representing such a large investment of time and effort is only the starting point. Nor is there any assurance that the information is accurate, up-to-date or consistent with the foundation or corporation's actual behavior.

The activities of government grant programs are determined by legislation and regulations. While many people resent the bureaucratic structure and excessive paperwork associated with federal grants, it is true in most cases that government programs can be held accountable for adherence to articulated priorities.

No such accountability mechanism exists for foundation and corporate grant programs. Although held fiscally accountable for their actions through the Internal Revenue Service, foundations and corporations are free to change or deviate from their published priorities. Sometimes the public is not informed of changes.

The potential applicant, therefore, must go far beyond the information found in the directories. Direct contact is extremely important. Many foundations publish guidelines, annual reports and application forms. The Foundation Center has available the tax returns of the foundations, including corporate foundations (but not direct corporate giving programs). The applicant should obtain as much information as is available. This should be supplemented with a phone call or personal visit, where possible.

All this information helps in identifying those funding sources whose interests most closely coincide with the applicant's. Only by concentrating on funders who share mutual concerns will there be the possibility of a grant. There is, however, one notable exception to this rule; it will be discussed in a subsequent section. Once the research is complete, resulting in a short list of very appropriate foundations and corporations, the proposal writing process can begin.

The Proposal...Or How to Offer to Make an Exchange

The most common error in proposal writing is failing to identify the request with the funder's interest. Many applicants become so involved with their causes or projects, they assume that everyone else will recognize the merit of the proposal. Proposal writing involves the art of persuasion. Winning proposals present well conceived projects in clear, simple English. They link their cause with the funder's agenda. They make no assumptions.

A proposal assuming the reader will identify with the project simply because of the severity of the need will surely be rejected. Rather, the proposal must demonstrate why it is in the funder's interest to support it.

There is much too much competition for funding to assume that projects will sell themselves. The linkages between applicant and funder interests have to be established in the proposal's first paragraphs.

Once this context of common interest, or potential for exchange, has been established, many other items of information must be addressed. Since most corporate and foundation proposals are contained in letters of two to three pages, clarity of thought and brevity of language are essential. The following questions will serve as a guide to the information that should be contained in a proposal letter.

1. Who is the applicant?
2. Why is the applicant the most able to conduct the project?
3. What is the project?
4. How much will it cost?
5. Who are the beneficiaries?
6. What lasting benefits will be realized through the project?
7. Who will do the work?
8. Where will it take place?
9. Why is it important to conduct this project?
10. Who else, if anybody, is supporting it?

That's a large amount of information to get into two or three pages, but it can be done. Applicants should consult any of a number of available proposal writing manuals. It's also not a bad idea to keep a general style manual and guide to writing close at hand. My favorite is the fifth edition of William K. Zinsser's, *On Writing Well*.

The Value of Contacts

The competition for grants is intense. Government funding of domestic social programs is diminishing. Foundations and corporations have become the focus of many fund-raising organizations. The needs of nonprofit organizations greatly exceed the capacity of the philanthropic community. Applicants have become much more sophisticated in seeking funds. Instructional materials and seminars have sharply reduced the number of inadequate proposals. Funders are finding it increasingly more difficult to differentiate among equally good proposals presenting worthy projects.

To complicate the scenario, the community of organizations representing similar populations compete with each other. Rather than presenting a unified approach, groups with common interests appear balkanized in their fund-raising strategies. Funders face the problem of choosing one over another.

Why is it that some of these groups achieve funding success and others of equal merit, can't seem to get a hearing? The answer, assuming all other factors to be equal, lies in the contact base of the successful organizations. The difference between successful and unsuccessful applicants often resides in the board room rather than with the fund-raising or proposal writing staff.

If a foundation or corporation is considering two proposals of equal interest, it will fund the one that has a contact. The use of personal contacts helps the funder to make difficult choices. An organization that is known is less of a risk than one that makes a "cold" approach.

These are high-level contacts among board members, not contacts made between applicant and funder staff members. Board members of grant making organizations usually are people of social position. They may be from prominent families or be executives and/or trustees of large corporations. Generally, they will support organizations known to them or to people whom they know and respect.

Nonprofit organizations often overlook development of their own boards as a fund-raising strategy. If one of the applicant's board members is on or knows someone on the board of a grant making organization, his or her support of the proposal will play a significant role in obtaining funding. This can be true even where the proposal falls outside the funder's articulated areas of interest, and represents the exception noted above.

It is exceptionally important, therefore, to survey the board of trustees to see if they have relationships with people associated with grant making organizations. Developing the nonprofit organization's board to include such individuals is a vital, albeit difficult, task. Without such contacts, even the best proposals are disadvantaged. Although the system of personal contacts may violate the concepts of equity and objectivity, it is unrealistic to disregard or dismiss it. While not all contacts produce results and not all funders can be influenced this way, the organizations with strong contacts generally will win more grants than the organization making a cold approach.

Even with a strong contact, however, it is important to submit a compelling proposal that describes a good project. The last thing an applicant should do is to embarrass a board member by submitting a poor proposal. In fact, project planning and proposal writing are more important when a prominent contact is involved.

Organizations without strong contacts might consider becoming members of consortia. A more unified approach will help reduce fragmentation among organizations representing similar populations. It also increases the possibility that a contact exists among the members of the group.

Some Random Thoughts In Closing

This essay deviates from the traditional advice found in books about funding. It is less optimistic than the frequent pep talks presented at the beginning of funding directories. It seeks to present a realistic perspective and set expectations at a generally low level. It may be more helpful in the long run by focusing attention on the important area of contacts. Grant making and seeking is serious business. Responsible grant seekers are those who understand the factors influencing how funds are distributed. They use that understanding to win grants that can be applied to the solution of problems. These people help formulate and implement the nation's social agenda.

My aim is not to be discouraging, but realistic. Most proposals are rejected, even good ones. This does not mean that organizations should not seek grants. They should, however, focus their efforts on the most productive means of approaching funders. This may mean expanding their boards and/or cooperating with other organizations. Working with grant funds to reach common goals is an exciting and rewarding enterprise. Approaching it with a measure of realism will make the rejections less frustrating.

FOUNDATIONS

ALABAMA

1
Alabama Power Foundation, Inc.
600 N. 18th Street
Birmingham, AL 35291
(205) 250-2393

Mentally and physically disabled;
Special Olympics

Grants awarded to organizations located
in Alabama.

2
J.L. Bedsole Foundation
c/o AmSouth Bank, N.A.
P.O. Box 1628
Mobile, AL 36629
(205) 432-3369

United Cerebral Palsy; Alabama Special
Camp for Children and Adults

Most grants awarded to organizations
located in the Mobile vicinity.

3
Blount Foundation, Inc.
4520 Executive Park Drive
Montgomery, AL 36116
(205) 244-4348

Physically disabled; mental health;
Alabama Institute for Deaf and Blind

Typical grant range: $2,000 to $75,000

4
Central Bank Foundation
701 S. 20th Street
Birmingham, AL 35233

Hard-of-hearing; visually impaired;
physically and mentally disabled;
mental health

Grants awarded to organizations located
in Alabama.

Most grants awarded to preselected
organizations.

Typical grant range: $500 to $4,000

5
Daniel Foundation of Alabama
820 Shades Creek Parkway, Suite 1200
Birmingham, AL 35209
(205) 879-0902

Mental health; hard-of-hearing; United
Cerebral Palsy; Helen Keller Eye
Research

Grants awarded to organizations located
in Alabama.

6
Greater Birmingham Foundation
P.O. Box 131027
Birmingham, AL 35213
(205) 871-0735

Mentally and physically disabled

Grants awarded to organizations located
in the Birmingham vicinity.

7
Hill Crest Foundation, Inc.
310 N. 19th Street
Bessemer, AL 35020
(205) 425-5800

Mentally disabled; Alabama Institute
for the Deaf and Blind; Mental Health
Association; United Cerebral Palsy

Grants awarded to organizations located
in Alabama.

Typical grant range: $3,000 to $25,000

8
Robert R. Meyer Foundation
c/o AmSouth Bank, N.A. Trust Dept.
P.O. Box 11426
Birmingham, AL 35202
(205) 326-5396

Glenwood Mental Health; Alabama
Institute for the Deaf and Blind; Eye
Foundation

Grants awarded to organizations located
in the Birmingham vicinity.

Typical grant range: $10,000 to $50,000

9
Mitchell Foundation, Inc.
2405 First National Bank Bldg.
P.O. Box 1126
Mobile, AL 36633
(205) 432-1711

Visually impaired; physically disabled

Grants awarded to organizations located
in Alabama.

10
Mobile Community Foundation
P.O. Box 990
Mobile, AL 36601
(205) 438-5591

Hard-of-hearing; visually impaired;
Mobile Preschool for the Sensory
Impaired

Grants awarded to organizations located
in the Mobile vicinity.

11
M.W. Smith, Jr. Foundation
c/o AmSouth Bank, N.A.
P.O. Drawer 1628
Mobile, AL 36629

Association for Retarded Citizens;
Preschool for the Sensory Impaired

Grants awarded to organizations located
in the Mobile vicinity.

Typical grant range: $1,000 to $15,000

12
Sonat Foundation, Inc.
1900 Fifth Avenue North
P.O. Box 2563
Birmingham, AL 35202
(205) 325-7460

Physically disabled; visually impaired;
hard-of-hearing; youth

Grants awarded to organizations located
in areas of company operations.

Typical grant range: $3,000 to $20,000

13
**William H. and Kate F. Stockham
Foundation, Inc.**
c/o Stockham Valves & Fittings, Inc.
4000 N. Tenth Avenue, P.O. Box 10326
Birmingham, AL 35202

Alabama Institute for the Deaf and Blind

Most grants awarded to organizations
located in Alabama.

Typical grant range: $1,000 to $10,000

14
Susan Mott Webb Charitable Trust
c/o AmSouth Bank, N.A.
P.O. Box 11426
Birmingham, AL 35202
(205) 326-5396

United Cerebral Palsy; Glenwood Mental
Health Services

Most grants awarded to organizations
located in the Birmingham vicinity.

Typical grant range: $2,000 to $25,000

ALASKA

15
Z.J. Loussac Trust
c/o National Bank of Alaska
P.O. Box 100600
Anchorage, AK 99510

Visually impaired; mentally and
physically disabled

Most grants awarded to organizations
located in the Anchorage vicinity.

Typical grant range: $1,000 to $7,000

16
Rasmuson Foundation
c/o National Bank of Alaska
P.O. Box 100600
Anchorage, AK 99510

Physically disabled; Very Special Arts

Most grants awarded to organizations
located in the Anchorage vicinity.

Typical grant range: $400 to $5,000

17
Skaggs Foundation
P.O. Box 20510
Juneau, AK 99802
(907) 463-4843

Physically disabled; recreation; Glacier
Swim Club (for people with disabilities)

Grants awarded to organizations located
in Alaska.

Typical grant range: $1,000 to $6,000

ARIZONA

18
Arizona Community Foundation
2122 E. Highland Avenue, Suite 400
Phoenix, AZ 85016
(602) 381-1400

Foundation for Blind Children; Center for
the Handicapped; Valley Center for the
Deaf; Multiple Sclerosis Society; Mental
Health Association

Grants awarded to organizations located
in Arizona.

Typical grant range: $500 to $14,000

19
Bidstrup Foundation
7511 N. Eucalyptus Drive
Paradise Valley, AZ 85253

Mentally and physically disabled; elderly

20
**First Interstate Bank of Arizona, N.A.
Charitable Foundation**
P.O. Box 29743
Phoenix, AZ 85038
(602) 229-4544

Mentally and physically disabled;
recreation

Grants awarded to organizations located
in Arizona.

Typical grant range: $300 to $8,000

21
**Charles and Gertrude Gordon
Foundation**
111 S. Church Avenue
Tucson, AZ 85701
(602) 624-9983

Muscular Dystrophy Association;
Special Olympics

Grants awarded to organizations located
in the Tucson vicinity.

Typical grant range: $3,000 to $10,000

22
J.W. Kieckhefer Foundation
116 E. Gurley Street
P.O. Box 750
Prescott, AZ 86302
(602) 445-4010

Mentally and physically disabled;
visually impaired

Typical grant range: $2,000 to $20,000

23
Margaret T. Morris Foundation
P.O. Box 592
Prescott, AZ 86302
(602) 445-4010

Mental health; mentally disabled;
Foundation for Blind Children

Grants awarded to organizations located
in Arizona.

Typical grant range: $1,000 to $21,000

24
Phelps Dodge Foundation
2600 N. Central Avenue
Phoenix, AZ 85004
(602) 234-8100

Mentally and physically disabled; youth

Grants awarded to organizations located
in areas of company operations.

Typical grant range: $5,000 to $20,000

25
Tucson Community Foundation
6601 E. Grant Road, Suite 111
Tucson, AZ 85715
(602) 772-1707

Physically disabled; cultural programs

Most grants awarded to organizations
located in the Tucson vicinity.

26
Del E. Webb Foundation
2023 W. Wickenburg Way
P.O. Box 20519
Wickenburg, AZ 85358
(602) 684-7223

Deaf; youth; dental care; Recreation
Center for the Handicapped (van equipped
with wheelchair lift); Center for the
Partially Sighted; Foundation for Blind
Children; Center for the Handicapped
(speech therapy program)

Typical grant range: $5,000 to $75,000

ARKANSAS

27
Beasley Foundation
550 Beddit Lane
Heber Springs, AR 72543

Visually impaired

28
**William C. and Theodosia Murphy
Nolan Foundation**
200 N. Jefferson, Suite 308
El Dorado, AR 71730
(501) 863-7118

Eye research; physically disabled

Grants awarded to organizations located
in Arkansas.

Typical grant range: $500 to $8,000

29
Ross Foundation
1039 Henderson Street
Arkadelphia, AR 71923
(501) 246-9881

Mentally and physically disabled

Grants awarded to organizations located
in the Arkadelphia vicinity.

Typical grant range: $2,500 to $10,000

CALIFORNIA

30
Ahmanson Foundation
9215 Wilshire Blvd.
Beverly Hills, CA 90210
(310) 278-0770

Disabled (all areas); education; youth

Most grants awarded to organizations
located in the Los Angeles vicinity.

Typical grant range: $8,000 to $45,000

31
Aidlin Foundation
5143 Sunset Blvd.
Los Angeles, CA 90027

Foundation for the Junior Blind

Grants awarded to organizations located
in California.

Typical grant range: $500 to $5,000

32
Maurice Amado Foundation
3600 Wilshire Blvd., Suite 1228
Los Angeles, CA 90010

Foundation for the Junior Blind

33
American Honda Foundation
P.O. Box 2205
Torrance, CA 90509
(310) 781-4090

Education program for children with
dyslexia.

Typical grant range: $15,000 to $75,000

34
ARCO Foundation
515 S. Flower Street
Los Angeles, CA 90071
(213) 486-3342

Physically disabled; job training;
Goodwill Industries

Grants awarded to organizations located
in areas of company operations.

35
Atkinson Foundation
1100 Grundy Lane, Suite 140
San Bruno, CA 94066
(415) 876-1359

Mentally disabled; developmentally
disabled; accessibility project; Mental
Health Association

Grants awarded to organizations located
in San Mateo County.

Typical grant range: $2,000 to $12,000

36
Myrtle L. Atkinson Foundation
101 Alma Street, Suite 1207
Palo Alto, CA 94301

Physically disabled; visually impaired

Most grants awarded to organizations
located in California.

37
R.C. Baker Foundation
P.O. Box 6150
Orange, CA 92613
(714) 750-8987

Hard-of-hearing; mentally and physically
disabled; Help for Brain Injured Children;
Special Olympics; Braille Institute of
America

Typical grant range: $500 to $30,000

38
**Solomon R. & Rebecca D. Baker
Foundation, Inc.**
1900 Avenue of the Stars, Suite 630
Los Angeles, CA 90067
(213) 552-9822

Autism Society of America; Foundation
for the Junior Blind

Grants awarded to organizations located
in California.

39
BankAmerica Foundation
Bank of America Center, Dept. 3246
P.O. Box 37000
San Francisco, CA 94137
(415) 953-3175

Foundation for Blind Children; Dole
Foundation for Employment of People
with Disabilities; Special Olympics;
Museum of Natural History (accessibility
project); Audio Vision Radio Reading
Service for the Blind

Grants awarded to organizations located
in areas of company operations.

Typical grant range: $1,000 to $15,000

40
William C. Bannerman Foundation
4720 Lincoln Blvd., Suite 250
Marina del Rey, CA 90292

Foundation for the Junior Blind;
Association for Retarded Citizens;
Crippled Children's Society; Cystic
Fibrosis Foundation

Grants awarded to organizations located
in the Los Angeles vicinity.

Typical grant range: $2,000 to $15,000

41
Donald R. Barker Foundation
11661 San Vicente Blvd., Suite 300
Los Angeles, CA 90049

Mental health; hard-of-hearing; Council
for Retarded Children; Shriner's Hospital
for Crippled Children

Typical grant range: $2,000 to $11,000

42
Lowell Berry Foundation
Four Orinda Way, Suite 140B
Orinda, CA 94563
(512) 254-1944

Physically disabled; hard-of-hearing;
youth

Typical grant range: $1,000 to $15,000

43
Bireley Foundation
130 N. Brand Blvd.
Glendale, CA 91203
(818) 500-7755

March of Dimes; Exceptional Children's
Foundation; Braille Institute; Foundation
for the Junior Blind; Crippled Children's
Society; Goodwill Industries

44
Charles Bloom Foundation, Inc.
240 Eucalyptus Hill Drive
Santa Barbara, CA 93108

Visually impaired; hard-of-hearing

Grants awarded to organizations located
in California.

45
Bothin Foundation
873 Sutter Street, Suite B
San Francisco, CA 94109
(415) 771-4300

Physically and mentally disabled; learning
disabled; visually impaired

Typical grant range: $1,000 to $20,000

46
**Alphonse A. Burnand Medical and
Educational Foundation**
P.O. Box 59
593 Palm Canyon Drive
Borrego Springs, CA 92004
(714) 767-5314

Braille Institute; Guide Dog for the Blind

Typical grant range: $2,000 to $7,000

47
Fritz B. Burns Foundation
4001 W. Alameda Avenue, Suite 201
Burbank, CA 91505
(818) 840-8802

Visually impaired; physically disabled;
youth

Most grants awarded to organizations
located in Los Angeles vicinity.

Typical grant range: $10,000 to $150,000

48
California Community Foundation
606 S. Olive Street, Suite 2400
Los Angeles, CA 90014
(213) 413-4042

Physically and mentally disabled; autism;
employment programs; Guide Dogs for
the Blind

Grants awarded to organizations located
in the Los Angeles County.

Typical grant range: $3,000 to $30,000

49
Callison Foundation
1493 Beach Park Blvd., Suite 295
Foster City, CA 94404
(415) 349-0557

Center for Handicapped Children and
Teenagers; Recreation Center for the
Handicapped; San Francisco Hearing
Dog Program

Grants awarded to organizations located
in the San Francisco vicinity.

Typical grant range: $5,000 to $20,000

50
Capital Fund Foundation
1250 4th Street, 6th Floor
Santa Monica, CA 90401

Visually impaired; physically disabled;
recreation

Typical grant range: $2,000 to $75,000

51
Clorox Company Foundation
1221 Broadway
Oakland, CA 94612
(510) 271-7747

Mentally and physically disabled

Grants awarded to organizations located in areas of company operations, with an emphasis in the Oakland vicinity.

Typical grant range: $2,000 to $8,000

52
Community Foundation for Monterey County
P.O. Box 1384
Monterey, CA 93942
(408) 375-9712

Physically disabled; mental health

Grants awarded to organizations located in Monterey County.

53
Community Foundation of Santa Clara County
960 W. Hedding, Suite 220
San Jose, CA 95126
(408) 241-2666

Physically disabled; mental health services

Grants awarded to organizations located in Santa Clara County.

Typical grant range: $2,000 to $10,000

54
James S. Copley Foundation
7776 Ivanhoe Avenue
P.O. Box 1530
La Jolla, CA 92038
(619) 454-0411

Mental health; Easter Seals Rehabilitation Center; Special Olympics

Typical grant range: $1,000 to $8,000

55
S.H. Cowell Foundation
120 Montgomery Street, Suite 2570
San Francisco, CA 94104
(415) 397-0285

Mentally and physically disabled; developmentally disabled; education; youth; independent living programs; Goodwill Industries; Association for Retarded Citizens

Grants awarded to organizations located in Northern California.

Typical grant range: $15,000 to $70,000

56
Darrow Foundation
1000 Fourth Street, Suite 375
San Rafael, CA 94901
(415) 453-0534

Mentally and physically disabled; visually impaired; recreation

Most grants awarded to organizations located in the San Rafael vicinity.

Most grants awarded to Christian organizations.

Typical grant range: $500 to $2,000

57
Lyda-Rico DeLuca Foundation, Inc.
832 Barron Avenue
Redwood City, CA 94063

Physically disabled; recreation

Grants awarded to organizations located in California.

58
Joseph Drown Foundation
1999 Ave. of the Stars, Suite 1930
Los Angeles, CA 90067
(213) 277-4488

Special Olympics; Guide Dogs for the
Blind; Blind Sports International; Center
for the Partially Sighted; Exceptional
Children Foundation; Hearing & Speech
Center

Grants awarded to organizations located
in California.

Typical grant range: $10,000 to $75,000

59
East Bay Community Foundation
501 Wickson Avenue
Oakland, CA 94610
(510) 836-3223

National Institute for Art and Disabilities;
Disabled Children's Computer Group;
Down Syndrome League

Grants awarded to organizations located
in Alameda and Contra Costa Counties.

Typical grant range: $500 to $10,000

60
Freeman E. Fairfield Foundation
3610 Long Beach Blvd.
P.O. Box 7798
Long Beach, CA 90807
(213) 427-7219

Physically disabled; mental health;
Crippled Children's Society

Grants awarded to organizations located
in the Long Beach vicinity.

Typical grant range: $4,000 to $25,000

61
Fireman's Fund Foundation
777 San Marin Drive
P.O. Box 777
Novato, CA 94998
(415) 899-2757

Autism; hard-of-hearing; visually
impaired; Special Olympics

Typical grant range: $1,000 to $5,000

62
Fleishhacker Foundation
One Maritime Plaza, Suite 830
San Francisco, CA 94111
(415) 788-2909

San Francisco Hearing Services; World
Institute of Disabilities; Youth in Arts (for
children with disabilities)

Grants awarded to organizations located
in the San Francisco vicinity.

Typical grant range: $1,000 to $15,000

63
Foundation of the Litton Industries
360 N. Crescent Drive
Beverly Hills, CA 90210
(310) 859-5423

Autism Society; Center for Partially
Sighted; March of Dimes

Typical grant range: $1,000 to $20,000

64
Friedman Family Foundation
204 E. Second Avenue, No. 719
San Mateo, CA 94401
(415) 342-8750

Assistance Dog Institute; Hearing Society;
Recording for the Blind

Most grants awarded to organizations
located in the San Francisco vicinity.

65

**Georges and Germaine Fusenot
Charity Foundation**
7060 Hollywood Blvd., Suite 912
Hollywood, CA 90028

Braille Institute; Canine Companions for
Independence; Foundation for the Junior
Blind; House Ear Institute

Grants awarded to organizations located
in California.

66

Gallo Foundation
P.O. Box 1130
Modesto, CA 95353

Mentally and physically disabled;
Foundation for Exceptional Children;
United Cerebral Palsy

Grants awarded to organizations located
in California.

Typical grant range: $3,000 to $15,000

67

**John Jewett and H. Chandler Garland
Foundation**
P.O. Box 550
Pasadena, CA 91102

Visually impaired; hard-of-hearing

Typical grant range: $3,000 to $25,000

68

Carl Gellert Foundation
2222 19th Avenue
San Francisco, CA 94116
(415) 566-4420

Association for Retarded Citizens;
Recreation Center for the Handicapped;
Children with Disabilities; Center for the
Blind and Handicapped; Lighthouse for
the Blind; Special Olympics; Peninsula
Center for Retarded Children and Adults

Grants awarded to organizations located
in the San Francisco vicinity.

Typical grant range: $1,500 to $9,000

69

Celia Berta Gellert Foundation
2222 19th Avenue
San Francisco, CA 94116
(415) 566-4420

Association for Retarded Citizens;
Edgewood Children's Center (support
services for children who are emotionally
disturbed); Freewheelers Association (to
improve quality of life of people in
wheelchairs); Foundation for Hearing
Research; Recreation Center for the
Handicapped

Grants awarded to organizations located
in the San Francisco vicinity.

Typical grant range: $1,500 to $8,000

70

Fred Gellert Foundation
One Embarcadero Center, Suite 2480
San Francisco, CA 94111
(415) 433-6174

Disabled (all areas); recreation;
child welfare

Typical grant range: $2,000 to $8,000

71

Glendale Community Foundation
100 N. Brand Blvd., Suite 316
Glendale, CA 91203
(818) 241-8040

Physically disabled; employment
programs

Grants awarded to organizations located
in the Glendale vicinity.

72

Stella B. Gross Charitable Trust
Bank of the West
P.O. Box 1121
San Jose, CA 95108

Mentally disabled; visually impaired

Grants awarded to organizations located
in Santa Clara County.

73

Evelyn and Walter Haas, Jr. Fund
One Lombard Street, Suite 305
San Francisco, CA 94111
(415) 398-3744

National Multiple Sclerosis Society;
Recording for the Blind

Typical grant range: $3,000 to $30,000

74

Walter and Elise Haas Fund
One Lombard Street, Suite 305
San Francisco, CA 94111
(415) 398-4474

Mental health; visually impaired;
physically disabled; youth

Grants awarded to organizations located
in the San Francisco vicinity.

Typical grant range: $2,000 to $60,000

75

Harden Foundation
P.O. Box 779
Salinas, CA 93902
(408) 442-3005

Mental health; hard-of-hearing; physically
disabled; visually impaired; youth;
Special Olympics

Grants awarded to organizations located
in the Salinas vicinity.

Typical grant range: $8,000 to $40,000

76

Herbst Foundation, Inc.
Three Embarcadero Center., 21st Fl.
San Francisco, CA 94111
(415) 951-7508

Physically and mentally disabled; visually
impaired; recreation

Grants awarded to organizations located
in the San Francisco vicinity.

Typical grant range: $5,000 to $45,000

77

**Margaret W. and Herbert Hoover, Jr.
Foundation**
200 S. Los Robles Avenue, Suite 520
Pasadena, CA 91101
(818) 796-4014

Research (hearing and eye research)

Typical grant range: $10,000 to $100,000

78

**Lucile Horton Howe and Mitchell B.
Howe Foundation**
180 S. Lake Avenue
Pasadena, CA 91101
(818) 792-0514

Deaf; Canine Companions for
Independence; Braille Institute

79

Humboldt Area Foundation
P.O. Box 632
Eureka, CA 95502
(707) 442-2993

Developmentally disabled; mentally and
physically disabled; Easter Seal Society;
Arcata Christian School (learning
disabled)

Typical grant range: $1,000 to $11,000

80

Jaquelin Hume Foundation
600 Montgomery Street, Suite 2800
San Francisco, CA 94111
(415) 705-5112

Guide Dogs for the Blind; Hearing
Society; Hearing and Speech Center

Grants awarded to organizations located
in the San Francisco vicinity.

81
Irvine Health Foundation
18301 Von Karman Avenue, Suite 440
Irvine, CA 92715

Speech and hearing impaired; learning
disabled; United Cerebral Palsy; Mental
Health Association

Grants awarded to organizations located
in Orange County.

Typical grant range: $5,000 to $50,000

82
William G. Irwin Charity Foundation
711 Russ Building
235 Montgomery Street
San Francisco, CA 94104
(415) 362-6954

Visually impaired; hard-of-hearing

Typical grant range: $15,000 to $90,000

83
Ann Jackson Family Foundation
P.O. Box 5580
Santa Barbara, CA 93150

Dyslexia; mental health; Association for
Retarded Children; Direct Link for the
Disabled; Blind Babies Foundation;
Braille Institute

Grants awarded to organizations located
in Santa Barbara.

84
Jacobs Family Foundation, Inc.
P.O. Box 261519
San Diego, CA 92196
(619) 578-7256

Mental health; Near East Foundation for
the Blind

Typical grant range: $2,000 to $30,000

85
Jerome Foundation
7439 La Palma, Suite 153
Buena Park, CA 90620
(714) 522-6548

Physically disabled; visually impaired;
youth

86
W.M. Keck Foundation
555 S. Flower Street, Suite 3230
Los Angeles, CA 90071

Foundation for the Junior Blind; Goodwill
Industries; Junior Arts Center (children
with disabilities); Exceptional Children
Foundation (developmentally disabled)

Most grants awarded to preselected
organizations.

Typical grant range: $150,000 to
$700,000

87
Karl Kirchgessner Foundation
c/o Greenberg, Glusker, Fields, Claman &
Machtinger
1900 Ave. of the Stars, Suite 2100
Los Angeles, CA 90067
(213) 553-3610

Eye research; Blind Children's Learning
Center; Recording for the Blind; Guide
Dogs for the Blind; Foundation for the
Junior Blind

Grants awarded to organizations located
in Southern California.

Typical grant range: $5,000 to $40,000

88
Tom and Valley Knudsen Foundation
900 Wilshire Blvd., Suite 1424
Los Angeles, CA 90017
(213) 614-1940

Visually impaired; mental health

Grants awarded to organizations located
in Southern California.

89
Komes Foundation
1801 Van Ness Avenue, Suite 300
San Francisco, CA 94109
(415) 441-6462

School for the Deaf; Center for
Handicapped Children and Teenagers;
Hearing Society; Guide Dogs for the
Blind

90
Koret Foundation
33 New Montgomery Street, Suite 1090
San Francisco, CA 94105
(415) 882-7740

Physically and mentally disabled; visually
impaired; independent living programs

Typical grant range: $1,000 to $50,000

91
Thomas and Dorothy Leavey
Foundation
4680 Wilshire Blvd.
Los Angeles, CA 90010
(213) 930-4252

Foundation for the Junior Blind;
Recording for the Blind

Grants awarded to organizations located
in the Los Angeles vicinity.

Typical grant range: $5,000 to $125,000

92
Levi Strauss Foundation
1155 Battery Street
San Francisco, CA 94111
(415) 544-2194

Mentally and physically disabled; mental
health; recreation; independent living
programs; employment programs

Grants awarded to organizations located
in areas of company operations.

Typical grant range: $3,000 to $30,000

93
General and Mrs. William Lyon
Family Foundation
P.O. Box 8858
Newport Beach, CA 92658
(714) 833-3600

Developmentally disabled

Typical grant range: $5,000 to $150,000

94
Bertha Ross Lytel Foundation
P.O. Box 893
Ferndale, CA 95536
(707) 786-4682

Easter Seal Society

Grants awarded to organizations located
in Humboldt County.

Typical grant range: $500 to $25,000

95
Margoes Foundation
57 Post Street, Suite 510
San Francisco, CA 94104
(415) 981-2966

Mental health; mentally disabled;
rehabilitation; employment programs;
Center for Independent Living

Grants awarded to organizations located
in the San Francisco vicinity.

Typical grant range: $1,000 to $14,000

96
Marin Community Foundation
17 E. Sir Francis Drake Blvd., Suite 200
Larkspur, CA 94939
(415) 461-3333

Mental health; independent living
programs; youth; Easter Seal Society

Grants awarded to organizations located
in Marin County.

Typical grant range: $5,000 to $200,000

97
Mattel Foundation
c/o Mattel Toys
333 Continental Blvd.
El Segundo, CA 90245
(310) 524-3530

National Multiple Sclerosis; Muscular
Dystrophy Association; E. Meadow
Cerebral Palsy; Activities for Retarded
Children; Easter Seal Society

98
McConnell Foundation
P.O. Box 991870
Redding, CA 96099
(916) 222-0696

Physically disabled; accessibility projects; visually impaired

Typical grant range: $3,000 to $80,000

99
McKesson Foundation, Inc.
One Post Street
San Francisco, CA 94104
(415) 983-8673

Easter Seal Society; March of Dimes; Special Olympics; Braille Institute

Grants awarded to organizations located in the San Francisco vicinity.

Typical grant range: $1,000 to $20,000

100
Mericos Foundation
1260 Huntington Drive, Suite 204
South Pasadena, CA 91030
(213) 259-0484

Physically disabled; visually impaired; recreation

Grants awarded to organizations located in California, with an emphasis in Santa Barbara.

Typical grant range: $5,000 to $85,000

101
Robert Stewart Odell and Helen Pfeiffer Odell Fund
c/o Wells Fargo Bank
P.O. Box 63002
San Francisco, CA 94163
(415) 396-3226

Blind Babies Foundation; Center for Handicapped Children and Teenagers; Lighthouse for the Blind; Recreation Center for the Handicapped; Rose Rednick Center for the Blind; Hebrew Home for Aged Disabled; Community Association for the Retarded; Association for Retarded Citizens

Grants awarded to organizations located in the San Francisco vicinity.

Typical grant range: $3,000 to $20,000

102
David and Lucile Packard Foundation
300 Second Street, Suite 200
Los Altos, CA 94022
(415) 948-7658

Mentally and physically disabled; emotionally disturbed; employment program; youth

Typical grant range: $5,000 to $100,000

103
George B. Page Foundation
P.O. Box 1299
Santa Barbara, CA 93102
(805) 963-1841

Braille Institute; Recording for the Blind; Santa Barbara Special Olympics

Grants awarded to organizations located in Santa Barbara.

Typical grant range: $500 to $5,000

104
Parker Foundation
1200 Prospect Street, Suite 575
La Jolla, CA 92037
(619) 456-3038

Visually impaired; mental health;
learning disabled

Grants awarded to organizations located
in San Diego County.

Typical grant range: $2,000 to $15,000

105
Ralph M. Parsons Foundation
1055 Wilshire Blvd., Suite 1701
Los Angeles, CA 90017
(213) 482-3185

Mentally and physically disabled; visually
impaired; youth; recreation; employment
programs

Grants awarded to organizations located
in the Los Angeles vicinity.

Typical grant range: $15,000 to $85,000

106
Pasadena Child Health Foundation
35 N. Lake Avenue, Suite 800
Pasadena, CA 91101

Child welfare; Pasadena Mental Health
Association

107
Ann Peppers Foundation
P.O. Box 50146
Pasadena, CA 91105
(818) 449-0793

Visually impaired; hard-of-hearing;
physically and mentally disabled

Grants awarded to organizations located
in the Los Angeles vicinity.

Typical grant range: $2,000 to $11,000

108
**Gustavus and Louise Pfeiffer
Research Foundation**
P.O. Box 1153
Redlands, CA 92373
(714) 792-6269

Clark School for the Deaf (research)

Typical grant range: $10,000 to $50,000

109
Roberts Foundation
873 Sutter Street
San Francisco, CA 94109
(415) 771-4300

Learning disabled; hard-of-hearing;
visually impaired; employment programs;
youth

Typical grant range: $8,000 to $35,000

110
San Diego Community Foundation
Wells Fargo Bank Building
101 W. Broadway, Suite 1120
San Diego, CA 92101
(619) 239-8815

Hard-of-hearing; physically and mentally
disabled; Association for Retarded
Citizens

Grants awarded to organizations located
in San Diego County.

Typical grant range: $1,000 to $15,000

111
San Francisco Foundation
685 Market Street, Suite 910
San Francisco, CA 94105
(415) 495-3100

Disabled (all areas); developmentally
disabled; independent living programs;
education; youth; elderly; Berkeley
Mental Health; Hearing Society for the
Bay Area

Grants awarded in Alameda, Contra
Costa, Marin, San Francisco, and San
Mateo counties.

Typical grant range: $2,000 to $40,000

112
George H. Sandy Foundation
P.O. Box 591717
San Francisco, CA 94159

Disabled (all areas)

Grants awarded to organizations located
in the San Francisco vicinity.

113
Annunziata Sanguinetti Foundation
c/o Wells Fargo Bank, N.A.
420 Montgomery Street, MAC #0101-056
San Francisco, CA 94163
(415) 396-3215

Lighthouse for the Blind; Blind Babies
Foundation; United Cerebral Palsy
Association; Easter Seal Society;
Recreation Center for the Handicapped;
Hearing Society for the Bay Area; St.
Francis Hearing and Speech Center;
Center for Handicapped Children and
Teenagers

Grants awarded to organizations located
in San Francisco.

Typical grant range: $3,000 to $10,000

114
Santa Barbara Foundation
15 E. Carrillo Street
Santa Barbara, CA 93101
(805) 963-1873

Mentally and physically disabled;
Dyslexia Awareness and Resource Center

Grants awarded to organizations located
in Santa Barbara County.

Typical grant range: $5,000 to $25,000

115
Frances Schermer Charitable Trust
c/o Security Pacific National Bank
P.O. Box 3189, Terminal Annex
Los Angeles, CA 90051

Physically disabled; Multiple Sclerosis
Service Agency; Recording for the Blind

Typical grant range: $1,000 to $6,500

116
Shea Foundation
655 Brea Canyon Road
Walnut, CA 91789

Braille Institute; Recording for the Blind;
Portland Center for Hearing and Speech;
Angels for Autistic Children

Grants awarded to organizations located
in California.

117
Milton Shoong Foundation
321 10th Street
Oakland, CA 94607

Mentally disabled; March of Dimes;
Pacific Vision Foundation; Recreation
Center for the Handicapped

Grants awarded to organizations located
in California.

118
May and Stanley Smith Trust
49 Geary Street, Suite 244
San Francisco, CA 94108
(415) 391-0292

Physically disabled; independent living;
mental health; Foundation for Hearing
Research (parent infant program);
Lighthouse for the Visually Impaired

Most grants awarded to organizations
located in the San Francisco vicinity.

Typical grant range: $1,500 to $6,000

119
**Sonoma County Community
Foundation**
3550 Round Barn Boulevard, No. 212
Santa Rosa, CA 95403
(707) 579-4073

Visually impaired; physically disabled

Grants awarded to organizations located
in Sonoma County.

120
Edward L. & Addie M. Soule Foundation
P.O. Drawer SS
Walnut Creek, CA 94596

Guide Dogs for the Blind; Reader's Digest Fund for the Blind; Goodwill Industries

121
Jules and Doris Stein Foundation
P.O. Box 30
Beverly Hills, CA 90213
(310) 276-2101

Visually impaired; eye research; physically disabled; youth

Typical grant range: $2,000 to $15,000

122
Sidney Stern Memorial Trust
P.O. Box 893
Pacific Palisades, CA 90272

Physically and mentally disabled; youth

Grants awarded to organizations located in California.

Typical grant range: $1,000 to $8,000

123
Glen and Dorothy Stillwell Charitable Trust
301 N. Lake Avenue, 10th Floor
Pasadena, CA 91101
(818) 793-9400

Physically disabled; hard-of-hearing; speech impaired

Grants awarded to organizations located in Orange County.

Typical grant range: $7,000 to $12,000

124
Swift Memorial Health Care Foundation
1355 Del Norte Road
Camarillo, CA 93010
(805) 988-0196

Mentally disabled; Easter Seals; Multiple Sclerosis

Grants awarded to organizations located in Ventura County.

Typical grant range: $1,000 to $5,000

125
Teledyne Charitable Trust Foundation
1901 Avenue of the Stars, Suite 1800
Los Angeles, CA 90067

Physically disabled, visually impaired; Goodwill Industries

Typical grant range: $3,000 to $15,000

126
Flora L. Thornton Foundation
c/o Edward A. Landry
4444 Lakeside Drive, Suite 300
Burbank, CA 91505
(818) 842-1645

Visually impaired; National Multiple Sclerosis Society

127
Alice Tweed Tuohy Foundation
205 E. Carrillo Street
Santa Barbara, CA 93101
(805) 962-6430

Mentally disabled

Grants awarded to organizations located in the Santa Barbara vicinity.

Typical grant range: $1,000 to $15,000

128
Valley Foundation
333 W. Santa Clara Street
San Jose, CA 95113
(508) 292-1124

Autism; visually impaired; Rehabilitation
Mental Health Services; United Cerebral
Palsy Association

Grants awarded to organizations located
in the Santa Clara vicinity.

Typical grant range: $15,000 to $85,000

129
Wayne and Gladys Valley Foundation
1939 Harrison Street, Suite 510
Oakland, CA 94612

Visually impaired; hard-of-hearing;
mentally disabled

Typical grant range: $15,000 to $100,000

130
J.B. and Emily Van Nuys Charities
P.O. Box 33
Palos Verdes Estates, CA 90274
(310) 373-8521

Mentally and physically disabled; visually
impaired; youth

Grants awarded to organizations located
in the Los Angeles vicinity.

131
**Ventura County Community
Foundation**
1355 Del Norte Road
Camarillo, CA 93010
(805) 988-0196

Physically disabled; hard-of-hearing;
education

Grants awarded to organizations located
in Ventura County.

Typical grant range: $500 to $7,000

132
Alexander F. Victor Foundation
P.O. Box Law
Monterey, CA 93942
(408) 649-1100

Visually impaired

133
Weingart Foundation
1055 W. Seventh Street, Suite 3050
Los Angeles, CA 90017
(213) 688-7799

Developmentally disabled; Visually
Handicapped Adults of the Valley; Angel
View Crippled Children's Foundation;
Prentice Day School (learning disabled)

Grants awarded to organizations located
in Southern California.

Typical grant range: $5,000 to $150,000

134
WELfund, Inc.
152 N. Almont Drive
Los Angeles, CA 90048
(213) 276-6163

Association for Retarded Citizens; Autism
Research Institute; California Spinal Cord
Injury Network; Dogs for the Deaf;
Special Olympics; Easter Seal Society;
Foundation for the Junior Blind; Guide
Dogs for the Blind; Learning Disabilities
Association of California; March of
Dimes; National Multiple Sclerosis
Society; Recording for the Blind

Grants awarded to organizations located
in California.

Typical grant range: $200 to $3,000

135
Wood-Claeyssens Foundation
P.O. Box 99
Santa Barbara, CA 93102
(805) 962-0011

Association for Retarded Citizens;
National Multiple Sclerosis Society;
Recording for the Blind; March of Dimes
Birth Defects Foundation

COLORADO

136
Boettcher Foundation
600 17th Street, Suite 2210 South
Denver, CO 80202
(303) 534-1937

Physically disabled; developmentally
disabled; visually impaired; youth;
recreation

Grants awarded to organizations located
in Colorado.

Typical grant range: $5,000 to $45,000

137
Bonfils-Stanton Foundation
1601 Arapahoe Street, Suite 5
Denver, CO 80202
(303) 825-3774

Physically disabled; visually impaired;
employment programs

Grants awarded to organizations located
in Colorado.

Typical grant range: $2,000 to $25,000

138
Chamberlain Foundation
P.O. Box 5003
Pueblo, CO 81002
(719) 543-8596

Pueblo County Board for Developmental
Disabilities

Grants awarded to organizations located
in Pueblo County.

Typical grant range: $2,000 to $8,000

139
Collins Foundation
c/o Norwest Bank, Boulder
P.O. Box 299
Boulder, CO 80306
(303) 441-0309

Mentally and physically disabled;
employment programs; recreation

Grants awarded to organizations located
in Boulder County.

Typical grant range: $500 to $3,500

140
Adolph Coors Foundation
3773 Cherry Creek North Drive, Suite 955
Denver, CO 80209
(303) 388-1636

Disabled (all areas); accessibility project;
recreation

Grants awarded to organizations located
in Colorado.

Typical grant range: $5,000 to $45,000

141
Ben C. Delatour Foundation
P.O. Box 96
Fort Collins, CO 80522

Visually impaired; hard-of-hearing;
speech impaired; education

Most grants awarded to organizations
located in Colorado.

Typical grant range: $600 to $2,500

142
Denver Foundation
455 Sherman Street, Suite 220
Denver, CO 80203
(303) 778-7587

Disabled (all areas); emotionally
disturbed; learning disabled; cultural
programs; employment programs

Grants awarded to organizations located
in the Denver vicinity.

Typical grant range: $2,000 to $20,000

143
John G. Duncan Trust
c/o First Interstate Bank of Denver, N.A.
P.O. Box 5825 TA
Denver, CO 80217
(303) 293-5324

Colorado Foundation of Dentistry for the
Handicapped; International Hearing Dog
Association

Grants awarded to organizations located
in Colorado.

144
El Pomar Foundation
Ten Lake Circle
P.O. Box 158
Colorado Springs, CO 80901
(719) 633-7733

Physically disabled; accessibility projects;
recreation; Goodwill Industries

Grants awarded to organizations located
in Colorado.

Typical grant range: $3,000 to $50,000

145
Gates Foundation
3200 Cherry Creek South Dr., #630
Denver, CO 80209
(303) 722-1881

Physically disabled; visually impaired;
learning disabled; accessibility projects;
recreation; youth

Grants awarded to organizations located
in Colorado.

Typical grant range: $5,000 to $30,000

146
Humphreys Foundation
555 17th Street, Suite 2900
Denver, CO 80202
(303) 295-8461

National Sports Center for the Disabled

Grants awarded to organizations located
in Colorado.

Typical grant range: $500 to $4,500

147
A. V. Hunter Trust, Inc.
55 Madison Street, Suite 225
Denver, CO 80206
(303) 399-5450

Rocky Mountain Multiple Sclerosis
Center; Easter Seals; Colorado
Foundation of Dentistry for the
Handicapped; Families of the Blind;
Recording for the Blind

Most grants awarded to organizations
located in Denver.

Typical grant range: $3,000 to $30,000

148
**Helen K. and Arthur E. Johnson
Foundation**
1700 Broadway, Room 2302
Denver, CO 80290
(303) 861-4127

Physically disabled; visually impaired;
hard-of-hearing; youth; employment
programs; recreation

Grants awarded to organizations located
in Colorado.

Typical grant range: $12,000 to $100,000

149
**Carl W. and Carrie Mae Joslyn
Charitable Trust**
c/o Bank One, Colorado Springs, N.A.
P.O. Box 1699, Trust Dept.
Colorado Springs, CO 80942
(719) 471-5115

Physically disabled; visually impaired;
deaf; education; employment programs

Grants awarded to organizations located
in El Paso County.

Typical grant range: $500 to $4,000

150
Lowe Foundation
Colorado Judicial Center
Two E. 14th Avenue
Denver, CO 80203
(303) 837-3750

Physically and mentally disabled; child welfare; independent living programs; United Cerebral Palsy

Grants awarded to organizations located in Colorado.

151
Needmor Fund
1730 15th Street
Boulder, CO 80302
(303) 449-5801

Physically disabled; visually impaired

Typical grant range: $2,000 to $20,000

152
Aksel Nielsen Foundation
13115 North Melody Lane
Parker, CO 80134
(303) 841-3581

National Sports Center for the Disabled

Grants awarded to organizations located in Colorado.

Typical grant range: $1,000 to $10,000

153
Carl A. Norgren Foundation
2696 S. Colorado Blvd., Suite 585
Denver, CO 80222
(303) 758-8393

Visually impaired; physically disabled; employment programs

Grants awarded to organizations located in the Denver vicinity.

Typical grant range: $500 to $3,000

154
Herbert E. Parker Trust
c/o First Interstate Bank of Denver, N.A.
633 17th Street
Denver, CO 80270

Physically disabled; developmentally disabled; recreation; employment programs

Grants awarded to organizations located in Colorado.

155
Schramm Foundation
8528 W. 10th Avenue
Lakewood, CO 80215
(303) 232-1772

Hard-of-hearing; Society to Prevent Blindness

Grants awarded to organizations located in Colorado.

Typical grant range: $1,000 to $15,000

156
St. John's Foundation
1419 Pine Street
Boulder, CO 80302

Mental Health Center

Grants awarded to organizations located in Boulder County.

157
H. Chase Stone Trust
c/o Bank One
P.O. Box 1699
Colorado Springs, CO 80942
(719) 471-5000

Center for Hearing, Speech and Language; Easter Seal Society; Performing Arts for Youth (children who are physically disabled)

Grants awarded to organizations located in El Paso County.

Typical grant range: $1,000 to $15,000

158
Bal F. and Hilda N. Swan Foundation
The First Interstate Bank of Denver, N.A.
P.O. Box 5825, Terminal Annex
Denver, CO 80217
(303) 293-5275

Colorado Special Olympics; Society to
Prevent Blindness; Recording for the
Blind; Muscular Dystrophy Association;
International Hearing Dog

Grants awarded to organizations located
in Colorado.

CONNECTICUT

159
Beatrice Fox Auerbach Foundation
25 Brookside Blvd.
West Hartford, CT 06107
(203) 232-5854

Connecticut Braille Association, Inc.;
Fidelco Guide Dog Foundation; Greater
Hartford Easter Seal Rehabilitation
Center; American School for the Deaf

Grants awarded to organizations located
in the Hartford vicinity.

Typical grant range: $2,000 to $60,000

160
Barnes Foundation, Inc.
P.O. Box 1560
Bristol, CT 06011
(203) 583-7070

Hard-of-hearing; education

Grants awarded to organizations located
in Connecticut.

161
**Community Foundation for Greater
New Haven**
70 Audubon Street
New Haven, CT 06510
(203) 777-2386

Visually impaired; hard-of-hearing;
mental health; physically disabled;
youth; Special Olympics

Grants awarded to organizations located
in the New Haven vicinity.

Typical grant range: $2,000 to $40,000

162
**Community Foundation of
Southeastern Connecticut**
302 State Street
P.O. Box 769
New London, CT 06320
(203) 442-3572

Employment projects; Easter Seal
Rehabilitation Center; Association
for Retarded Citizens;

Grants awarded to organizations located
in Southeastern Connecticut.

163
**Connecticut Mutual Life
Foundation, Inc.**
140 Garden Street
Hartford, CT 06154
(203) 727-6500

Physically disabled; visually impaired;
hard-of-hearing; rehabilitation

Grants awarded to organizations located
in the Hartford vicinity.

Typical grant range: $1,000 to $20,000

164
Charles E. Culpeper Foundation, Inc.
Financial Centre
695 E. Main Street, Suite 404
Stamford, CT 06901
(203) 975-1240

Physically disabled; emotionally disturbed

Typical grant range: $3,000 to $55,000

165
Daphne Seybolt Culpeper Memorial Foundation, Inc.
129 Musket Ridge Road
Norwalk, CT 06850
(203) 762-3984

Physically disabled; hard-of-hearing

Typical grant range: $500 to $15,000

166
Marie G. Dennett Foundation
c/o Whitman & Ransom
Two Greenwich Plaza, P.O. Box 2250
Greenwich, CT 06836
(203) 862-2361

Hard-of-hearing; visually impaired

Typical grant range: $1,000 to $7,000

167
EIS Foundation, Inc.
19 West Walk
Clinton, CT 06413
(203) 669-5367

Physically disabled; hard-of-hearing; education

Typical grant range: $500 to $7,000

168
Greater Bridgeport Area Foundation, Inc.
280 State Street
Bridgeport, CT 06604
(203) 334-7511

Learning disabled; physically disabled; cultural programs; employment programs

Grants awarded to organizations located in the Bridgeport vicinity.

Typical grant range: $100 to $5,000

169
Hartford Foundation for Public Giving
85 Gillett Street
Hartford, CT 06105
(203) 548-1888

Speech impaired; mentally disabled; hard-of-hearing; education; accessibility projects; youth; Mental Health Center; Learning Disabilities Association; United Cerebral Palsy

Grants awarded to organizations located in the Hartford vicinity.

Typical grant range: $25,000 to $50,000

170
Heublein Foundation, Inc.
P.O. Box 388
Farmington, CT 06034
(203) 231-5000

Mentally and physically disabled; mental health; recreation; child welfare

Grants awarded to organizations located in areas of company operations.

Typical grant range: $5,000 to $30,000

171
ITT Hartford Insurance Group Foundation, Inc.
Hartford Plaza
Hartford, CT 06115
(203) 547-5000

Physically disabled; visually impaired; deaf; recreation; education

Most grants awarded to organizations located in the Hartford vicinity.

Typical grant range: $1,000 to $15,000

172
Koopman Fund, Inc.
17 Brookside Blvd.
W. Hartford, CT 06107
(203) 232-6406

Mental Health Association; visually
impaired; learning disabled; hard-of-
hearing; cultural programs; education

Most grants awarded to organizations
located in Connecticut.

173
Newman's Own Foundation, Inc.
246 Post Road East
Westport, CT 06880
(203) 222-0136

Visually impaired; deaf; youth

Typical grant range: $10,000 to $25,000

174
Panwy Foundation, Inc.
Greenwich Office Park IX
10 Valley Drive
Greenwich, CT 06831
(203) 661-6616

Physically disabled; hard-of-hearing;
visually impaired

175
Swindells Charitable Foundation Trust
c/o Shawmut Bank, N.A.
777 Main Street
Hartford, CT 06115
(203) 728-2274

Physically disabled; rehabilitation

Grants awarded to organizations located
in Connecticut.

176
R.T. Vanderbilt Trust
30 Winfield Street
Norwalk, CT 06855

Mentally disabled; March of Dimes;
Shriner's Hospital for Crippled Children

Typical grant range: $250 to $7,000

177
Waterbury Foundation
P.O. Box 252
Waterbury, CT 06720
(203) 753-1315

Mentally and physically disabled;
rehabilitation

Grants awarded to organizations located
in the Waterbury vicinity.

Typical grant range: $2,500 to $45,000

178
**E. Matilda Ziegler Foundation
for the Blind, Inc.**
250 Harbor Drive
P.O. Box 10128
Stamford, CT 06904
(203) 356-9000

Visually impaired; eye research

Typical grant range: $2,000 to $10,000

DELAWARE

179
Borkee-Hagley Foundation, Inc.
P.O. Box 4590
Greenville, DE 19807
(302) 652-8616

Delaware Special Olympics

Grants awarded to organizations located
in Delaware.

Typical grant range: $1,000 to $5,000

180
Crestlea Foundation, Inc.
1004 Wilmington Trust Center
Wilmington, DE 19801
(302) 654-2489

United Cerebral Palsy

Grants awarded to organizations located
in Delaware.

Typical grant range: $1,000 to $20,000

181
Crystal Trust
1088 DuPont Building
Wilmington, DE 19898
(302) 774-8421

Delaware Special Olympics; United
Cerebral Palsy of Delaware; Paralyzed
Veterans Association (prosthetic aid
program)

Grants awarded to organizations located
in Delaware, with an emphasis in
Wilmington.

Typical grant range: $5,000 to $75,000

182
Delaware Community Foundation
P.O. Box 25207
Wilmington, DE 19899
(302) 571-8004

Physically disabled; mental health

Grants awarded to organizations located
in Delaware.

Typical grant range: $2,000 to $15,000

183
Good Samaritan, Inc.
600 Center Mill Road
Wilmington, DE 19807
(302) 654-7558

Dyslexia; learning disabled; Cambridge
College (for students with learning
disabilities)

184
Laffey-McHugh Foundation
1220 Market Building
P.O. Box 2207
Wilmington, DE 19899
(302) 658-9141

Delaware Special Olympics; National
Multiple Sclerosis Society; Recording
for the Blind; United Cerebral Palsy

Grants awarded to organizations located
in Delaware, with an emphasis in
Wilmington.

Typical grant range: $4,000 to $40,000

185
Longwood Foundation, Inc.
1004 Wilmington Trust Center
Wilmington, DE 19801
(302) 654-2477

Mentally and physically disabled;
accessibility project; youth

Grants awarded to organizations located
in Delaware, with an emphasis in
Wilmington.

Typical grant range: $20,000 to $325,000

186
Lovett Foundation, Inc.
82 Governor Printz Blvd.
Claymont, DE 19703
(302) 798-6604

Physically disabled; Montgomery County
Association for the Blind; Overbrook
School for the Blind

187
**Raskob Foundation for Catholic
Activities, Inc.**
P.O. Box 4019
Wilmington, DE 19807
(302) 655-4440

Learning disabled; mental health

Grants awarded to Catholic organizations.

Typical grant range: $3,000 to $15,000

DISTRICT OF COLUMBIA

188
Appleby Foundation
Crestar Bank, N.A., Trust Division
1445 New York Avenue, N.W.
Washington, DC 20005
(202) 879-6341

Recording for the Blind; Multiple
Sclerosis Society

189
Walter A. Bloedorn Foundation
c/o Reasoner, Davis & Fox
888 Seventeenth St., N.W., Suite 800
Washington, DC 20006
(202) 463-8282

Visually impaired; physically disabled

Grants awarded to organizations located
in the Washington, DC vicinity.

Typical grant range: $500 to $3,500

190
**Morris and Gwendolyn Cafritz
Foundation**
1825 K Street, N.W., 14th Floor
Washington, DC 20006
(202) 223-3100

Physically disabled; visually impaired;
mental health; youth; cultural programs;
employment programs

Grants awarded to organizations located
in the Washington, DC vicinity.

Typical grant range: $15,000 to $60,000

191
Queene Ferry Coonley Foundation, Inc.
P.O. Box 3722
Washington, DC 20007
(202) 333-3046

Recording for the Blind

Grants awarded to organizations located
in the Washington, DC vicinity.

Typical grant range: $500 to $6,000

192
Charles Delmar Foundation
918 16th Street, N.W., No. 203
Washington, DC 20006
(202) 393-2494

Physically disabled; visually impaired

Grants awarded to organizations located
in Washington, DC.

193
**Dole Foundation for Employment of
People with Disabilities**
1819 H Street, N.W., Suite 340
Washington, DC 20006
(202) 457-0318

World Institute on Disability; Disability
Rights Education and Defense Fund;
International Center for the Disabled;
National Rehabilitation Association; most
grants are associated with employment
programs

Typical grant range: $1,000 to $25,000

194
**Foundation for the National
Capital Region**
1002 Wisconsin Avenue, N.W.
Washington, DC 20007
(202) 338-8993

Physically disabled; visually impaired;
hard-of-hearing; recreation

Grants awarded to organizations located
in the Washington, DC vicinity.

195
**John Edward Fowler Memorial
Foundation**
1725 K Street N.W., Suite 1201
Washington, DC 20006
(202) 728-9080

Mentally and physically disabled; learning
disabled; independent living programs;
education; Plan of MD-DC (helping adults
with mental illness)

Grants awarded to organizations located
in the Washington, DC vicinity.

Typical grant range: $4,000 to $15,000

196
Freed Foundation
3050 K Street, N.W., Suite 335
Washington, DC 20007
(202) 337-5487

National Mental Health Association;
Information for the Partially Sighted;
Clubhouse Project (Deaf Interpreter
Program); D.C. Institute for Mental
Health

Typical grant range: $2,000 to $30,000

197
GEICO Philanthropic Foundation
c/o GEICO Corporation
One GEICO Plaza
Washington, DC 20076
(301) 986-2055

Physically disabled; visually impaired;
dyslexia; recreation; education

Grants awarded to organizations located
in areas of company operations.

Typical grant range: $150 to $2,500

198
Philip L. Graham Fund
c/o The Washington Post Co.
1150 Fifteenth Street, N.W.
Washington, DC 20071
(202) 334-6640

Mental health; hard-of-hearing;
employment programs

Grants awarded to organizations located
in the Washington, DC vicinity.

Typical grant range: $10,000 to $40,000

199
Joseph P. Kennedy, Jr. Foundation
1350 New York Ave., N.W., Suite 500
Washington, DC 20005
(202) 393-1250

Mentally and physically disabled;
research; higher education; Down's
Syndrome Adoption Exchange; Eunice
Kennedy Shriver Foundation (mentally
disabled)

Typical grant range: $10,000 to $70,000

200
Kiplinger Foundation
1729 H Street, N.W.
Washington, DC 20006
(202) 887-6559

Visually impaired; physically disabled;
employment programs

Grants awarded to organizations located
in the Washington, DC vicinity.

Typical grant range: $1,000 to $3,000

201
**Anthony Francis Lucas-Spindletop
Foundation**
c/o Crestar Bank, N. A.
1445 New York Avenue, N. W.
Washington, DC 20005
(202) 879-6294

Gallaudet University (hearing impaired)

Grants awarded to organizations located
in Washington, DC.

Typical grant range: $1,000 to $5,000

202
**Eugene and Agnes E. Meyer
Foundation**
1400 Sixteenth Street, N.W., Suite 360
Washington, DC 20036
(202) 483-8294

Mental health; developmentally disabled;
visually impaired; youth

Grants awarded to organizations located
in the Washington, DC vicinity.

Typical grant range: $12,000 to $35,000

203
**Mitsubishi Electric America
Foundation**
1150 Connecticut Ave., NW, Suite 1020
Washington, DC 20036
(202) 857-0031

Foundation for Exceptional Children;
National Technical Institute for the Deaf;
Foundation on Employment for
Disabilities; Special Education Technical
Resource Center; Clairbrook Center for
the Handicapped; Special Olympics; St.
Rita's School for the Deaf; March of
Dimes; Alternative Education for the
Hearing Impaired; Canine Companions
for Handicapped; Multiple Sclerosis
Society; Crippled Children's Society;
Easter Seal Society; Blind Children
Learning Center

Most grants awarded to organizations
located in areas of company operations.

Typical grant range: $5,000 to $25,000

204
Public Welfare Foundation, Inc.
2600 Virginia Ave., N.W., Room 505
Washington, DC 20037
(202) 965-1800

Mentally disabled; developmentally
disabled; youth; Gallaudet University
(hearing impaired)

205
RJR Nabisco Foundation
1455 Pennsylvania Ave., N.W., Suite 525
Washington, DC 20004
(202) 626-7200

Special Children's School; Children's
Center for the Physically Handicapped

Typical grant range: $50,000 to $250,000

206
Walter G. Ross Foundation
c/o ASB Capital Management Inc.
1101 Pennsylvania Avenue, N.W.
Washington, DC 20004

Mentally and physically disabled;
Gallaudet University (hard-of-hearing)

Most grants awarded to organizations
located in the Washington, DC vicinity.

Typical grant range: $10,000 to $65,000

207
**Alexander and Margaret Stewart Trust
u/w of the late Helen S. Devore**
First American Bank, N.A., Trust Dept.
740 Fifteenth Street, N.W.
Washington, DC 20005
(202) 637-7887

Washington Hearing and Speech Society;
Children's Hearing and Speech Center;
Easter Seal Society; D.C. Institute for
Mental Health; Recording for the Blind;
Center for the Handicapped; Hospital for
Sick Children; Jewish Social Service
Agency (children with disabilities); St.
John's Community Services (children
with autism)

Grants awarded to organizations located
in the Washington, DC vicinity.

Typical grant range: $15,000 to $100,000

FLORIDA

208
Anthony R. Abraham Foundation, Inc.
6600 S.W. 57th Avenue
Miami, FL 33143
(305) 665-2222

Cystic Fibrosis Foundation; School for the
Deaf and Blind

Grants awarded to organizations located
in Miami.

209
Myron H. Ackerman Foundation, Inc.
7209 Promenade Drive, Suite D-201
Boca Raton, FL 33433

Visually impaired; physically disabled

210
Amaturo Foundation
2929 E. Commercial Blvd., PH-C
Fort Lauderdale, FL 33308
(305) 776-7815

Physically disabled; multiple sclerosis
(research)

Grants awarded to organizations located
in Florida.

Typical grant range: $1,000 to $5,000

211
Ruth Anderson Foundation
2511 Ponce De Leon Blvd., Suite 320
Coral Gables, FL 33134
(305) 444-6121

Physically disabled; cultural programs;
youth

Grants awarded to organizations located
in the Miami vicinity.

Typical grant range: $2,500 to $15,000

212
John E. and Nellie J. Bastien
Memorial Foundation
100 E. Sample Road, Suite 240
Pompano Beach, FL 33064
(305) 942-3203

Recording for the Blind; United Cerebral
Palsy; Association for Retarded Citizens;
Goodwill Industries

Grants awarded to organizations located
in Florida.

Typical grant range: $1,000 to $10,000

213
Batchelor Foundation, Inc.
950 S.E. 12th Street
Hialeah, FL 33010

Physically and mentally disabled; youth;
recreation; employment programs

Grants awarded to organizations located
in Florida.

Typical grant range: $500 to $15,000

214
BCR Foundation, Inc.
P.O. Box 13307
Pensacola, FL 32591
(904) 438-2509

Physically disabled; independent living
programs

Grants awarded to organizations located
in Florida.

Typical grant range: $1,000 to $5,000

215
Margaret R. Binz Foundation, Inc.
1825 S. Riverview Drive
Melbourne, FL 32901

Visually impaired; physically disabled;
youth; hospitals

Grants awarded to organizations located
in Florida.

Typical grant range: $1,000 to $15,000

216
Broward Community Foundation, Inc.
2601 E. Oakland Park Blvd., Suite 202
Ft. Lauderdale, FL 33306
(305) 563-4483

Habilitation Center for the Handicapped;
Horses and Handicapped; Mental Health
Association; Lighthouse for the Blind

Grants awarded to organizations located
in Broward County.

Typical grant range: $2,000 to $6,000

217
**Edyth Bush Charitable
Foundation, Inc.**
199 E. Welbourne Avenue
P.O. Box 1967
Winter Park, FL 32790
(407) 647-4322

Mentally and physically disabled

Grants awarded to organizations located
in central Florida.

Typical grant range: $15,000 to $65,000

218
Isaac W. Byrd Family Foundation, Inc.
3310 S. Harbour Circle
Panama City, FL 32405

Physically disabled; mental health

Grants awarded to organizations located
in Panama City.

Typical grant range: $1,000 to $7,000

219
Chatlos Foundation, Inc.
P.O. Box 915048
Longwood, FL 32791
(407) 862-5077

Visually impaired; eye research

Typical grant range: $3,000 to $30,000

220
Barron Collier, Jr. Foundation, Inc.
2600 Golden Gate Parkway, Suite 200
Naples, FL 33942
(813) 262-2600

Training and Education Center for the
Handicapped

Most grants awarded to organizations
located in Collier County.

Typical grant range: $4,000 to $10,000

221
**Community Foundation of
Collier County**
4949 Tamiami Trail North, Suite 202
Naples, FL 33940
(813) 649-5000

Mentally and physically disabled;
recreation; Meals on Wheels (deaf)

Grants awarded to organizations located
in Collier County.

222
**Community Foundation of
Greater Tampa**
315 E. Madison, Suite 600
Tampa, FL 33602
(813) 221-1776

Visually impaired; Goodwill Industries;
National Multiple Sclerosis Society

Grants awarded to organizations located
in the Tampa vicinity.

Typical grant range: $1,500 to $5,000

223
**Community Foundation of Sarasota
County, Inc.**
P.O. Box 49587
Sarasota, FL 34230
(813) 955-3000

Disabled (all areas); recreation; youth

Grants awarded to organizations located
in Sarasota County.

Typical grant range: $500 to $5,000

224
Conn Memorial Foundation, Inc.
5401 Kennedy Blvd. West, Suite 530
Tampa, FL 33609
(813) 282-4922

Visually impaired; physically disabled;
rehabilitation

Grants awarded to organizations located
in the Tampa vicinity.

Typical grant range: $2,000 to $20,000

225
Dade Community Foundation
200 S. Biscayne Blvd., Suite 4770
Miami, FL 33131
(305) 371-2711

Physically and mentally disabled

Grants awarded to organizations located
in Dade County.

Typical grant range: $1,000 to $20,000

226
Alfred I. duPont Foundation
P.O. Box 1380
Jacksonville, FL 32201
(904) 396-6600

Physically disabled; rehabilitation

Typical grant range: $3,000 to $10,000

227
Jessie Ball duPont Fund
225 Water Street, Suite 1200
Jacksonville, FL 32202
(904) 353-0890

Physically and mentally disabled; visually
impaired; accessibility projects

Only previous grant recipients from this
foundation are eligible to apply for
another grant.

Typical grant range: $5,000 to $85,000

228
Jack Eckerd Corporation Foundation
P.O. Box 4689
Clearwater, FL 34618
(813) 398-8318

Disabled (all areas); youth

Grants awarded to organizations located
in areas of company operations.

229
David Falk Foundation, Inc.
c/o SunBank of Tampa Bay
P.O. Box 1498
Tampa, FL 33601
(813) 224-2626

Hard-of-hearing; visually impaired;
Tampa Lighthouse for the Blind;
Easter Seal Society

Grants awarded to organizations located
in the Tampa vicinity.

230
**Jefferson Lee Ford III Memorial
Foundation, Inc.**
c/o Sun Bank
9600 Collins Avenue
P.O. Box 546487
Bal Harbour, FL 33154
(305) 868-2630

Lighthouse for the Blind; Cystic Fibrosis;
Speech Center and Hearing Center;
Crippled Children's Hospital

Grants awarded to organizations located
in Florida.

231
A. Friends' Foundation Trust
9100 Hubbard Place
Orlando, FL 32819
(407) 363-4621

United Cerebral Palsy

232
Charles A. Frueauff Foundation, Inc.
307 E. Seventh Avenue
Tallahassee, FL 32303
(904) 561-3508

Visually impaired; hard-of-hearing;
mental health; physically disabled;
employment programs; education;
Goodwill Industries

Typical grant range: $10,000 to $35,000

233
James P. Gills Foundation, Inc.
P.O. Box 1608
Tarpon Springs, FL 34688
(813) 942-2591

March of Dimes; Pinellas Center for
the Visually Impaired

Typical grant range: $4,000 to $12,000

234
Gore Family Memorial Foundation
4747 N. Ocean Drive, Suite 204
Fort Lauderdale, FL 33302

Physically disabled; accessibility projects;
many grants awarded to individuals with
disabilities

Most grants awarded to organizations
located in Broward County.

235
Grace Foundation, Inc.
One Town Center Road
Boca Raton, FL 33486
(407) 362-1487

Disabled (all areas); independent living
programs; youth; rehabilitation; education

Grants awarded to organizations located
in areas of company operations (W.R.
Grace & Co.).

Typical grant range: $1,000 to $15,000

236
Greenburg-May Foundation, Inc.
P.O. Box 54-6119
Miami Beach, FL 33154
(305) 864-8639

Research to Prevent Blindness; Cerebral
Palsy; March of Dimes

Typical grant range: $3,000 to $10,000

237
Harry J. Heeb Foundation
P.O. Box 3838
Orlando, FL 32802

Visually impaired; mentally disabled;
hard-of-hearing

Grants awarded to organizations located
in Florida.

Typical grant range: $1,000 to $7,500

238
William M. & Nina B. Hollis
Foundation, Inc.
P.O. Box 8847
Lakeland, FL 33806
(813) 646-3980

Central Florida Speech and Hearing
Center; SE Guide Dogs; Goodwill
Industries

Most grants awarded to organizations
located in Lakeland.

Typical grant range: $2,000 to $40,000

239
George W. Jenkins Foundation, Inc.
1936 George Jenkins Blvd.
P.O. Box 407
Lakeland, FL 33802
(813) 688-1188

Disabled (all areas); recreation; youth;
employment programs

Grants awarded to organizations located
in Florida.

Typical grant range: $500 to $25,000

240
John S. and James L. Knight Foundation
One Biscayne Tower, Suite 3800
2 S. Biscayne Blvd.
Miami, FL 33131
(305) 539-0009

Visually impaired; Carolina Computer Access Center (preschool children with disabilities); Special Olympics; Goodwill Industries

Grants awarded to organizations located in areas of company operations (Knight-Ridder Newspapers).

Typical grant range: $10,000 to $125,000

241
Forrest C. Lattner Foundation, Inc.
777 E. Atlantic Avenue, Suite 317
Delray Beach, FL 33483
(407) 278-3781

Mental health; deaf; physically disabled; recreation; Association for Retarded Citizens

Typical grant range: $5,000 to $35,000

242
Joe and Emily Lowe Foundation, Inc.
249 Royal Palm Way
Palm Beach, FL 33480
(407) 655-7001

Mentally and physically disabled; visually impaired; independent living programs

Typical grant range: $1,000 to $7,500

243
Mary E. Parker Foundation
1215 Manatee Avenue West
Bradenton, FL 34205
(813) 748-3666

Special Olympics; March of Dimes Birth Defects Foundation; Southeastern Guide Dogs; Association for Retarded Citizens

Grants awarded to organizations located in Florida.

Typical grant range: $1,000 to $25,000

244
Dr. P. Phillips Foundation
60 W. Robinson Street
P.O. Box 3753
Orlando, FL 32802
(407) 422-6105

Physically disabled; mental health; Russell Home for Atypical Children

Grants awarded to organizations located in Orange County.

Typical grant range: $1,000 to $30,000

245
John E. & Aliese Price Foundation, Inc.
1279 Lavin Lane
P.O. Box 4607
North Fort Myers, FL 33918
(813) 656-0196

Mentally and physically disabled; visually impaired

Typical grant range: $500 to $8,000

246
William G. Selby and Marie Selby Foundation
Southeast Bank
P.O. Box 267
Sarasota, FL 34230
(813) 957-0442

Visually impaired; physically disabled; Association for Retarded Citizens

Typical grant range: $5,000 to $45,000

247
Jimmie Sikes Foundation
One Sikes Blvd.
P.O. Box 447
Lakeland, FL 33802
(813) 687-7171

Physically and mentally disabled; recreation

Typical grant range: $200 to $5,000

248
Southwest Florida Community Foundation, Inc.
P.O. Box 9326
Fort Myers, FL 33902
(813) 334-0377

Mental health; independent living program; Deaf Service Center; Easter Seal Society

Grants awarded to organizations located in Southwest Florida.

Typical grant range: $3,000 to $12,000

249
George B. Storer Foundation, Inc.
91551 Overseas Highway
P.O. Box 1427
Tavernier, FL 33070
(305) 852-3323

Visually impaired; physically disabled

Grants awarded to organizations located in Florida.

Typical grant range: $5,000 to $50,000

250
Robert Lee Turner Foundation, Inc.
300 S. Ocean Blvd.
Palm Beach, FL 33480
(407) 655-0755

Goodwill Industries; Hough Ear Institute

Typical grant range: $500 to $2,000

251
United States Sugar Corporation Charitable Trust
c/o United States Sugar Corporation
P.O. Drawer 1207
Clewiston, FL 33440
(813) 983-8121

Mentally and physically disabled; hard-of-hearing; eye research

Grants awarded to organizations located in Florida.

252
Wahlstrom Foundation, Inc.
2855 Ocean Drive, Suite D-4
Vero Beach, FL 32963
(407) 231-0373

Mentally and physically disabled

Grants awarded to organizations located in Indian River County.

Typical grant range: $500 to $5,000

253
Walter Foundation
1500 N. Dale Mabry Highway
P.O. Box 31601
Tampa, FL 33631
(813) 871-4168

Helen Keller Eye Research Foundation; Crippled Children's Foundation

Most grants awarded to organizations located in Florida.

Typical grant range: $250 to $7,500

254
Joseph Weintraub Family Foundation, Inc.
200 S.E. First Street, Suite 901
Miami, FL 33131

Miami Lighthouse for the Blind

Grants awarded to organizations located in Florida.

Typical grant range: $1,000 to $12,000

255
Hugh and Mary Wilson Foundation, Inc.
7188 Beneva Road South
Sarasota, FL 34238
(813) 921-2856

Goodwill Industries; Pinellas Center for the Visually Impaired; Southeastern Guide Dogs; Lighthouse for the Blind

Typical grant range: $1,000 to $20,000

GEORGIA

256
Bradley-Turner Foundation
P.O. Box 140
Columbus, GA 31902
(404) 571-6040

Mental health; hard-of-hearing;
physically disabled

Grants awarded to organizations located
in Georgia, with an emphasis in
Columbus.

Typical grant range: $2,500 to $45,000

257
Callaway Foundation, Inc.
209 Broome Street
P.O. Box 790
LaGrange, GA 30241
(706) 884-7348

Disabled (all areas); youth; hospitals;
research; mental health; recreation

Most grants awarded to organizations
located in the La Grange vicinity.

Typical grant range: $1,000 to $85,000

258
Fuller E. Callaway Foundation
209 Broome Street
P.O. Box 790
LaGrange, GA 30241
(404) 884-7348

Georgia Chapter of National Multiple
Sclerosis Society; Scottish Rite Hospital
for Crippled Children

Most grants awarded to organizations
located in the La Grange vicinity.

Typical grant range: $500 to $20,000

259
Equifax Foundation
c/o Equifax Inc.
1600 Peachtree Street, N.W.
Atlanta, GA 30309
(404) 885-8301

Mentally and physically disabled

Grants awarded to organizations located
in Georgia.

260
Exposition Foundation, Inc.
520 E. Paces Ferry Road, N.E.
Atlanta, GA 30305
(404) 233-6404

Atlanta Speech School; Friends of
Disabled Adults; Canine Assistants

Grants awarded to organizations located
in Georgia.

Typical grant range: $1,000 to $4,000

261
**Isobel A. Fraser & Nancy F. Parker
Charitable Trust**
1530 Trust Co. Tower
Atlanta, GA 30303
(404) 658-9980

Atlanta Speech School; Shepherd Spinal
Center; Stuttering Foundation of America

Most grants awarded to organizations
located in Atlanta.

Typical grant range: $3,000 to $20,000

262
**Lenora and Alfred Glancy
Foundation, Inc.**
One Atlantic Center, Suite 4200
1201 W. Peachtree Street
Atlanta, GA 30309
(404) 881-7000

Canine Assistance

263
John H. and Wilhelmina D. Harland Charitable Foundation, Inc.
Two Piedmont Center, Suite 106
Atlanta, GA 30305
(404) 264-9912

Center for the Visually Impaired; Hillside Psychiatry Hospital; Friends of Disabled Adults; Cystic Fibrosis Camp of Georgia; Society to Prevent Blindness; Easter Seal Society; Lions Eye Bank

Grants awarded to organizations located in Georgia, with an emphasis in Atlanta.

Typical grant range: $5,000 to $35,000

264
John P. and Dorothy S. Illges Foundation, Inc.
945 Broadway
Columbus, GA 31901

Special Olympics; Lions Eye Bank

Typical grant range: $2,000 to $15,000

265
Ray M. and Mary Elizabeth Lee Foundation, Inc.
c/o NationsBank
P.O. Box 4446
Atlanta, GA 30302
(404) 607-4530

Visually impaired; Goodwill Industries; Shepherd Spinal Center; National Multiple Sclerosis Society; Special Olympics; Epilepsy Foundation; Society to Prevent Blindness

Most grants awarded to organizations located in the Atlanta vicinity.

Typical grant range: $2,000 to $25,000

266
Loretta Haley McKnight Charitable Trust Fund
First State Bank and Trust Co.
P.O. Box 8
Albany, GA 31702

Easter Seal Society

Grants awarded to organizations located in Albany.

Typical grant range: $500 to $5,000

267
Metropolitan Atlanta Community Foundation, Inc.
The Hurt Building, Suite 449
Atlanta, GA 30303
(404) 688-5525

Developmentally disabled; mental health; rehabilitation; education

Grants awarded to organizations located in the Atlanta vicinity.

Typical grant range: $2,000 to $15,000

268
Albert N. Parker Charitable Trust
c/o Trust Company Bank
P.O. Box 4655
Atlanta, GA 30302
(404) 588-8449

Speech impaired; education

Most grants awarded to organizations located in Atlanta.

269
James Hyde Porter Testamentary Trust
Trust Co. Bank of Middle Georgia, N.A.
606 Cherry Street, P.O. Box 4248
Macon, GA 31208
(912) 741-2265

Mentally disabled; Trust for Historic Preservation (construction of restrooms for people with disabilities)

Typical grant range: $5,000 to $25,000

270
Rich Foundation, Inc.
10 Piedmont Center, Suite 802
Atlanta, GA 30305
(404) 262-2266

Shepherd's Spinal Clinic; Cystic
Fibrosis Camp

Grants awarded to organizations located
in the Atlanta vicinity.

Typical grant range: $1,500 to $20,000

271
South Atlantic Foundation, Inc.
428 Bull Street
Savannah, GA 31401
(912) 231-3288

Hearing impaired; learning disabled

272
Joseph B. Whitehead Foundation
50 Hurt Plaza, Suite 1200
Atlanta, GA 30303
(404) 522-6755

Mentally and physically disabled;
employment programs; recreation;
education; Easter Seal Society

Grants awarded to organizations located
in the Atlanta vicinity.

Typical grant range: $50,000 to $400,000

273
Frances Wood Wilson Foundation, Inc.
1501 Clairmont Road, Suite 104
Decatur, GA 30033
(404) 634-3363

Shepherd's Spinal Center; Special
Olympics

Most grants awarded to organizations
located in Georgia.

Typical grant range: $5,000 to $25,000

274
**David, Helen and Marian Woodward
Fund-Atlanta**
Wachovia Bank of Georgia, N.A.
191 Peachtree Street
Atlanta, GA 30303
(404) 332-6677

Georgia Eye Bank; Shepherd's Spinal
Center; Auditory Education Center;
Cystic Fibrosis Camp

Grants awarded to organizations located
in the Atlanta vicinity.

Typical grant range: $5,000 to $40,000

HAWAII

275
Barbara Cox Anthony Foundation
1132 Bishop Street, No. 120
Honolulu, HI 96813

Easter Seal Society; Hawaii Mental
Health Center; National Multiple
Sclerosis Society; March of Dimes

Grants awarded to organizations located
in Hawaii.

276
Atherton Family Foundation
c/o Hawaii Community Foundation
222 Merchant Street
Honolulu, HI 96813
(808) 537-6333

Physically disabled; Learning Disabilities
Association

Grants awarded to organizations located
in Hawaii.

Typical grant range: $2,000 to $20,000

277

Harold K.L. Castle Foundation
146 Hekili Street
Kailua, HI 96734
(808) 262-9413

Special education; Therapeutic
Horsemanship for the Handicapped

Grants awarded to organizations located
in Hawaii.

Typical grant range: $20,000 to $175,000

278

Samuel N. and Mary Castle Foundation
222 Merchant Street
Honolulu, HI 96813
(808) 537-6333

Physically disabled; independent living
programs; Special Education Center
(recreation)

Grants awarded to organizations located
in Hawaii.

Typical grant range: $2,500 to $20,000

279

Cooke Foundation, Limited
c/o Hawaiian Trust Co., Ltd.
P.O. Box 3170
Honolulu, HI 96802
(808) 537-6333

Developmentally disabled; physically
disabled; youth; Learning Disabilities
Association; Mental Health Association

Grants awarded to organizations located
in Hawaii.

Typical grant range: $2,000 to $15,000

280

**Mary D. and Walter F. Frear
Eleemosynary Trust**
c/o Bishop Trust Co., Ltd.
1000 Bishop Street
Honolulu, HI 96813
(808) 523-2234

Mentally and physically disabled;
learning disabled

Grants awarded to organizations located
in Hawaii.

Typical grant range: $1,000 to $8,000

281

Hawaii Community Foundation
222 Merchant Street
Honolulu, HI 96813
(808) 537-6333

Learning Disabilities Association
(education program for children); Waikiki
Health Center (accessibility project);
Mental Health Association; Persons-In-
Need (physically disabled); Autism
Society of Hawaii

Grants awarded to organizations located
in Hawaii.

Typical grant range: $3,000 to $40,000

282

McInerny Foundation
c/o Bishop Trust Co., Ltd.
1000 Bishop Street
Honolulu, HI 96813
(808) 523-2234

Mentally and physically disabled; hard-of-
hearing; learning disabled

Grants awarded to organizations located
in Hawaii.

Typical grant range: $5,000 to $20,000

283
O. L. Moore Foundation
100 Ridge Road
Lahaina, HI 96761

Mentally and physically disabled

Most grants awarded to organizations
located in Hawaii.

284
Sophie Russell Testamentary Trust
c/o Bishop Trust Co., Ltd.
1000 Bishop Street
Honolulu, HI 96813
(808) 523-2233

Physically disabled; rehabilitation;
education; employment programs

Grants awarded to organizations located
in Hawaii.

Typical grant range: $5,000 to $10,000

285
A. & E. Vidinha Charitable Trust
c/o Bishop Trust Co., Ltd.
1000 Bishop Street
Honolulu, HI 96813
(808) 523-2234

Easter Seal Society; Hawaii Special
Olympics

Grants awarded to organizations located
in Kauai.

Typical grant range: $6,000 to $30,000

IDAHO

286
**Laura Moore Cunningham
Foundation, Inc.**
510 Main
Boise, ID 83702
(208) 347-7852

Mentally disabled

Grants awarded to organizations located
in Idaho.

Typical grant range: $2,000 to $15,000

287
Daugherty Foundation
c/o West One Bank, Idaho, N.A.
P.O. Box 7928
Boise, ID 83707

Special Olympics; Elks Rehabilitation

288
Idaho Community Foundation
205 N. 10th Street, Suite 625
Boise, ID 83702
(208) 342-3535

Multiple Sclerosis Society; Resources for
the Blind; Special Olympics; Glenns Ferry
Historical Museum (accessibility project)

Grants awarded to organizations located
in Idaho.

Typical grant range: $500 to $5,000

289
Harry W. Morrison Foundation, Inc.
3505 Crescent Rim Drive
Boise, ID 83706

Special Olympics

Grants awarded to organizations located
in Boise.

Typical grant range: $500 to $10,000

290
Ray Foundation
P.O. Box 2156
Ketchum, ID 83340

NW School for Hearing Impaired
Children; Community Psychiatric Clinic

Typical grant range: $3,000 to $30,000

ILLINOIS

291
G.J. Aigner Foundation, Inc.
5617 Dempster Street
Morton Grove, IL 60053
(708) 966-5782

Mentally disabled; independent living;
vocational training; Easter Seal Society;
Christian League for the Handicapped

Typical grant range: $1,000 to $5,000

292
Amoco Foundation, Inc.
200 E. Randolph Drive
Chicago, IL 60601
(312) 856-6305

Disabled (all areas); youth; recreation;
employment programs; Cystic Fibrosis
Foundation

Grants awarded to organizations located
in areas of company operations.

Typical grant range: $4,000 to $60,000

293
Francis Beidler Charitable Trust
53 W. Jackson Blvd., Suite 530
Chicago, IL 60604
(312) 922-3792

Hadley School for the Blind; Illinois
Society to Prevent Blindness

Grants awarded to organizations located
in Illinois.

294
Bersted Foundation
c/o Continental National Bank, N.A.
30 N. LaSalle Street
Chicago, IL 60697
(312) 828-8026

Physically disabled; mental health

Grants awarded to organizations located
in McHenry, DeKalb, Kane and DuPage
Counties.

295
Blowitz-Ridgeway Foundation
2700 River Road, Suite 211
Des Plaines, IL 60018
(708) 298-2378

Mentally disabled; independent living
programs; Special Olympics; Housing
Options for the Mentally Ill

Grants awarded to organizations located
in Illinois.

Typical grant range: $2,000 to $25,000

296
Blum-Kovler Foundation
919 N. Michigan Avenue
Chicago, IL 60611
(312) 664-5050

Mentally and physically disabled;
visually impaired

Grants awarded to organizations located
in the Chicago vicinity.

Typical grant range: $1,000 to $10,000

297
Helen Brach Foundation
55 W. Wacker Drive, Suite 701
Chicago, IL 60601
(312) 372-4417

Physically and mentally disabled

Typical grant range: $1,000 to $65,000

298
Caterpillar Foundation
100 N.E. Adams Street
Peoria, IL 61629

Physically disabled; Easter Seal Center

Grants awarded to organizations located
in areas of company operations.

Typical grant range: $5,000 to $50,000

299
Chicago Community Trust
222 N. LaSalle Street, Suite 1400
Chicago, IL 60601
(312) 372-3356

Visually impaired; youth; Mental Health
Association; Alliance for the Mentally Ill;
Center for the Rehabilitation and Training
of Persons with Disabilities

Grants awarded to organizations located
in the Chicago vicinity.

Typical grant range: $15,000 to $70,000

300
Coleman Foundation, Inc.
575 W. Madison, Suite 4605-II
Chicago, IL 60661
(312) 902-7120

Mentally disabled; Rehabilitation Institute of Chicago; Family Services and Mental Health Center

Grants awarded to organizations located in the Chicago vicinity.

Typical grant range: $1,000 to $50,000

301
Arie and Ida Crown Memorial
222 N. LaSalle Street
Chicago, IL 60601
(312) 236-6300

Mentally and physically disabled; hard-of-hearing

Most grants awarded to organizations located in the Chicago vicinity.

Typical grant range: $1,000 to $20,000

302
Doris and Victor Day Foundation, Inc.
1705 Second Avenue, Suite 424
Rock Island, IL 61201
(309) 788-2300

Physically disabled (recreation); Association for Retarded Citizens

Grants awarded to organizations located in the Illinois/Iowa Quad Cities.

Typical grant range: $1,000 to $15,000

303
Evanston Community Foundation
828 Davis Street, Suite 300
Evanston, IL 60201
(708) 475-2402

Mental health; physically disabled

Grants awarded to organizations located in Evanston.

Typical grant range: $1,000 to $12,000

304
Field Foundation of Illinois, Inc.
200 S. Wacker Drive, Suite 4
Chicago, IL 60606
(312) 831-0910

Visually impaired; developmentally disabled; mentally disabled; independent living

Grants awarded to organizations located in the Chicago vicinity.

Typical grant range: $5,000 to $45,000

305
Frankel Foundation
c/o Harris Trust & Savings Bank
111 W. Monroe Street
Chicago, IL 60603

Hard-of-hearing; visually impaired

Grants awarded to organizations located in Illinois.

306
Lloyd A. Fry Foundation
135 S. LaSalle Street, Suite 1910
Chicago, IL 60603
(312) 580-0310

Physically disabled; learning disabled; employment programs; youth

Grants awarded to organizations located in the Chicago vicinity.

Typical grant range: $2,000 to $40,000

307
Robert W. Galvin Foundation
1303 E. Algonquin Road
Schaumburg, IL 60196
(708) 576-5300

Ecker Center for Mental Health; Association for the Handicapped

Grants awarded to organizations located in Illinois.

308
Harris Family Foundation
P.O. Box 2279
Northbrook, IL 60065
(708) 498-1261

Visually impaired; speech impaired;
education; rehabilitation; Foundation for
Hearing and Speech Rehabilitation;
Special Olympics; Chicago Lighthouse
for the Blind

Most grants awarded to organizations
located in Chicago.

Typical grant range: $1,000 to $10,000

309
Grover Hermann Foundation
c/o Schiff, Hardin & Waite
7200 Sears Tower, 233 S. Wacker Drive
Chicago, IL 60606
(312) 876-1000

Visually impaired; hard-of-hearing

Typical grant range: $1,000 to $40,000

310
Illinois Tool Works Foundation
3600 W. Lake Avenue
Glenview, IL 60025
(708) 724-7500

Physically disabled

Grants awarded to organizations located
in areas of company operations, with an
emphasis in Chicago.

Typical grant range: $1,000 to $15,000

311
Joyce Foundation
135 S. LaSalle Street, Suite 4010
Chicago, IL 60603
(312) 782-2464

Mentally and physically disabled;
education

Typical grant range: $5,000 to $75,000

312
**Mayer and Morris Kaplan
Family Foundation**
191 Waukegan Road
Northfield, IL 60093
(708) 441-6630

Hadley School for the Blind

313
**Donald P. and Byrd M. Kelly
Foundation**
701 Harger Road, Suite 150
Oak Brook, IL 60521

Residence for Retarded and Autistic
Families

Most grants awarded to organizations
located in the Chicago vicinity.

Typical grant range: $1,000 to $12,000

314
**Charles G. and Rheta Kramer
Foundation**
c/o The Ross Group, Inc.
101 W. Grand Avenue, Suite 500
Chicago, IL 60610
(312) 527-4747

Chicago Hearing Society; School for
Autistic Children; Chicago Club for
Crippled Children

Grants awarded to organizations located
in Chicago.

Typical grant range: $250 to $4,000

315
Otto W. Lehmann Foundation
P.O. Box 11194
Chicago, IL 60611

Association for Retarded Citizens; Hadley
School for the Blind; Illinois Society to
Prevent Blindness; Mental Health
Association; Peacock Camp for Crippled
Children

Grants awarded to organizations located
in the Chicago vicinity.

316
Leslie Fund, Inc.
One Northfield Plaza
Northfield, IL 60093
(708) 441-2613

Hard-of-hearing; visually impaired;
education

Grants awarded to organizations located
in Illinois.

Typical grant range: $1,000 to $10,000

317
**Robert R. McCormick Tribune
Foundation**
435 N. Michigan Avenue, Suite 770
Chicago, IL 60611
(312) 222-3512

Mentally and physically disabled; visually
impaired; emotionally disturbed;
rehabilitation; employment programs;
youth; recreation; United Cerebral Palsy
Association; DuPage Easter Seal
Treatment Center; National Down
Syndrome Congress; Chicago Lighthouse
for the Blind; Association for Retarded
Citizens; Boy Scouts of America
(program for children with disabilities)

Grants awarded to organizations located
in the Chicago vicinity.

Typical grant range: $5,000 to $75,000

318
Motorola Foundation
1303 E. Algonquin Road
Schaumburg, IL 60196
(708) 576-6200

Physically and mentally disabled;
visually impaired; recreation

Grants awarded to organizations located
in areas of company operations.

Typical grant range: $500 to $12,000

319
Nalco Foundation
One Nalco Center
Naperville, IL 60563
(708) 305-1556

Disabled (all areas); mental health; youth;
United Cerebral Palsy; Lighthouse for the
Blind

Grants awarded to organizations located
in areas of company operations.

Typical grant range: $1,000 to $12,000

320
OMRON Foundation, Inc.
1375 E. Woodfield Road, Suite 520
Schaumburg, IL 60173
(708) 240-5330

Muscular Dystrophy Association;
National Multiple Sclerosis; Illinois
Special Olympics

Most grants awarded to organizations
located in Chicago.

321
**Frank E. Payne and Seba B. Payne
Foundation**
c/o Continental Bank, N.A.
30 N. LaSalle Street
Chicago, IL 60697
(312) 828-1785

Physically disabled; Recording for the
Blind

Typical grant range: $10,000 to $95,000

322
Polk Bros. Foundation, Inc.
420 N. Wabash Avenue, Suite 204
Chicago, IL 60611
(312) 527-4684

Physically and mentally disabled; mental
health; developmentally disabled;
emotionally disturbed; independent living
programs; education

Grants awarded to organizations located
in the Chicago vicinity.

Typical grant range: $2,000 to $35,000

323
Regenstein Foundation
8600 W. Bryn Mawr Ave., Suite 705N
Chicago, IL 60631
(312) 693-6464

Recording for the Blind; Bureau for the Blind and Physically Handicapped

Grants awarded to organizations located in the Chicago vicinity.

Typical grant range: $500 to $100,000

324
Rockford Community Trust
321 W. State Street, 13th Floor
Rockford, IL 61101
(815) 962-2110

Mentally and physically disabled; speech impaired; youth; recreation; Center for Sight and Hearing Impaired; New American Theatre (equipment for hearing impaired)

Grants awarded to organizations located in the Rockford vicinity.

Typical grant range: $500 to $8,000

325
Rockford Products Corporation Foundation
707 Harrison Avenue
Rockford, IL 61104
(815) 397-6000

Center for Sight and Hearing; United Cerebral Palsy

Grants awarded to organizations located in Rockford.

Typical grant range: $500 to $5,000

326
Dr. Scholl Foundation
11 S. LaSalle Street, Suite 2100
Chicago, IL 60603
(312) 782-5210

Deaf; physically disabled; visually impaired; developmentally disabled; employment programs; youth; recreation

Typical grant range: $5,000 to $40,000

327
Fred B. Snite Foundation
550 Frontage Road, Suite 3082
Northfield, IL 60093
(312) 446-7705

Hadley School for the Blind

328
Solo Cup Foundation
1700 Old Deerfield Road
Highland Park, IL 60035

Visually impaired; physically disabled

Typical grant range: $5,000 to $25,000

329
Donna Wolf Steigerwaldt Foundation, Inc.
200 N. LaSalle Street, Suite 2100
Chicago, IL 60601

Easter Seal Society; Cerebral Palsy Respite Assistance Program; Association for Retarded Citizens

Most grants awarded to preselected organizations.

330
Irvin Stern Foundation
116 W. Illinois Street
Chicago, IL 60610
(312) 321-9402

Mental health; physically disabled

Typical grant range: $4,000 to $20,000

331
Sunstrand Corporation Foundation
4949 Harrison Avenue
P.O. Box 7003
Rockford, IL 61125
(815) 226-6000

Association for Retarded Citizens; Goodwill Industries; Special Olympics

Grants awarded to organizations located in areas of company operations.

Typical grant range: $1,000 to $15,000

332
Walgreen Benefit Fund
200 Wilmot Road
Deerfield, IL 60015
(708) 940-2931

Physically disabled; mental health

Typical grant range: $500 to $3,000

333
**Washington Square Health
Foundation, Inc.**
875 N. Michigan Avenue, Suite 3516
Chicago, IL 60611
(312) 664-6488

Physically disabled; visually impaired

Grants awarded to organizations located
in the Chicago vicinity.

334
Howard L. Willet Foundation, Inc.
111 W. Washington Street, Suite 1900
Chicago, IL 60602
(312) 407-7800

Mentally and physically disabled;
visually impaired; youth

Grants awarded to organizations located
in the Chicago vicinity.

335
Woods Charitable Fund, Inc.
Three First National Plaza, Suite 2010
Chicago, IL 60602
(312) 782-2698

Physically disabled; vocational training

Typical grant range: $10,000 to $35,000

INDIANA

336
John W. Anderson Foundation
402 Wall Street
Valparaiso, IN 46383
(219) 462-4611

Disabled (all areas); recreation;
employment programs; rehabilitation;
Cerebral Palsy of Northwest Indiana

Typical grant range: $5,000 to $30,000

337
Arvin Foundation, Inc.
One Noblitt Plaza
Box 3000
Columbus, IN 47202
(812) 379-3285

United Cerebral Palsy; Multiple Sclerosis
Society; March of Dimes; Special
Olympics; Mental Health Association;
Eye-Sight Hospital-Lions Club; Cystic
Fibrosis; School for the Deaf and Blind;
Muscular Dystrophy Association

Grants awarded to organizations located
in areas of company operations (Arvin
Industries).

Typical grant range: $100 to $4,000

338
Ball Brothers Foundation
222 S. Mulberry Street
P.O. Box 1408
Muncie, IN 47308

Mentally and physically disabled;
Therapeutic Riding

Grants awarded to organizations located
in Indiana.

Typical grant range: $1,500 to $30,000

339
George and Frances Ball Foundation
P.O. Box 1408
Muncie, IN 47308
(317) 741-5500

Indiana Therapeutic Riding; Indiana
Special Olympics; Very Special Arts

Grants awarded to organizations located
in Muncie.

Typical grant range: $10,000 to $70,000

340
Robert Lee Blaffer Trust
P.O. Box 581
New Harmony, IN 47631
(812) 682-4431

Very Special Arts

Grants awarded to organizations located
in Indiana.

341
Clowes Fund, Inc.
250 E. 38th Street
Indianapolis, IN 46205
(317) 923-3264

Visually impaired; employment programs;
Bosma Industries for the Blind; Delaware
County Special Education; Recording for
the Blind

Typical grant range: $3,000 to $40,000

342
Olive B. Cole Foundation, Inc.
6207 Constitution Drive
Fort Wayne, IN 46804
(219) 436-2182

Radio Reading Service; Chamber of
Commerce (accessibility project)

Typical grant range: $3,000 to $15,000

343
**Community Foundation of Muncie and
Delaware County, Inc.**
P.O. Box 807
Muncie, IN 47308
(317) 747-7181

Physically disabled

Grants awarded to organizations located
in Muncie and Delaware County.

Typical grant range: $2,000 to $12,000

344
Foellinger Foundation
520 E. Berry Street
Ft. Wayne, IN 46802
(219) 422-2900

Visually impaired; mentally and
physically disabled; rehabilitation

Grants awarded to organizations located
in the Ft. Wayne vicinity.

Typical grant range: $8,000 to $150,000

345
Ford Meter Box Foundation, Inc.
775 Manchester Avenue
P.O. Box 443
Wabash, IN 46992

Indiana Society to Prevent Blindness

Typical grant range: $500 to $10,000

346
**Fort Wayne Community
Foundation, Inc.**
709 S. Clinton Street
Fort Wayne, IN 46802
(219) 426-4083

Mentally and physically disabled;
mental health

Grants awarded to organizations located
in the Ft. Wayne vicinity.

Typical grant range: $2,000 to $10,000

347
**Eugene and Marilyn Glick
Foundation Corporation**
P.O. Box 40177
Indianapolis, IN 46240
(317) 469-5858

Dyslexia Institute of Indiana; Central
Indiana Radio Reading; Indiana Society
to Prevent Blindness

Grants awarded to organizations located
in the Indianapolis vicinity.

348
W.C. Griffith Foundation
c/o National City Bank, Indiana
P.O. Box 5031
Indianapolis, IN 46255
(317) 267-7281

Visually impaired; Goodwill Industries

Most grants awarded to organizations
located in Indianapolis.

349
Hook Drug Foundation
2800 Enterprise Street
Indianapolis, IN 46219

Physically disabled; mental health; youth;
recreation; cultural programs

Typical grant range: $500 to $10,000

350
Indianapolis Foundation
615 N. Alabama Street
Indianapolis, IN 46204
(317) 634-7497

Dyslexia; employment programs;
accessibility projects; Very Special Arts;
Indiana Alliance for the Mentally Ill;
Indiana Foundation of Dentistry for the
Handicapped

Grants awarded to organizations located
in the Indianapolis vicinity.

Typical grant range: $5,000 to $75,000

351
Journal Gazette Foundation, Inc.
701 S. Clinton Street
Fort Wayne, IN 46802
(219) 461-8202

Very Special Arts

Typical grant range: $500 to $5,000

352
Eli Lilly and Company Foundation
Lilly Corporate Center
Indianapolis, IN 46285
(317) 276-5342

Mentally disabled; mental health;
recreation; Special Olympics

Grants awarded to organizations located
in areas of company operations, with an
emphasis in Indianapolis.

Typical grant range: $5,000 to $100,000

353
Martin Foundation, Inc.
500 Simpson Avenue
Elkhart, IN 46515
(219) 295-3343

Physically disabled; mental health

Grants awarded to organizations located
in Indiana.

Typical grant range: $1,000 to $20,000

354
**Nicholas H. Noyes, Jr. Memorial
Foundation, Inc.**
Lilly Corporate Center
Indianapolis, IN 46285
(317) 276-3171

American Foundation for the Blind;
Rehabilitation Center; Indiana Foundation
of Dentistry for the Handicapped; Indiana
Society to Prevent Blindness

Grants awarded to organizations located
in Indiana.

355
M.E. Raker Foundation
6207 Constitution Drive
Fort Wayne, IN 46804
(219) 436-2182

Mentally disabled; St. Francis College
(accessibility project)

Grants awarded to organizations located
in Indiana, with an emphasis in Fort
Wayne.

356
Vanderburgh Community Foundation
c/o Community Foundation Alliance
123 N.W. 4th Street, Suite 216
Evansville, IN 47708
(812) 429-1191

Goodwill Industries; The Rehabilitation
Center; Association for Retarded Citizens

IOWA

357
Roy J. Carver Charitable Trust
P.O. Box 76
Muscatine, IA 52761
(319) 263-4010

Mentally disabled; visually impaired;
higher education; recreation

Grants awarded to organizations located
in Iowa.

Typical grant range: $25,000 to $200,000

358
**John K. and Luise V. Hanson
Foundation**
P.O. Box 450
Forest City, IA 50436

Physically disabled; visually impaired

359
Hawley Foundation
1530 Financial Center
666 Walnut
Des Moines, IA 50309
(515) 280-7071

Mentally and physically disabled; visually
impaired; youth; recreation

Grants awarded to organizations located
in the Des Moines vicinity.

Typical grant range: $2,500 to $6,000

360
Kinney-Lindstrom Foundation, Inc.
P.O. Box 520
Mason City, IA 50401
(515) 896-3888

Mentally and physically disabled;
cultural programs

Grants awarded to organizations located
in Iowa.

Typical grant range: $1,000 to $20,000

361
Fred Maytag Family Foundation
200 First Street South
P.O. Box 426
Newton, IA 50208
(515) 792-1800

Mentally and physically disabled;
visually impaired

Most grants awarded to organizations
located in Newton and Des Moines.

Typical grant range: $2,000 to $30,000

362
Mid-Iowa Health Foundation
550 39th Street, Suite 104
Des Moines, IA 50312
(515) 277-6411

Physically disabled; autism; mental
health; housing

Most grants awarded to organizations
located in Polk County.

363
Pella Rolscreen Foundation
c/o Rolscreen Corporation
102 Main Street
Pella, IA 50219
(515) 628-1000

National Multiple Sclerosis Society;
Easter Seal Society

Grants awarded to organizations located
in areas of company operations.

Typical grant range: $300 to $8,000

364
Hobart A. and Alta V. Ross Family Foundation
P.O. Box AK
Spirit Lake, IA 51360

Physically disabled; employment programs; youth; Iowa Special Olympics

Grants awarded to organizations located in Dickinson County.

Typical grant range: $500 to $5,000

365
Wahlert Foundation
c/o FDL Foods, Inc.
P.O. Box 898
Dubuque, IA 52001
(319) 588-5400

Physically disabled; Gannon Center for Mental Health

Grants awarded to organizations located in the Dubuque vicinity.

Typical grant range: $500 to $10,000

KANSAS

366
Bank IV Charitable Trust
c/o Bank IV Kansas, N.A.
P.O. Box 1122
Wichita, KS 67201
(316) 261-4361

Starkey Development Center for the Retarded; Kansas Elks Training Center for Handicapped

Grants awarded to organizations located in areas of company operations (Kansas).

Typical grant range: $1,000 to $15,000

367
Beech Aircraft Foundation
9709 E. Central Avenue
Wichita, KS 67201
(316) 681-8177

Cystic Fibrosis Research Foundation; Guide Dog Foundation for the Blind; Special Olympics; Goodwill Industries; Easter Seal Society

Grants awarded to organizations located in areas of company operations, with an emphasis in Kansas.

Typical grant range: $1,500 to $75,000

368
Charles E. Carey Foundation, Inc.
P.O. Box 1488
Hutchinson, KS 67504

County Mental Health Association; Horizons Mental Health Center

Grants awarded to organizations located in the Hutchinson vicinity.

369
Cessna Foundation, Inc.
P.O. Box 7704
Wichita, KS 67277
(316) 941-6000

Physically disabled; employment programs; research

Grants awarded to organizations located in areas of company operations, with an emphasis in Kansas.

Typical grant range: $1,000 to $15,000

370
DeVore Foundation, Inc.
P.O. Box 118
Wichita, KS 67201
(316) 267-3211

Physically disabled; National Multiple Sclerosis Society; Special Olympics; Association for Retarded Citizens

Grants awarded to organizations located in the Wichita vicinity.

Typical grant range: $100 to $1,500

371
Garvey Foundation
300 W. Douglas Street
Wichita, KS 67202

Physically disabled; employment projects;
Special Olympics; Recording for the
Blind

372
Olive White Garvey Trust
300 W. Douglas Street, Suite 1000
Wichita, KS 67202

American Printing House for the Blind;
Cerebral Palsy; National Federation for
the Blind; Society for Crippled Children;
Paralyzed Veterans of America

Most grants awarded to preselected
organizations.

373
Gault-Hussey Charitable Trust
c/o Bank IV Topeka, N.A., Trust Dept.
P.O. Box 88
Topeka, KS 66601
(913) 295-3463

Physically disabled; Kansas Specialty
Dog Services; Kansas Head Injury
Association

Typical grant range: $500 to $5,000

374
Dane G. Hansen Foundation
P.O. Box 187
Logan, KS 67646
(913) 689-4832

Cystic Fibrosis Foundation; Kansas Elks
Training for the Handicapped; National
Multiple Sclerosis Society; Kansas
Special Olympics; Kansas Society for
Crippled Children

Typical grant range: $3,000 to $25,000

375
David H. Koch Charitable Foundation
4111 E. 37th Street, North
Wichita, KS 67220

Physically disabled; House Ear Institute
(research)

Typical grant range: $15,000 to $120,000

376
Henry Krause Charitable Foundation
P.O. Box 2707
Hutchinson, KS 67504
(316) 663-6161

Special Olympics; Training Center for the
Handicapped; Mental Health Association

Grants awarded to organizations located
in Kansas.

Typical grant range: $1,000 to $10,000

377
Marley Fund
1900 Shawnee Mission Parkway
Mission Woods, KS 66205
(913) 362-1818

Children's Center for Visually Impaired;
Cerebral Palsy

Grants awarded to organizations located
in areas of company operations.

378
Price R. and Flora A. Reid Foundation
P.O. Box 1122
Wichita, KS 67201

Cerebral Palsy Research Foundation;
National Multiple Sclerosis Society;
Association for Retarded Citizens;
Goodwill Industries; Easter Seal Society;
Wichita Industries and Services for the
Blind

Most grants awarded to organizations
located in the Wichita vicinity.

Typical grant range: $100 to $1,500

379
Ethel and Raymond F. Rice Foundation
700 Massachusetts Street
Lawrence, KS 66044
(913) 843-0420

Mentally and physically disabled; mental health; recreation; youth

Grants awarded to organizations located in the Lawrence vicinity.

Typical grant range: $1,000 to $8,000

KENTUCKY

380
James Graham Brown Foundation, Inc.
132 E. Gray Street
Louisville, KY 40202
(502) 583-4085

American Printing House for the Blind; Louisville Deaf Oral School; Kentucky Lions Eye Foundation; Easter Seal Society; March of Dimes; Visually Impaired Preschool Services

Grants awarded to organizations located in Kentucky.

Typical grant range: $10,000 to $200,000

381
V.V. Cooke Foundation Corp.
4350 Brownsboro Road, Suite 110
Louisville, KY 40207
(502) 893-4598

Visually impaired; Deaf Oral School

Grants awarded to organizations located in Louisville.

Typical grant range: $500 to $12,000

382
Gheens Foundation, Inc.
One Riverfront Plaza, Suite 705
Louisville, KY 40202
(502) 584-4650

Mentally disabled; Kentucky Society to Prevent Blindness; Schizophrenia Foundation; Spina Bifida Association; Audio Studio for the Reading Impaired; Muscular Dystrophy Association; Louisville Deaf Oral School

Most grants awarded to organizations located in the Louisville vicinity.

Typical grant range: $5,000 to $60,000

383
Louisville Community Foundation, Inc.
325 W. Main Street, Suite 1110
Louisville, KY 40202
(502) 585-4649

Visually Impaired Preschool Services; Louisville Deaf Oral School

Grants awarded to organizations located in Louisville.

Typical grant range: $3,000 to $10,000

384
Norton Foundation, Inc.
4350 Brownsboro Road, Suite 133
Louisville, KY 40207
(502) 893-9549

Learning Disabilities Association; Louisville Deaf Oral School; Visually Impaired Preschool

Grants awarded to organizations located in the Louisville vicinity.

Typical grant range: $3,000 to $25,000

385
E.O. Robinson Mountain Fund
P.O. Box 54930
Lexington, KY 40555
(606) 233-0817

Speech Clinic, Inc.

Typical grant range: $3,000 to $25,000

386
Fred B. and Opal Woosley Foundation
900 Kentucky Home Life Building
Louisville, KY 40202

Easter Seal Society; Cerebral Palsy
School; Deaf Oral School; Special
Olympics; School for the Blind

Grants awarded to organizations located
in the Louisville vicinity.

Typical grant range: $1,000 to $3,000

LOUISIANA

387
Baton Rouge Area Foundation
One American Place, Suite 610
Baton Rouge, LA 70825
(504) 387-6126

Mentally and physically disabled;
emotionally disturbed; mental health

Grants awarded to organizations located
in Baton Rouge.

388
Charles T. Beaird Foundation
P.O. Box 31110
Shreveport, LA 71130
(318) 459-3242

Association for the Blind; Hearing Aid
Fund

Grants awarded to organizations located
in the Shreveport vicinity.

389
Boh Foundation
730 S. Tonti Street
New Orleans, LA 70119

Lighthouse for the Blind; Radio for the
Blind; Cystic Fibrosis; Special Olympics

Grants awarded to organizations located
in New Orleans.

Typical grant range: $1,000 to $10,000

390
**Community Foundation of
Shreveport-Bossier**
401 Edwards Street, Suite 517
Shreveport, LA 71101
(318) 221-0582

Mentally and physically disabled;
speech impaired

391
**Sybil M. and D. Blair Favrot
Family Fund**
2825 St. Charles Avenue
New Orleans, LA 70115
(504) 482-4357

Visually impaired; mental health

Grants awarded to organizations located
in the New Orleans vicinity.

392
**German Protestant Orphan
Asylum Association**
5342 St. Charles Avenue
New Orleans, LA 70115
(504) 895-2361

Physically disabled; employment
programs; recreation; Goodwill Industries

Grants awarded to organizations located
in Louisiana.

393
Greater New Orleans Foundation
2515 Canal Street, Suite 401
New Orleans, LA 70119
(504) 822-4906

Learning disabled; Children's Hospital
(for people who are physically disabled)

Grants awarded to organizations located
in the New Orleans vicinity.

Typical grant range: $500 to $15,000

394
Magale Foundation, Inc.
First National Bank of Shreveport
P.O. Box 21116
Shreveport, LA 71154
(318) 226-2382

Association for Retarded Citizens;
Louisiana Association for the Blind;
Louisiana Special Olympics

395
J. Edgar Monroe Foundation
228 St. Charles Street, Suite 1402
New Orleans, LA 70130
(504) 529-3539

Eye research; Multiple Sclerosis Society

Grants awarded to organizations located
in Louisiana.

396
Poindexter Foundation, Inc.
P.O. Box 1692
Shreveport, LA 71165
(318) 226-1040

Visually impaired; mental health; deaf

Grants awarded to organizations located
in Louisiana.

397
Fred B. and Ruth B. Zigler Foundation
P.O. Box 986
Jennings, LA 70546
(318) 824-2413

Louisiana Special Olympics; Lions Club
(camp for children with disabilities)

Typical grant range: $500 to $8,000

MAINE

398
Kenduskeag Foundation
c/o Dead River Company
One Dana Street
Portland, ME 04101
(207) 773-5841

Multiple Handicapped Center

Grants awarded to organizations located
in Maine.

399
Simmons Foundation, Inc.
One Canal Plaza
Portland, ME 04101
(207) 774-2635

Mental Health Services; Mental Health
Coalition; School for the Deaf

Grants awarded to organizations located
in Portland, Maine.

Typical grant range: $1,500 to $5,000

400
UNUM Charitable Foundation
2211 Congress Street
Portland, ME 04122
(207) 770-2211

Mentally and physically disabled; mental
health; developmentally disabled;
employment programs

Grants awarded to organizations located
in Maine.

MARYLAND

401
Charles S. Abell Foundation, Inc.
8401 Connecticut Avenue
Chevy Chase, MD 20815
(301) 652-2224

Developmentally disabled; employment
programs; St. Gertrude's School (for girls
who are mentally disabled); Alliance for
the Mentally Ill

Typical grant range: $5,000 to $30,000

402
Abell Foundation, Inc.
111 S. Calvert Street, Suite 2300
Baltimore, MD 21202
(410) 547-1300

Maryland Association for Dyslexic Adults
and Youths; National Multiple Sclerosis
Society

Grants awarded to organizations located
in Maryland, with an emphasis in
Baltimore.

Typical grant range: $3,000 to $50,000

403
Baltimore Community Foundation
The Latrobe Building
Two E. Read Street
Baltimore, MD 21202
(301) 332-4171

Physically and mentally disabled;
employment projects; Baltimore
Partnership for Mental Health; Goodwill
Industries; Disabled in Action

Grants awarded to organizations located
in the Baltimore vicinity.

404
Thomas W. Bradley Foundation, Inc.
c/o Pierson, Pierson & Nolan
217 E. Redwood Street, Suite 1600
Baltimore, MD 21202
(301) 727-4136

Mentally and physically disabled; learning
disabled; youth; recreation; education

Most grants awarded to organizations
located in Maryland.

Typical grant range: $1,000 to $3,000

405
**Alex Brown and Sons Charitable
Foundation, Inc.**
c/o Alex Brown and Sons, Inc.
135 E. Baltimore Street
Baltimore, MD 21202

Cystic Fibrosis Foundation; Depression
Related Affective Disorders Association;
Maryland Association for Dyslexic
Adults; Maryland Special Olympics

Grants awarded to organizations located
in Maryland.

406
Campbell Foundation, Inc.
100 W. Pennsylvania Avenue
Baltimore, MD 21204

Maryland School for the Blind

Grants awarded to organizations located
in the Baltimore vicinity.

Typical grant range: $1,500 to $7,000

407
Eugene B. Casey Foundation
800 S. Frederick Avenue, Suite 100
Gaithersburg, MD 20877

Georgetown University Medical Center
(spinal disorder research); Metropolitan
Washington Ear (audio services for people
who are visually impaired)

Typical grant range: $15,000 to $120,000

408
Clark-Winchcole Foundation
4550 Montgomery Ave., Suite 345N
Bethesda, MD 20814
(301) 654-3607

Physically disabled; learning disabled;
youth; employment projects; recreation;
research; Goodwill Industries; Recording
for the Blind; Columbia Lighthouse for
the Blind

Typical grant range: $2,000 to $25,000

409
Columbia Foundation
10221 Wineopin Circle
Columbia, MD 21044
(301) 730-7840

Physically disabled; Association for
Retarded Citizens

Grants awarded to organizations located
in Howard County.

410
**Community Foundation of the Eastern
Shore, Inc.**
200 W. Main Street
Salisbury, MD 21801
(410) 742-9911

March of Dimes; United Cerebral Palsy;
Easter Seal Society

Grants awarded to organizations located
in the Salisbury vicinity.

411
**Jacob and Annita France
Foundation, Inc.**
The Exchange, Suite 118
1122 Kenilworth Drive
Baltimore, MD 21204
(410) 832-5700

Mentally and physically disabled; blind;
education; recreation

Grants awarded to organizations located
in Maryland, with an emphasis in
Baltimore.

Typical grant range: $3,000 to $35,000

412
**Homer and Martha Gudelsky Family
Foundation, Inc.**
11900 Tech Road
Silver Spring, MD 20904
(301) 622-0100

Mentally and physically disabled

413
Emmert Hobbs Foundation, Inc.
c/o Friedman & Friedman
409 Washington Ave., Suite 900
Towson, MD 21204

Dental program; Mental Health Center;
League for Handicapped; Learning
Independence Through Computers;
Maryland Trust for the Retarded

Grants awarded to organizations located
in the Baltimore vicinity.

Typical grant range: $2,000 to $10,000

414
Hoffberger Foundation
800 Garrett Building
233 E. Redwood Street
Baltimore, MD 21202
(301) 576-4258

Mental health; physically disabled;
visually impaired

Grants awarded to organizations located
in the Baltimore vicinity.

Typical grant range: $500 to $20,000

415
**Marion I. and Henry J. Knott
Foundation, Inc.**
3904 Hickory Avenue
Baltimore, MD 21211
(410) 235-7068

Physically disabled; dental program;
accessibility projects; Special Olympics

Typical grant range: $1,000 to $25,000

416
John J. Leidy Foundation
217 E. Redwood Street, Suite 1600
Baltimore, MD 21202
(301) 727-4136

Mentally and physically disabled; visually impaired; recreation; employment programs

Grants awarded to organizations located in Maryland.

Typical grant range: $300 to $5,000

417
Morton and Sophia Macht Foundation
II E. Fayette Street
Baltimore, MD 21202
(301) 539-2370

Recording for the Blind; United Cerebral Palsy; Association for Retarded Citizens; Maryland School for the Blind

Grants awarded to organizations located in Maryland.

Typical grant range: $100 to $1,500

418
George Preston Marshall Foundation
35 Wisconsin Circle, Suite 525
Chevy Chase, MD 20815
(301) 654-7774

Association for Retarded Citizens of Montgomery County; Easter Seal Society; Information Center for Handicapped Individuals; Maryland School for the Blind

419
Middendorf Foundation, Inc.
Five E. Read Street
Baltimore, MD 21202
(410) 752-7088

Driving for the Disabled

Grants awarded to organizations located in Maryland.

Typical grant range: $1,000 to $25,000

420
W. O'Neil Foundation
5454 Wisconsin Avenue, Suite 750
Chevy Chase, MD 20815

Visually impaired; physically disabled; accessibility projects

421
Aaron Straus and Lillie Straus Foundation, Inc.
101 W. Mt. Royal Avenue
Baltimore, MD 21201
(301) 539-8308

Mentally and physically disabled; recreation; United Cerebral Palsy

Grants awarded to organizations located in the Baltimore vicinity.

Typical grant range: $1,500 to $50,000

422
Tate Industries Foundation, Inc.
601 W. West Street
Baltimore, MD 21230
(410) 539-0787

Dyslexia; Maryland Special Olympics; Alliance for the Mentally Ill of Baltimore; Maryland School for the Blind; Maryland School for the Deaf; Maryland Special Olympics

Grants awarded to organizations located in the Baltimore vicinity.

Typical grant range: $300 to $3,000

423
Weir Foundation Trust
1320 Fenwick Lane, Suite 700
Silver Spring, MD 20910

March of Dimes; National Sports Center for the Disabled; United Cerebral Palsy

Most grants awarded to preselected organizations.

MASSACHUSETTS

424
Adelaide Breed Bayrd Foundation
28 Pilgrim Road
Melrose, MA 02176
(617) 662-7342

Mental Health Center; Easter Seal Society

Grants awarded to organizations located
in the Malden vicinity.

Typical grant range: $1,000 to $15,000

425
Boston Foundation, Inc.
One Boston Place, 24th Floor
Boston, MA 02108
(617) 723-7415

Visually impaired; hard-of-hearing; youth;
cultural programs; Boston Aid to the
Blind; Information Center for Individuals
with Disabilities; Goodwill Industries;
Mental Health Association

Grants awarded to organizations located
in the Boston vicinity.

Typical grant range: $10,000 to $55,000

426
John W. Boynton Fund
c/o State Street Bank & Trust Co.
P.O. Box 351
Boston, MA 02101

Boston Aid for the Blind

427
Harold Brooks Foundation
c/o South Shore Bank
1400 Hancock Street
Quincy, MA 02169
(617) 847-3301

South Shore Association for Retarded
Citizens; King Solomon Humanitarian
Foundation for Handicapped Children;
Massachusetts Cerebral Palsy

Grants awarded to organizations located
in Massachusetts.

428
**Bushrod H. Campbell and Adah F. Hall
Charity Fund**
c/o Palmer & Dodge
One Beacon Street
Boston, MA 02108
(617) 573-0328

Physically disabled; youth; Boston Guild
for the Hard of Hearing; Clarke School
for the Deaf/Center for Oral Education;
Horace Mann School for the Deaf; Carroll
Center for the Blind; Recording for the
Blind

Grants awarded to organizations located
in the Boston vicinity.

Typical grant range: $2,000 to $10,000

429
**Roberta M. Childs Charitable
Foundation**
P.O. Box 639
North Andover, MA 01845

Guide Dog Foundation; Guiding Eyes for
the Blind; Easter Seal Society; Learning
Center for Deaf Children; Humanitarian
Foundation for Handicapped Children;
Clarke School for the Deaf

Grants awarded to organizations located
in Massachusetts.

Typical grant range: $1,000 to $5,000

430
Clipper Ship Foundation, Inc.
c/o Hill & Barlow, 100 Oliver Street
One International Plaza, 20th Floor
Boston, MA 02110
(617) 439-3555

Physically disabled; visually impaired;
mental health; rehabilitation

Grants awarded to organizations located
in the Boston vicinity.

Typical grant range: $2,000 to $15,000

431
Community Foundation of Western Massachusetts
1500 Main Street, Suite 1814
P.O. Box 15769
Springfield, MA 01115
(413) 732-2858

Mentally disabled; developmentally disabled; accessibility projects

432
Coolidge Hill Foundation
c/o Laurie Sturma
73 Birch Grove Drive
Pittsfield, MA 01201

Visually impaired; United Cerebral Palsy

Grants awarded to organizations located in Berkshire County.

Typical grant range: $2,000 to $8,000

433
Lillian L. and Harry A. Cowan Foundation Corporation
20 Chapel Street, #412-B
Brookline, MA 02146
(617) 738-1461

Physically disabled; emotionally disturbed; youth; Vision Foundation; Sight-Loss Services

Grants awarded to organizations located in the Boston vicinity.

Typical grant range: $3,000 to $7,000

434
Jessie B. Cox Charitable Trust
c/o Grants Management Associates
230 Congress Street, 3rd Floor
Boston, MA 02110
(617) 426-7172

Easter Seal Society; Mental Health Center

Typical grant range: $10,000 to $65,000

435
Frances R. Dewing Foundation
10 Kearney Road, Suite 301
Needham, MA 02194
(617) 449-2110

Physically disabled; blind; cultural programs; Learning Center for Deaf Children

436
Eugene A. Dexter Charitable Fund
Community Foundation of Western Massachusetts
BayBank Valley Tower
1500 Main Street, P.O. Box 15769
Springfield, MA 01115

Mentally and physically disabled

Most grants awarded to organizations located in the Springfield vicinity.

Typical grant range: $3,000 to $30,000

437
Ruth H. and Warren A. Ellsworth Foundation
370 Main Street, 12th Floor
Worcester, MA 01608
(508) 798-8621

Easter Seal Society

Grants awarded to organizations located in the Worcester vicinity.

Typical grant range: $2,000 to $25,000

438
Charles H. Farnsworth Trust
c/o State Street Bank & Trust Co.
P.O. Box 351
Boston, MA 02101

Center for the Blind; New England Home for the Deaf; Mental Health and Retardation Center

Grants awarded to organizations located in the Boston vicinity.

Typical grant range: $7,000 to $15,000

439
George F. and Sybil H. Fuller Foundation
P.O. Box 252
Boylston, MA 01505

Mental health; physically disabled;
National Braille Press

Typical grant range: $5,000 to $20,000

440
GenRad Foundation
300 Baker Avenue
Concord, MA 01742
(508) 369-4400

Mental Health Association; Red Acre
Hearing Dog Center; Friends of Action
Disabled; Learning Center for the
Multiple Handicapped

Grants awarded to organizations located
in the Concord vicinity.

441
Greater Worcester Community Foundation, Inc.
44 Front Street, Suite 530
Worcester, MA 01608
(508) 755-0980

Youth; Very Special Arts; Association
for Retarded Citizens

Grants awarded to organizations located
in the Worcester vicinity.

Typical grant range: $2,000 to $25,000

442
Nan and Matilda Heydt Fund
c/o BayBank Valley Trust Company
P.O. Box 3422
Burlington, MA 01803
(617) 273-1700

Physically disabled; mental health

Grants awarded to organizations located
in Hampden County.

443
Massachusetts Charitable Mechanic Association
353 Southern Artery
Quincy, MA 02169
(617) 479-1795

Physically disabled; visually impaired

Grants awarded to organizations located
in Massachusetts.

Typical grant range: $2,000 to $15,000

444
Morgan-Worcester, Inc.
15 Belmont Street
Worcester, MA 01605
(508) 755-6111

Easter Seal Society; Very Special Arts;
Special Olympics

Grants awarded to organizations located
in the Worcester vicinity.

Typical grant range: $100 to $4,000

445
Thomas Anthony Pappas Charitable Foundation, Inc.
P.O. Box 463
Belmont, MA 02178
(617) 862-2802

Association for Retarded Citizens; N.E.
Center for Autism; Perkins School for the
Blind

Grants awarded to organizations located
in Massachusetts.

446
Theodore Edson Parker Foundation
Grants Management Associates, Inc.
230 Congress Street
Boston, MA 02110
(617) 426-7172

Goodwill Industries

447
Perpetual Trust for Charitable Giving
c/o Fleet Bank of Massachusetts, N.A.
75 State Street, 7th Floor
Boston, MA 02109
(617) 346-2467

Perkins School for the Blind; Recording
for the Blind

Grants awarded to organizations located
in Massachusetts.

448
Edwin Phillips Trust
c/o Fleet Investment Services
Endowment & Foundations Management
75 State Street
Boston, MA 02109
(617) 346-2467

Mental health; recreation; youth; Perkins
School for the Blind; Easter Seal Society;
National Speech and Language Therapy;
Association for Retarded Citizens

Grants awarded to organizations located
in Plymouth County.

Typical grant range: $3,000 to $30,000

449
Polaroid Foundation, Inc.
750 Main Street, 2M
Cambridge, MA 02139
(617) 577-4035

Disabled (all areas); autism; recreation;
youth

Grants awarded to organizations located
in Massachusetts.

Typical grant range: $1,000 to $12,000

450
Rowland Foundation, Inc.
P.O. Box 13
Cambridge, MA 02238

National Society for the Prevention of
Blindness; Recording for the Blind

Typical grant range: $10,000 to $50,000

451
Sawyer Charitable Foundation
142 Berkeley Street
Boston, MA 02116
(617) 267-2414

Fidelco Guide Dog Foundation; Carroll
Center for the Blind; Association for
Retarded Citizens; Massachusetts Easter
Seal Society; Massachusetts Special
Olympics; Perkins School for the Blind;
National Braille Press

452
Stoddard Charitable Trust
370 Main Street
Worcester, MA 01608
(617) 798-8621

Clarke School for the Deaf

Grants awarded to organizations located
in the Worcester vicinity.

Typical grant range: $5,000 to $30,000

453
Stop & Shop Charitable Foundation
One Bradlee Circle
Braintree, MA 02184

Very Special Arts; Guild for the Hard of
Hearing; Hebrew Rehabilitation Center;
Special Olympics; Association for
Retarded and Handicapped Citizens

Grants awarded to organizations located
in areas of company operations.

Typical grant range: $1,000 to $5,000

454
Edwin S. Webster Foundation
Grants Management Associates, Inc.
230 Congress Street, 3rd Floor
Boston, MA 02110
(617) 426-7172

Physically disabled; rehabilitation

Most grants awarded to organizations
located in the Boston vicinity.

455
Wyman-Gordon Foundation
244 Worcester Street
P.O. Box 8001
North Grafton, MA 01536
(508) 756-5111

Association for Retarded Children

Grants awarded to organizations located in areas of company operations.

Typical grant range: $500 to $3,500

MICHIGAN

456
Ann Arbor Area Community Foundation
121 W. Washington, Suite 400
Ann Arbor, MI 48104

Washtenaw Area Self Help for Hard of Hearing People; Center for Independent Living

Grants awarded to organizations located in the Ann Arbor vicinity.

457
Battle Creek Community Foundation
One Riverwalk Center
34 W. Jackson Street
Battle Creek, MI 49017
(616) 962-2181

Physically disabled; vocational training

Grants awarded to organizations located in the Battle Creek vicinity.

Typical grant range: $1,000 to $20,000

458
Clarence and Grace Chamberlin Foundation
600 Woodbridge Place
Detroit, MI 48226
(313) 567-1000

Foundation for Exceptional Children; Hadley School for the Blind; Leader Dogs for the Blind; Rehabilitation Center; Newspapers for the Blind

Most grants awarded to organizations located in Michigan.

459
Community Foundation for Northeast Michigan
123 Water Street
Alpena, MI 49707
(517) 354-6881

Michigan Association for Emotionally Disturbed Children; Northland Library Cooperative (accessibility project)

Grants awarded to organizations located in the Alpena county vicinity.

Typical grant range: $400 to $5,000

460
Community Foundation for Southeastern Michigan
333 W. Fort Street, Suite 2010
Detroit, MI 48226
(313) 961-6675

Mental health; independent living programs; Recording for the Blind; Goodwill Industries; Deaf, Hearing and Speech Center

Grants awarded in the following Counties: Wayne, Oakland, Macomb, Washtenaw, St. Clair, Monroe, Livingston.

Typical grant range: $1,000 to $25,000

461
Dorothy U. Dalton Foundation, Inc.
c/o Arcadia Bank
P.O. Box 50566
Kalamazoo, MI 49003

Mental health; physically disabled; visually impaired

Grants awarded to organizations located in Kalamazoo County.

Typical grant range: $5,000 to $30,000

462
Earl-Beth Foundation
Nine Mack Center
23223 Nine Mack Drive
St. Clair Shores, MI 48080
(313) 776-8030

Foundation for Exceptional Children;
Good Sports for Special Needs Program;
Special Olympics; National Multiple
Sclerosis Society

463
Fibre Converters Foundation, Inc.
P.O. Box 117
125 East Broadway
Three Rivers, MI 49093

Braille Bible Foundation; Disabled
American Veterans; March of Dimes;
Parkinson's Disease Foundation;
Association for Emotionally Disturbed
Children

Grants awarded to organizations located
in Michigan.

464
Frey Foundation
48 Fountain Street, N.W.
Grand Rapids, MI 49503
(616) 451-0303

Mentally disabled; Michigan Dyslexia
Institute; Indian Trails Camp (physically
disabled)

Typical grant range: $10,000 to $30,000

465
Rollin M. Gerstacker Foundation
P.O. Box 1945
Midland, MI 48640
(517) 631-6097

Emotionally disturbed; child welfare;
Michigan Society for Mental Health;
Research to Prevent Blindness; Kresge
Hearing Research Institute

Typical grant range: $5,000 to $50,000

466
**Grand Haven Area Community
Foundation, Inc.**
One South Harbor
Grand Haven, MI 49417
(616) 842-6378

Mental health; mentally disabled

Grants awarded to organizations located
in the Grand Haven vicinity.

Typical grant range: $1,000 to $12,000

467
Grand Rapids Foundation
209-C Waters Building
161 Ottawa, N.W.
Grand Rapids, MI 49503
(616) 454-1751

Deaf; speech impaired; mentally and
physically disabled

Grants awarded to organizations located
in the Grand Rapids vicinity.

Typical grant range: $5,000 to $75,000

468
Greater Lansing Foundation
First of America Bank-Central
P.O. Box 21007
Lansing, MI 48909
(517) 334-5437

Physically disabled; visually impaired

469
Herrick Foundation
150 W. Jefferson, Suite 2500
Detroit, MI 48226
(313) 496-7656

Guide Dog Foundation for the Blind;
Readings for the Blind; Michigan Special
Olympics; Association for Retarded
Citizens of Monroe County

Most grants awarded to organizations
located in Michigan.

Typical grant range: $5,000 to $75,000

470
James and Lynelle Holden Fund
802 E. Big Beaver
Troy, MI 48083

Physically disabled; Society for the Blind

Grants awarded to organizations located
in Michigan.

Typical grant range: $4,000 to $30,000

471
Hurst Foundation
105 E. Michigan Avenue
P.O. Box 449
Jackson, MI 49204
(517) 787-6503

Speech and Hearing Clinic

Grants awarded to organizations located
in Jackson County.

472
Kalamazoo Foundation
151 S. Rose Street, Suite 332
Kalamazoo, MI 49007
(616) 381-4416

Community Advocates for Persons with
Developmental Disabilities; Specific
Language Disability Center

Grants awarded to organizations located
in Kalamazoo County.

473
Kresge Foundation
P.O. Box 3151
3215 W. Big Beaver Road
Troy, MI 48007
(313) 643-9630

Physically and mentally disabled; visually
impaired; Clarke School for the Deaf

Emphasis on building grants.

Typical grant range: $125,000 to
$600,000

474
McGregor Fund
333 W. Fort Street, Suite 1380
Detroit, MI 48226
(313) 963-3495

Dyslexia; visually impaired

Grants awarded to organizations located
in Detroit.

Typical grant range: $20,000 to $60,000

475
Midland Foundation
812 W. Main Street
P.O. Box 289
Midland, MI 48640
(517) 839-9661

Dyslexia; higher education; Special
Olympics

Grants awarded to organizations located
in Midland County.

476
Frances Goll Mills Fund
Second National Bank of Saginaw
101 N. Washington Avenue
Saginaw, MI 48607
(517) 776-7582

Saginaw County Special Olympics

Grants awarded to organizations located
in Saginaw County.

Typical grant range: $1,000 to $9,000

477
William M. and Mary E. Pagel Trust
c/o NBD Bank, N.A.
611 Woodward Avenue
Detroit, MI 48226
(313) 225-3124

Shriner's Hospital for Crippled Children

Grants awarded to organizations located
in Michigan.

478
Herbert & Elsa Ponting Foundation
600 Woodbridge Place
Detroit, MI 48226
(313) 567-1000

Michigan Dyslexia; Recording for
the Blind

Grants awarded to organizations located
in Michigan.

479
May Mitchell Royal Foundation
c/o Comerica Bank-Midland
201 McDonald Street
Midland, MI 48640

Hawaii Lyons Eye Bank; Kresge Eye
Institute; Leader Dogs for the Blind;
Shriner's Hospital for Crippled Children

Typical grant range: $2,000 to $15,000

480
Sage Foundation
10315 Grand River Road, Suite 204
Brighton, MI 48116

Physically disabled; visually impaired;
vocational training; education

Grants awarded to organizations located
in Michigan.

Typical grant range: $2,500 to $50,000

481
Skillman Foundation
333 W. Fort Street, Suite 1350
Detroit, MI 48226
(313) 961-8850

Mentally and physically disabled;
emotionally disturbed; sheltered
workshop; child welfare

Typical grant range: $25,000 to $150,000

482
Steelcase Foundation
P.O. Box 1967
Grand Rapids, MI 49507
(616) 246-4695

Lakeshore Center for Independent Living;
Western North Carolina Radio Reading
Service

Grants awarded to organizations located
in areas of company operations.

Typical grant range: $2,000 to $30,000

483
Charles J. Strosacker Foundation
P.O. Box 471
Midland, MI 48640

Muscular Dystrophy Association; Special
Olympics; Midland-Gladwin Mental
Health

Grants awarded to organizations located
in Michigan, with an emphasis in
Midland.

Typical grant range: $3,000 to $45,000

484
A. Alfred Taubman Foundation
200 E. Long Lake Road
P.O. Box 200
Bloomfield Hills, MI 48303
(313) 258-6800

Association for Autistic Children;
Goodwill Industries; Leader Dogs
for the Blind; Special Olympics

Grants awarded to organizations located
in Michigan.

Typical grant range: $250 to $10,000

485
**Frank S. & Mollie S. VanDervoort
Memorial Foundation**
1784 Hamilton Road
Okemos, MI 48864
(517) 349-7232

Radio-Talking Books; United Cerebral
Palsy; Physically Impaired Association of
Michigan; Muscular Dystrophy
Association

Grants awarded to organizations located
in Ingham County.

Typical grant range: $500 to $3,500

486
Frederick A. Vollbrecht Foundation
31700 Telegraph Road, Suite 220
Birmingham, MI 48025
(313) 646-0627

Visually impaired; physically disabled

Grants awarded to organizations located
in Michigan.

487
Whiting Foundation
901 Citizens Bank Building
328 South Saginaw Street
Flint, MI 48502
(313) 767-3600

Braille Circulating Library; Foundation
for Exceptional Children; National
Multiple Sclerosis Society; Readings for
the Blind; Tapings for the Blind

Grants awarded to organizations located
in the Flint vicinity.

Typical grant range: $250 to $20,000

488
Lula C. Wilson Trust
c/o NBD Bank, N.A.
1116 W. Long Lake Road
Bloomfield Hills, MI 48013
(313) 645-7306

Readings for the Blind; Lighthouse for the
Blind; Blind Recreational Society

489
Matilda R. Wilson Fund
100 Renaissance Center, 33rd Floor
Detroit, MI 48243
(313) 259-7777

Readings for the Blind

Typical grant range: $15,000 to $50,000

490
Youth Foundation of America
300 Park Avenue
Petoskey, MI 49770
(616) 347-4195

Physically disabled; youth; recreation

Grants awarded to organizations located
in Michigan.

Typical grant range: $3,000 to $7,500

MINNESOTA

491
AHS Foundation
c/o First Trust, N.A.
P.O. Box 64704
St. Paul, MN 55164
(612) 291-5128

Physically disabled; Disability Awareness

Typical grant range: $2,000 to $8,000

492
Andersen Foundation
c/o Andersen Corporation
100 Fourth Avenue North
Bayport, MN 55003
(612) 439-5150

Mental health; deaf (research)

Typical grant range: $10,000 to $100,000

493
Baker Foundation
4900 IDS Center
Minneapolis, MN 55402
(612) 332-7479

Cystic Fibrosis Association

Grants awarded to organizations located
in Minnesota.

494
Beim Foundation
20450 Lakeview Avenue
Excelsior, MN 55331
(612) 474-2442

Canine Companions for Independence;
Hearing Dog Program of Minnesota

Grants awarded to organizations located
in the Minneapolis vicinity.

495
Bemis Company Foundation
222 S. Ninth Street, Suite 2300
Minneapolis, MN 55402
(612) 340-6198

Hard-of-hearing; learning disabled;
visually impaired

Grants awarded to organizations located
in areas of company operations.

496
Blandin Foundation
100 Pokegama Avenue North
Grand Rapids, MN 55744
(218) 326-0523

Developmentally disabled; mentally
disabled; visually impaired; employment
programs; recreation

Grants awarded to organizations located
in Minnesota.

Typical grant range: $5,000 to $75,000

497
Otto Bremer Foundation
445 Minnesota Street, Suite 2000
St. Paul, MN 55101
(612) 227-8036

Mentally and physically disabled; mental
health; education; recreation; accessibility
project; Association for Retarded Citizens

Grants awarded to organizations located
in areas of company operations (Bremer
Bank).

Typical grant range: $2,000 to $20,000

498
Bush Foundation
E. 900 First National Bank Bldg.
332 Minnesota Street
St. Paul, MN 55101
(612) 227-0891

Physically and mentally disabled; mental
health; independent living programs;
employment programs

Typical grant range: $30,000 to $100,000

499
**Patrick and Aimee Butler Family
Foundation**
First National Bank Building
332 Minnesota Street, E-1420
St. Paul, MN 55101
(612) 222-2565

Learning Disabilities Association

Grants awarded to organizations located
in the Minneapolis-St. Paul vicinity.

500
Carolyn Foundation
4800 First Bank Place
Minneapolis, MN 55402
(612) 339-7101

Mentally and physically disabled;
cultural programs

Typical grant range: $5,000 to $30,000

501
Deluxe Corporation Foundation
P.O. Box 64399
St. Paul, MN 55164
(612) 483-7842

Mental health; mentally and physically disabled; autism; recreation; employment programs; youth; American School for the Deaf

Grants awarded to organizations located in areas of company operations.

Typical grant range: $1,000 to $14,000

502
Duluth-Superior Area Community Foundation
618 Missabe Building
227 W. First Street
Duluth, MN 55802
(218) 726-0232

Visually impaired; deaf; mentally and physically disabled; accessibility projects; recreation

Typical grant range: $1,000 to $9,000

503
Edwin H. Eddy Family Foundation
c/o Norwest Bank Duluth
Capital Management and Trust Dept.
Duluth, MN 55802
(218) 723-2773

Speech impaired; deaf; research

Grants awarded to organizations located in the Duluth vicinity.

Few grants awarded.

504
First Bank System Foundation
P.O. Box 522
Minneapolis, MN 55480

Association for Retarded Citizens; Camp School for the Deaf; accessibility project

Grants awarded to organizations located in areas of company operations.

Typical grant range: $1,000 to $8,000

505
General Mills Foundation
P.O. Box 1113
Minneapolis, MN 55440
(612) 540-7891

Physically disabled; mental health; visually impaired; independent living programs; education; youth

Grants awarded to organizations located in areas of company operations, with an emphasis in Minneapolis.

Typical grant range: $3,000 to $25,000

506
Graco Foundation
P.O. Box 1441
Minneapolis, MN 55440
(612) 623-6684

Mentally and physically disabled; learning disabled

Grants awarded to organizations located in areas of company operations.

Typical grant range: $1,000 to $5,000

507
Grand Metropolitan Food Sector Foundation
Mail Station 37X5
200 S. Sixth Street
Minneapolis, MN 55402
(612) 330-5434

Physically disabled; mental health; learning disabled; recreation; March of Dimes

Grants awarded to organizations located in areas of company operations (Pillsbury Company).

Typical grant range: $1,000 to $20,000

508
Honeywell Foundation
Honeywell Plaza
P.O. Box 524
Minneapolis, MN 55440
(612) 951-2231

Mentally and physically disabled

Grants awarded to organizations located
in areas of company operations, with an
emphasis in Minneapolis.

Typical grant range: $1,000 to $25,000

509
Emma B. Howe Memorial Foundation
A200 Foshay Tower
821 Marquette Avenue
Minneapolis, MN 55402
(612) 339-7343

Physically and mentally disabled; deaf;
visually impaired; independent living
programs; employment programs; youth;
People Achieving Change Through
Technology (high-tech projects for people
with disabilities)

Grants awarded to organizations located
in Minnesota.

Typical grant range: $5,000 to $30,000

510
MAHADH Foundation
287 Central Avenue
Bayport, MN 55003
(612) 439-1557

Learning disabled; physically disabled

511
McKnight Foundation
600 TCF Tower
121 S. Eighth Street
Minneapolis, MN 55402
(612) 333-4220

Physically disabled; employment
programs; Very Special Arts

Grants awarded to organizations located
in Minnesota.

Typical grant range: $20,000 to $200,000

512
Minneapolis Foundation
A200 Foshay Tower
821 Marquette Avenue
Minneapolis, MN 55402
(612) 339-7343

People with Autism, Inc.; Cystic Fibrosis
Foundation; Minnesota Multiple Sclerosis
Society

Grants awarded to organizations located
in the Minneapolis-St. Paul vicinity.

Typical grant range: $1,000 to $25,000

513
Northwestern National Life Foundation
20 Washington Ave. South, Route 0941
Minneapolis, MN 55401
(612) 342-7443

Mentally and physically disabled; learning
disabled; vocational training; recreation

Grants awarded to organizations located
in the Minneapolis vicinity.

514
Alice M. O'Brien Foundation
324 Forest
Mahtomedi, MN 55115
(612) 426-2143

Goodwill Industries; Easter Seals; Project
Reach (camp for people with disabilities)

Grants awarded to organizations located
in Minnesota.

Typical grant range: $1,000 to $8,000

515
Ordean Foundation
501 Ordean Building
424 W. Superior Street
Duluth, MN 55802
(218) 726-4785

Mentally and physically disabled; visually
impaired; employment programs

Typical grant range: $500 to $25,000

516
Jay and Rose Phillips Family Foundation
2345 N.E. Kennedy Street
Minneapolis, MN 55413
(612) 623-1654

Physically disabled; visually impaired; mental health

Grants awarded to organizations located in Minnesota.

Typical grant range: $1,000 to $15,000

517
Rochester Area Foundation
1815 14th Street, NW
Rochester, MN 55901
(507) 282-0203

Hard-of-hearing; physically disabled; cultural programs; accessibility projects

Grants awarded to organizations located in Olmstead County.

Typical grant range: $1,000 to $11,000

518
Saint Paul Foundation, Inc.
600 Norwest Center
St. Paul, MN 55101
(612) 224-5464

Hard-of-hearing; visually impaired; physically disabled; recreation

Grants awarded to organizations located in the St. Paul vicinity.

Typical grant range: $1,000 to $30,000

519
Tennant Foundation
701 North Lilac Drive
P.O. Box 1452
Minneapolis, MN 55440
(612) 540-1207

Mental health; autism; visually impaired; learning disabled

520
James R. Thorpe Foundation
8085 Wayzata Blvd.
Minneapolis, MN 55426
(612) 545-1111

Twin Cities Autism Society; Alliance for the Mentally Ill of Minnesota; Blind, Inc.; Minnesota Head Injury Association; Learning Disabilities Association

Grants awarded to organizations located in the Minneapolis vicinity.

Typical grant range: $1,500 to $7,500

521
Archie D. and Bertha H. Walker Foundation
1121 Hennepin Avenue
Minneapolis, MN 55403
(612) 332-3556

Learning Disabled; hard-of-hearing; mental health

Grants awarded to organizations located in the Minneapolis-St. Paul vicinity.

522
Wasie Foundation
601 2nd Avenue S., Suite 4700
Minneapolis, MN 55402
(612) 332-3883

Mental health; mentally and physically disabled

MISSISSIPPI

523
Deposit Guaranty Foundation
One Deposit Guaranty Plaza
P.O. Box 730
Jackson, MS 39205

Dogwood Speech School; Easter Seal Society

Grants awarded to organizations located in Mississippi.

524
Phil Hardin Foundation
c/o Citizens National Bank
P.O. Box 911
Meridian, MS 39302
(601) 483-4282

Mentally disabled; Meridian Speech
and Hearing Center

Most grants awarded to organizations
located in Mississippi.

Typical grant range: $5,000 to $40,000

525
W.E. Walker Foundation
2829 Lakeland Drive, Suite 1600
Jackson, MS 39208
(601) 939-3003

National Society to Prevent Blindness;
Muscular Dystrophy; Multiple Sclerosis;
Epilepsy Foundation; March of Dimes;
Cystic Fibrosis Foundation

Grants awarded to organizations located
in Mississippi.

MISSOURI

526
H & R Block Foundation
4410 Main Street
Kansas City, MO 64111
(816) 753-6900

Visually impaired; mental health;
physically disabled; youth

Grants awarded to organizations located
in the Kansas City vicinity.

527
Community Foundation, Inc.
901 St. Louis Street, Suite 303
Springfield, MO 65806
(417) 864-6199

Physically disabled; learning disabled;
visually impaired; dyslexia; autism;
youth; recreation; Easter Seal Society

528
**Charles R. and Minnie K. Cook
Foundation**
919 E. 14th Avenue
N. Kansas City, MO 64116
(816) 391-6315

March of Dimes; Cystic Fibrosis
Foundation; Eye Bank

Most grants awarded to organizations
located in Kansas City.

529
CPI Corporation Philanthropic Trust
1706 Washington Avenue
St. Louis, MO 63103
(314) 231-1575

Physically and mentally disabled;
recreation

Grants awarded to organizations located
in areas of company operations.

Typical grant range: $1,000 to $7,000

530
Cross Foundation, Inc.
106 E. 31st Terrace, Suite 206
Kansas City, MO 64111
(816) 753-7119

Mentally disabled; United Cerebral Palsy;
Transitional Living Consortium (for
adults with mental illness)

Most grants awarded to organizations
located in Kansas City.

531
Enterprise Leasing Foundation
35 Hunter Avenue
St. Louis, MO 63124
(314) 863-7000

Multiple Sclerosis Society; St. Louis
Hearing and Speech Center; Talking
Tapes for the Blind; St. Louis Wheelchair
Association; St. Louis Society for
Crippled Children; Special Olympics

Typical grant range: $1,000 to $15,000

532
Catherine Manley Gaylord Foundation
314 N. Broadway, Room 1230
St. Louis, MO 63102
(314) 421-0181

Mentally and physically disabled;
deaf; youth

Grants awarded to organizations located
in the St. Louis vicinity.

Typical grant range: $300 to $3,500

533
**Greater Kansas City Community
Foundation and Its Affiliated Trusts**
1055 Broadway, Suite 130
Kansas City, MO 64105
(816) 842-0944

Visually impaired; mental health;
physically disabled; youth; vocational
training

Grants awarded to organizations located
in the Kansas City vicinity.

Typical grant range: $5,000 to $25,000

534
Kellwood Foundation
P.O. Box 14080
St. Louis, MO 63178
(314) 576-3431

St. Louis Association for Retarded
Citizens; Society for Crippled Children;
Council for Extended Care of Mentally
Retarded Citizens; Support Dogs for the
Handicapped; Central Institute for the
Deaf; Midwestern Braille Volunteers;
Cystic Fibrosis Association; United
Cerebral Palsy; Missouri Special
Olympics

Most grants awarded to organizations
located in St. Louis.

Typical grant range: $500 to $5,000

535
**John Allan Love Charitable
Foundation**
c/o Edgar G. Boedeker
231 S. Bemiston Avenue
St. Louis, MO 63105
(314) 727-5822

Mentally and physically disabled;
autism; medical research

Grants awarded to organizations located
in Missouri.

536
McGee Foundation
4900 Main Street, Suite 717
Kansas City, MO 64112
(816) 931-1515

Children's Center for the Visually
Impaired; Head Injury Association

Grants awarded to organizations located
in the Kansas City vicinity.

537
Finis M. Moss Charitable Trust
108 West Walnut
P.O. Box J
Nevada, MO 64772
(417) 667-5076

Shriner's Club Crippled Children's
Transportation Fund

Grants awarded to organizations located
in Nevada, Missouri.

538
Musgrave Foundation
600 Plaza Towers
1736 East Sunshine
Springfield, MO 65804
(417) 883-7154

Visually Impaired Pre-School; Springfield
Handicapped Workshop; Alliance for the
Mentally Ill

539
Oppenstein Brothers Foundation
911 Main Street, Suite 100
P.O. Box 13095
Kansas City, MO 64199
(816) 234-8671

Physically disabled; Alliance for
the Mentally Ill

Grants awarded to organizations located
in the Kansas City vicinity.

Typical grant range: $1,000 to $25,000

540
Ralston Purina Trust Fund
Checkerboard Square
St. Louis, MO 63164
(314) 982-3230

Central Institute for the Deaf; St. Louis
Association for Retarded Citizens;
Foundation for Special Education for
Children; Missouri Goodwill Industries;
Mental Health Association

Grants awarded to organizations located
in areas of company operations.

Typical grant range: $1,000 to $25,000

541
Roy W. Slusher Charitable Foundation
P.O. Box 10327
Springfield, MO 65808
(417) 882-9090

Shriners Hospital for Crippled Children

Grants awarded to organizations located
in Missouri.

Typical grant range: $500 to $20,000

542
Sosland Foundation
4800 Main Street, Suite 100
Kansas City, MO 64112
(816) 765-1000

Physically disabled; youth

Most grants awarded to organizations
located in the Kansas City vicinity.

Typical grant range: $1,000 to $15,000

543
John W. and Effie E. Speas
Memorial Trust
c/o Boatmen's First National Bank of
Kansas City
14 W. Tenth Street
Kansas City, MO 64183
(816) 691-7481

Mentally and physically disabled

Most grants awarded to organizations
located in the Kansas City vicinity.

Typical grant range: $5,000 to $80,000

544
St. Louis Community Foundation
818 Olive Street, Suite 935
St. Louis, MO 63101
(314) 241-2703

Mental health; learning disabled;
physically disabled

Grants awarded to organizations located
in the St. Louis vicinity.

Typical grant range: $500 to $9,000

545
Norman J. Stupp Foundation
c/o Commerce Bank of St. Louis, N.A.
8000 Forsyth, Suite 1305
St. Louis, MO 63105
(314) 746-8577

Central Institute for the Deaf; Shriner's
Hospital for Crippled Children; Eye
Institute; Association for Retarded
Children; Special Olympics

Most grants awarded to organizations
located in the St. Louis vicinity.

Typical grant range: $3,000 to $30,000

546
Union Electric Company
Charitable Trust
1901 Chouteau Street
P.O. Box 149
St. Louis, MO 63166
(314) 621-3222

Association for Retarded Citizens;
Gallaudet University; Society for
Crippled Children

Grants awarded to organizations located
in areas of company operations.

Typical grant range: $5,000 to $35,000

547
Webb Foundation
7711 Carondelet Avenue, Suite 810
St. Louis, MO 63105
(314) 862-6220

Deaf; autism; physically disabled;
youth; education

548
Lyndon C. Whitaker Charitable
Foundation
120 S. Central Street, Suite 1122
St. Louis, MO 63105
(314) 726-5734

Society for Crippled Children;
Wheelchair Athletic Association

Grants awarded to organizations located
in St. Louis.

MONTANA

549
Dufresne Foundation
P.O. Box 1484
Great Falls, MT 59403
(406) 452-9414

Montana Special Olympics; Montana
School for the Deaf and Blind

Grants awarded to organizations located
in Montana.

NEBRASKA

550
Lincoln Foundation, Inc.
215 Centennial Mall South, Suite 200
Lincoln, NE 68508
(402) 474-2345

Radio Talking Book (visually impaired)

Most grants awarded to organizations
located in the Lincoln vicinity.

Typical grant range: $1,000 to $6,000

551
Omaha Community Foundation
Two Central Park Plaza
222 S. 15th Street
Omaha, NE 68102
(402) 342-3458

Goodwill Industries; Children's Respite
Center (physically disabled); Youth Care,
Inc. (van for people who are mentally
disabled)

Grants awarded to organizations located
in the Omaha vicinity.

Typical grant range: $500 to $15,000

552
Pamida Foundation
P.O. Box 3856
Omaha, NE 68103
(402) 339-2400

Cystic Fibrosis Foundation

Grants awarded to organizations located
in areas of company operations.

Typical grant range: $300 to $1,500

553
**Physicians Mutual Insurance
Company Foundation**
2600 Dodge Street
Omaha, NE 68131
(402) 633-1000

Cystic Fibrosis Foundation; Goodwill,
Inc.; Easter Seal Society; Omaha Hearing
School; United Cerebral Palsy

Grants awarded to organizations located
in the Omaha vicinity.

Typical grant range: $250 to $5,000

NEVADA

554
Cord Foundation
200 Court Street
Reno, NV 89501
(702) 323-0373

Physically and mentally disabled;
cultural programs; recreation

Most grants awarded to organizations
located in Reno.

Typical grant range: $5,000 to $50,000

555
**First Interstate Bank of Nevada
Foundation**
P.O. Box 98588
Las Vegas, NV 89193
(702) 791-6462

Mentally and physically disabled; North
Nevada Center for Independent Living

Grants awarded to organizations located
in Nevada.

Typical grant range: $5,000 to $12,000

556
Robert Z. Hawkins Foundation
One E. Liberty Street, Suite 509
Reno, NV 89505
(702) 786-1105

Nevada Special Olympics; North Nevada
Braille Transcribers; Association for
Retarded Citizens

Grants awarded to organizations located
in Nevada.

557
Conrad N. Hilton Foundation
100 W. Liberty Street, Suite 840
Reno, NV 89501
(702) 323-4221

Mentally and physically disabled;
visually impaired; education

Typical grant range: $5,000 to $75,000

558
Nell J. Redfield Foundation
1755 E. Plumb Lane, Suite 212
Reno, NV 89504
(702) 323-1373

Mentally and physically disabled;
speech impaired; youth; recreation

Most grants awarded to organizations
located in Reno.

Typical grant range: $2,000 to $25,000

559
E.L. Wiegand Foundation
Wiegand Center
165 Liberty Street
Reno, NV 89501
(702) 333-0310

Physically and mentally disabled;
Special Olympics

Most grants awarded to Roman Catholic
organizations.

Typical grant range: $5,000 to $75,000

NEW HAMPSHIRE

560
Michael D. Dingman Foundation
1 Liberty Lane
Hampton, NH 03842
(603) 926-5911

Orton Dyslexia Society; Eye and Ear
Infirmary

561
Agnes M. Lindsay Trust
95 Market Street
Manchester, NH 03101
(603) 669-4140

Physically and mentally disabled;
mental health; youth

Typical grant range: $1,500 to $7,500

562
Mascoma Savings Bank Foundation
c/o Mascoma Savings Bank
67 North Park Street
Lebanon, NH 03766
(603) 448-3650

Alliance for the Mentally Ill

Typical grant range: $1,000 to $5,000

NEW JERSEY

563
AlliedSignal Foundation
P.O. Box 2245
Morristown, NJ 07962
(201) 455-5877

Visually impaired; mental health;
Occupational Training Center for
the Handicapped

Grants awarded to organizations located
in areas of company operations.

Typical grant range: $1,000 to $12,000

564
**Mary Owen Borden Memorial
Foundation**
160 Hodge Road
Princeton, NJ 08540
(609) 924-3637

Hard-of-hearing; mentally disabled;
United Cerebral Palsy; Association for
the Advancement of Mental Health

Typical grant range: $1,000 to $10,000

565
Charles Edison Fund
101 S. Harrison Street
East Orange, NJ 07018
(201) 675-9000

Eye research; Multiple Sclerosis;
Summit Speech School

Typical grant range: $500 to $10,000

566
Fund for the New Jersey Blind, Inc.
153 Halsey Street
P.O. Box 47017
Newark, NJ 07101
(201) 648-2324

New Jersey Camp for Blind Children;
Union County Association of the Blind;
National Federation of the Blind;
accessibility projects

Grants awarded to organizations located
in New Jersey.

Typical grant range: $500 to $5,000

567
E.J. Grassman Trust
P.O. Box 4470
Warren, NJ 07059
(908) 753-2440

Speech impaired; physically disabled;
education

Most grants awarded to organizations
located in Union County.

Typical grant range: $5,000 to $25,000

568
Hoyt Foundation
Half Acre Road
Cranbury, NJ 08512
(609) 655-6000

Deafness Research Foundation

569
Hyde and Watson Foundation
437 Southern Blvd.
Chatham, NJ 07928
(201) 966-6024

Visually impaired; physically disabled;
accessibility projects

Typical grant range: $5,000 to $25,000

570
Robert Wood Johnson Foundation
P.O. Box 2316
Princeton, NJ 08543
(609) 452-8701

Mental health; physically disabled;
independent living programs; youth;
Association for Retarded Citizens

571
F.M. Kirby Foundation, Inc.
17 DeHart Street
P.O. Box 151
Morristown, NJ 07963
(201) 538-4800

Visually impaired; mentally and
physically disabled; speech impaired;
employment programs; research; youth

Typical grant range: $10,000 to $25,000

572
Fanny & Svante Knistrom Foundation
c/o Carl A. Frahn
229 Main Street
Chatham, NJ 07928

Physically disabled; Association for
Retarded Citizens

Typical grant range: $3,000 to $15,000

573
Blanche and Irving Laurie Foundation
P.O. Box 53
Roseland, NJ 07068

Physically disabled; Mental Health
Association

Grants awarded to organizations located
in New Jersey.

Typical grant range: $500 to $30,000

574
Curtis W. McGraw Foundation
c/o Drinker, Biddle & Reath
P.O. Box 627
Princeton, NJ 08542
(609) 497-7011

Mental health; Recording for the Blind

Typical grant range: $1,000 to $7,500

575
**Aaron and Rachel Meyer Memorial
Foundation, Inc.**
340 North Avenue
Cranford, NJ 07016
(908) 272-7000

Foundation for the Handicapped

Grants awarded to organizations located
in Passaic County.

576
L.P. Schenck Fund
c/o Midlantic National Bank, Trust Dept.
41 Oak Street
Ridgewood, NJ 07450
(201) 652-8499

Mentally disabled; mental health;
Recording for the Blind

577
Arnold A. Schwartz Foundation
c/o Kunzman, Coley, Yospin & Bernstein
15 Mountain Blvd.
Warren, NJ 07060
(908) 757-7927

Visually impaired; speech impaired;
employment program; Edison Sheltered
Workshop; School for Exceptional
Children; National Multiple Sclerosis
Society

Typical grant range: $1,000 to $8,000

578
Standish Foundation
P.O. Box 4470
Warren, NJ 07059
(908) 753-2440

Summit Speech School

Typical grant range: $500 to $4,500

579
Ann Earle Talcott Fund
c/o First Fidelity Bank, N.A.
Philanthropic Services Group
765 Broad Street
Newark, NJ 07102
(201) 430-4533

Mental health; physically disabled

Most grants awarded to organizations
located in New Jersey.

580
Tomlinson Family Foundation, Inc.
P.O. Box 590
Morristown, NJ 07963

Recording for the Blind; Summit Speech
School

Grants awarded to organizations located
in New Jersey.

581
Union Foundation
31C Mountain Blvd.
P.O. Box 4470
Warren, NJ 07060
(908) 753-2440

Association of Schools and Agencies for
the Handicapped; Cerebral Palsy League
of Union County; Recording for the Blind

Grants awarded to organizations located
in Union County.

582
Westfield Foundation
301 North Avenue West
P.O. Box 2295
Westfield, NJ 07091
(908) 233-9787

Mentally disabled

Grants awarded to organizations located
in Westfield.

NEW MEXICO

583
Albuquerque Community Foundation
P.O. Box 36960
Albuquerque, NM 87176
(505) 883-6240

Physically disabled; autism; cultural
programs

Grants awarded to organizations located
in the Albuquerque vicinity.

584
Dale J. Bellamah Foundation
P.O. Box 36600, Station D
Albuquerque, NM 87176
(505) 293-1098

Mentally and physically disabled

Typical grant range: $5,000 to $80,000

585
R.D. and Joan Dale Hubbard Foundation
P.O. Box 1679
Ruidoso Downs, NM 88346
(505) 378-4142

Handicapped Skiers Association;
March of Dimes

Typical grant range: $5,000 to $75,000

586
J.F. Maddox Foundation
P.O. Box 5410
Hobbs, NM 88241
(505) 393-6338

Mentally and physically disabled; youth

Most grants awarded to organizations located in New Mexico.

Typical grant range: $5,000 to $75,000

587
Santa Fe Community Foundation
219 West Manhattan
Santa Fe, NM 87501
(505) 988-9715

Physically disabled; mental health; Las Cumbres Learning Services (care for children with disabilities)

Grants awarded to organizations located in Santa Fe.

NEW YORK

588
Joseph Alexander Foundation
400 Madison Avenue, Suite 906
New York, NY 10017
(212) 355-3688

Mental Health Center; Easter Seal Society; Friends of Guiding Eyes for the Blind; United Cerebral Palsy

Most grants awarded to organizations located in New York City.

Typical grant range: $3,000 to $30,000

589
Rita Allen Foundation, Inc.
550 Park Avenue
New York, NY 10021

Helen Keller Services for the Blind; Recording for the Blind; Cerebral Palsy; Multiple Sclerosis (research)

Typical grant range: $100 to $15,000

590
Altman Foundation
220 E. 42nd Street, Suite 411
New York, NY 10017
(212) 682-0970

Disabled (all areas); learning disabled; developmentally disabled; youth; rehabilitation; education

Grants awarded to organizations located in the New York vicinity.

Typical grant range: $5,000 to $100,000

591
AT&T Foundation
1301 Avenue of the Americas, Suite 3100
New York, NY 10019
(212) 841-4747

Blind; physically disabled; hard-of-hearing; youth; cultural programs; employment programs; March of Dimes Birth Defects Foundation

Grants awarded to organizations located in areas of company operations.

Typical grant range: $5,000 to $40,000

592
Rose M. Badgeley Residuary Charitable Trust
Marine Midland Bank, N.A.
250 Park Avenue
New York, NY 10177
(212) 503-2773

Hard-of-hearing; visually impaired; Recording for the Blind

Typical grant range: $5,000 to $20,000

593
Bodman Foundation
c/o Morris & McVeigh
767 Third Avenue, 22nd Floor
New York, NY 10017
(212) 418-0500

Physically disabled; employment
program; youth; International Center
for the Disabled

Grants awarded to organizations located
in the New York City vicinity.

Typical grant range: $15,000 to $50,000

594
Bristol-Myers Squibb Foundation, Inc.
345 Park Avenue, 43rd Floor
New York, NY 10154
(212) 546-4331

Physically disabled; rehabilitation;
education; Clarke School for the Deaf;
National Handicapped Sports; Easter Seal
Society

Grants awarded to organizations located
in areas of company operations.

Typical grant range: $3,000 to $25,000

595
Gladys Brooks Foundation
90 Broad Street
New York, NY 10004
(212) 943-3217

Mental health; National Center for
Disability Services

Typical grant range: $10,000 to $75,000

596
Buffalo Foundation
1601 Main-Seneca Building
237 Main Street
Buffalo, NY 14203
(716) 852-2857

Physically disabled; Buffalo Hearing
and Speech Center; D'Youville College
(accessibility project)

Grants awarded to organizations located
in Erie County.

Typical grant range: $1,000 to $15,000

597
**Central New York Community
Foundation, Inc.**
500 S. Salina Street, Suite 428
Syracuse, NY 13202
(315) 422-9538

Physically disabled; Mental Health
Association; Association for Retarded
Citizens; Disabled Americans of America;
Emmanuel Church (accessibility project)

Grants awarded to organizations located
in Onondaga and Madison Counties.

598
**Community Foundation for the Capital
Region, N.Y.**
P.O. Box 3198
Albany, NY 12203
(518) 273-8596

Visually impaired; physically disabled;
Center for the Disabled; Special Olympics

Grants awarded to organizations located
in Albany, Saratoga, and Rensselaer
Counties.

Typical grant range: $500 to $2,500

599
**Community Foundation of the Elmira-
Corning Area**
168 N. Main Street, Box 714
Elmira, NY 14902
(607) 734-6412

Emotionally disturbed; United Cerebral
Palsy; Multiple Sclerosis Association

Most grants awarded to organizations
located in Chemung County.

600
**Frances L. & Edwin L. Cummings
Memorial Fund**
501 Fifth Avenue, Suite 1208
New York, NY 10017
(212) 286-1778

Physically and mentally disabled; mental
health; employment programs

Grants awarded to organizations located
in the New York City vicinity.

Typical grant range: $15,000 to $40,000

601
Ira W. DeCamp Foundation
c/o Mudge Rose Guthrie Alexander &
Ferdon
630 Fifth Avenue, Suite 1650
New York, NY 10011
(212) 332-1612

Mentally and physically disabled; eye
research; employment programs

Typical grant range: $15,000 to $85,000

602
Eugene and Estelle Ferkauf Foundation
67 Allenwood Road
Great Neck, NY 11023
(516) 773-3269

National Center for Disability Services;
Jewish Braille Institute

Grants awarded to organizations located
in New York State.

603
Finch, Pruyn Foundation, Inc.
One Glen Street
Glen Falls, NY 12801
(518) 793-2541

Physically disabled; Special Olympics;
Association for Retarded Citizens

Grants awarded to organizations located
in Glen Falls.

604
D.E. French Foundation, Inc.
120 Genesee Street, Suite 503
Auburn, NY 13021
(315) 253-9321

Visually impaired; physically disabled;
recreation; youth

Grants awarded to organizations located
in the Auburn vicinity.

605
Arnold D. Frese Foundation, Inc.
10 Rockefeller Plaza, Suite 916
New York, NY 10020
(212) 373-1960

New York Association for the Blind;
Association for Retarded Citizens

606
Herman Goldman Foundation
61 Broadway, 18th Floor
New York, NY 10006
(212) 797-9090

Visually impaired; physically disabled;
March of Dimes Birth Defects Foundation

Grants awarded to organizations located
in the New York City vicinity.

Typical grant range: $5,000 to $40,000

607
Josephine Goodyear Foundation
1920 Liberty Building
Buffalo, NY 14202
(716) 856-2112

Physically disabled; Goodwill Industries;
St. Mary's School for the Deaf

Grants awarded to organizations located
in the Buffalo vicinity.

608
Greer Family Foundation
c/o Weiss, Peck & Greer
One New York Plaza, 30th Floor
New York, NY 10004
(212) 908-9500

Physically disabled; Helpers of the
Mentally Retarded

Typical grant range: $500 to $2,500

609
Hasbro Children's Foundation
32 W. 23rd Street
New York, NY 10010
(212) 645-2400

Mentally disabled; blind; hard-of-hearing;
youth

Typical grant range: $5,000 to $60,000

610
Charles Hayden Foundation
One Bankers Trust Plaza
130 Liberty Street
New York, NY 10006
(212) 938-0790

Deaf; physically disabled; education;
employment programs

Typical grant range: $15,000 to $125,000

611
Hearst Foundation, Inc.
888 Seventh Avenue, 45th Floor
New York, NY 10106
(212) 586-5404

Disabled (all areas); youth; research;
independent living programs; cultural
programs

Typical grant range: $10,000 to $40,000

612
The JM Foundation
60 E. 42nd Street, Room 1651
New York, NY 10165
(212) 687-7735

Physically disabled; independent living
programs; youth; Funding Partnership for
People with Disabilities; Association for
Retarded Citizens; Recording for the
Blind; Dole Foundation for Employment
of People with Disabilities; Goodwill
Industries

Typical grant range: $10,000 to $20,000

613
Julia R. and Estelle L. Foundation, Inc.
817 Washington Street
Buffalo, NY 14203
(716) 857-3325

Mentally and physically disabled; deaf;
Goodwill Industries

Grants awarded to organizations located
in the Buffalo vicinity.

Typical grant range: $3,000 to $30,000

614
Walter H. D. Killough Trust
c/o Marine Midland Bank, N.A.
250 Park Avenue, 4th Floor
New York, NY 10177
(212) 503-2768

Helen Keller Services for the Blind;
Jewish Guild for the Blind

615
L and L Foundation
c/o Mildred C. Brinn
570 Park Avenue, Suite 1A
New York, NY 10021

Jewish Guild for the Blind; Southampton
Fresh Air Home for Crippled Children

616
Frederick McDonald Trust
c/o Fleet Investment Services
69 State Street, 9th Floor
Albany, NY 12201
(518) 447-4189

Center for the Disabled; Association for
the Blind; United Cerebral Palsy

Grants awarded to organizations located
in Albany.

Typical grant range: $1,000 to $7,500

617
Edward S. Moore Foundation, Inc.
c/o Walter, Conston, Alexander and Green
90 Park Avenue
New York, NY 10016
(212) 210-9400

Recording for the Blind; Society to
Advance the Retarded

Typical grant range: $3,000 to $25,000

618
J. P. Morgan Charitable Trust
60 Wall Street, 46th Floor
New York, NY 10260
(212) 648-9673

Visually impaired; physically disabled;
cultural programs

Grants awarded to organizations located
in the New York City vicinity.

Typical grant range: $5,000 to $30,000

619
William T. Morris Foundation, Inc.
230 Park Avenue, Suite 622
New York, NY 10169
(212) 986-8036

Deafness Research Foundation; Goodwill
Industries; Recording for the Blind

Typical grant range: $5,000 to $50,000

620
Henry and Lucy Moses Fund, Inc.
c/o Moses & Singer
1301 Avenue of the Americas
New York, NY 10019
(212) 554-7800

Disabled (all areas); youth; education;
New York League for Hard of Hearing

Most grants awarded to organizations
located in the New York City vicinity.

Typical grant range: $3,000 to $12,000

621
NEC Foundation of America
c/o NEC America Inc.
Eight Old Sod Farm Road
Melville, NY 11747
(516) 753-7021

National Technical Institute for the Deaf;
Telecommunication for the Deaf; The
Stony Brook Foundation-Technology for
People with Disabilities

Typical grant range: $5,000 to $30,000

622
New York Community Trust
Two Park Avenue, 24th Floor
New York, NY 10016
(212) 686-0010

Mental health; developmentally disabled;
American Dance Theatre of the Deaf;
Goodwill Industries; National Society to
Prevent Blindness

Grants awarded to organizations located
in New York City, Long Island and
Westchester County.

Typical grant range: $5,000 to $45,000

623
Nichols Foundation, Inc.
630 Fifth Avenue, Room 1964
New York, NY 10111
(212) 581-1160

Physically disabled; Red Acre Farm
Hearing Dog Center; Recording for
the Blind

Grants awarded to organizations located
in the New York vicinity.

Typical grant range: $1,000 to $25,000

624
**Northern New York Community
Foundation, Inc.**
120 Washington Street
Watertown, NY 13601
(315) 782-7110

Disabled Persons Action Organization;
Croghan Library (accessibility project)

625
Moses L. Parshelsky Foundation
26 Court Street, Room 904
Brooklyn, NY 11242
(718) 875-8883

Hard-of-hearing; mental health; Helen
Keller Services for the Blind; Jewish
Braille Institute of America

Grants awarded to organizations located
in Queens and Brooklyn.

626
Peierls Foundation, Inc.
c/o Bankers Trust Company
P.O. Box 1297, Church Street Station
New York, NY 10008

American Foundation for the Blind;
Recording for the Blind; Deafness
Research Foundation

627
Pinkerton Foundation
725 Park Avenue
New York, NY 10021
(212) 772-6110

Speech impaired; physically disabled;
learning disabled; Alliance for
Mainstreaming Youth with Disabilities;
Resources for Children with Special
Needs

Grants awarded to organizations located
in New York City.

Typical grant range: $10,000 to $30,000

628
Prospect Hill Foundation, Inc.
420 Lexington Avenue, Suite 3020
New York, NY 10170
(212) 370-1144

National Multiple Sclerosis Society;
Easter Seal Society

Typical grant range: $3,000 to $30,000

629
Dorothea Haus Ross Foundation
1036 Monroe Avenue
Rochester, NY 14620
(716) 473-6006

Mentally and physically disabled

Typical grant range: $1,000 to $8,000

630
Helena Rubinstein Foundation, Inc.
405 Lexington Avenue
New York, NY 10174
(212) 986-0806

Physically disabled; independent living
programs; March of Dimes Birth Defects
Foundation (medical research); Fountain
House (mental health, rehabilitation);
Jewish Guild for the Blind

Grants awarded to organizations located
in New York City.

Typical grant range: $3,000 to $20,000

631
**Samuel and May Rudin
Foundation, Inc.**
345 Park Avenue
New York, NY 10154
(212) 407-2544

Visually impaired; physically disabled;
mental health

Grants awarded to organizations located
in New York City.

Typical grant range: $10,000 to $40,000

632
Scherman Foundation, Inc.
315 W. 57th Street, Suite 204
New York, NY 10019
(212) 489-7143

Mentally disabled; mental health; deaf;
cultural programs

Grants awarded to organizations located
in New York City.

Typical grant range: $10,000 to $30,000

633
Edith M. Schweckendieck Trusts
c/o Citibank, N.A.
One Court Square, 22nd Floor
Long Island City, NY 11120

Speech impaired; physically disabled;
education

634
John Ben Snow Memorial Trust
P.O. Box 378
Pulaski, NY 13142
(315) 298-6401

Physically disabled; Recording for
the Blind

Most grants awarded to organizations
located in Oswego County.

Typical grant range: $10,000 to $35,000

635
St. Giles Foundation
420 Lexington Avenue, Suite 1641
New York, NY 10170
(212) 338-9001

Physically disabled; visually impaired

Typical grant range: $30,000 to $125,000

636
Fred C. Trump Foundation
c/o Durben & Tosti
200 Garden City Plaza
Garden City, NY 11530

United Cerebral Palsy; Mental Health
Center; Association for the Help of
Retarded Children; United States
Organization for Disabled Athletes

Typical grant range: $500 to $2,500

637
Uris Brothers Foundation, Inc.
300 Park Avenue
New York, NY 10022
(212) 355-7080

Mentally disabled; New York League for
the Hard of Hearing

Grants awarded to organizations located
in the New York City vicinity.

Typical grant range: $10,000 to $27,000

638
van Ameringen Foundation, Inc.
509 Madison Avenue
New York, NY 10022
(212) 758-6221

Mental health; emotionally disturbed;
youth

Typical grant range: $20,000 to $50,000

639
Western New York Foundation
Main Seneca Building, Suite 1402
237 Main Street
Buffalo, NY 14203
(716) 847-6440

Goodwill Industries; Buffalo Hearing
and Speech

Typical grant range: $2,500 to $20,000

640
Robert W. Wilson Foundation
520 83rd Street, Suite 3R
Brooklyn, NY 11209
(718) 748-6113

American Paralysis Foundation;
International Center for Disabled;
National Multiple Sclerosis

Typical grant range: $2,500 to $25,000

NORTH CAROLINA

641
**Kathleen Price and Joseph M. Bryan
Family Foundation**
One North Pointe, Suite 170
3101 N. Elm Street
Greensboro, NC 27408
(910) 288-5455

Mentally and physically disabled; visually
impaired; Association for Retarded
Citizens

Grants awarded to organizations located
in North Carolina.

Typical grant range: $5,000 to $35,000

642
Community Foundation of Henderson County, Inc.
4th Avenue and Main Street
P.O. Box 1108
Hendersonville, NC 28793
(704) 697-6224

Visually impaired; mental health; physically disabled; recreation; YMCA (accessibility project)

Grants awarded to organizations located in Henderson County.

Typical grant range: $250 to $5,000

643
A.E. Finley Foundation, Inc.
P.O. Box 27785
Raleigh, NC 27611
(919) 782-0565

Special Olympics; United Cerebral Palsy; March of Dimes; Cystic Fibrosis

Grants awarded to organizations located in North Carolina.

644
Foundation for the Carolinas
301 S. Brevard Street
Charlotte, NC 28202
(704) 376-9541

Goodwill Industries; Special Olympics

Grants awarded to organizations located in North Carolina and South Carolina.

645
Foundation of Greater Greensboro, Inc.
P.O. Box 1207
Greensboro, NC 27402
(910) 379-9100

Learning disabled; mental health; hard-of-hearing; eye research; Special Olympics; Industries of the Blind; Piedmont Center for Therapeutic Horseback Riding

Most grants awarded to organizations located in the Greensboro vicinity.

646
Greater Triangle Community Foundation
P.O. Box 12834
Research Triangle Park, NC 27709
(919) 549-9840

Physically and mentally disabled

Grants awarded to organizations located in Wake, Durham and Orange Counties.

647
John W. and Anna H. Hanes Foundation
c/o Wachovia Bank of North Carolina, N.A.
P.O. Box 3099, MC 31022
Winston-Salem, NC 27150
(910) 770-5274

Lions Association for the Blind; Association for the Handicapped; United Cerebral Palsy

Grants awarded to organizations located in North Carolina.

Typical grant range: $2,000 to $22,000

648
Kate B. Reynolds Charitable Trust
128 Reynolda Village
Winston-Salem, NC 27106
(910) 723-1456

Physically disabled; developmentally disabled; youth; employment programs

Grants awarded to organizations located in North Carolina.

Typical grant range: $25,000 to $75,000

NORTH DAKOTA

649
Alex Stern Family Foundation
Bill Stern Building, Suite 205
609-1/2 First Avenue North
Fargo, ND 58102

Lutheran Social Services of Minnesota and North Dakota (care of adults with disabilities); American Lung Association (a camp for children with Cystic Fibrosis)

OHIO

650
Akron Community Foundation
Society Building, Suite 900
159 S. Main Street
Akron, OH 44308
(216) 376-8522

Physically disabled; recreation; Akron
Blind Center and Workshop

Grants awarded to organizations located
in the Akron vicinity.

Typical grant range: $1,000 to $20,000

651
William H. Albers Foundation, Inc.
P.O. Box 58360
Cincinnati, OH 45258

Cincinnati Association for the Blind;
Cerebral Palsy Service Center

Most grants awarded to organizations
located in Cincinnati.

Typical grant range: $1,000 to $7,000

652
**Elsie and Harry Baumker Charitable
Foundation, Inc.**
2828 Barrington Drive
Toledo, OH 43606
(419) 535-6969

Visually impaired; hard-of-hearing;
speech impaired; recreation; The Sight
Center

Grants awarded to organizations located
in Ohio, with an emphasis in Toledo.

Typical grant range: $500 to $7,000

653
Bicknell Fund
c/o Advisory Services, Inc.
1422 Euclid Avenue, Suite 1010
Cleveland, OH 44115
(216) 363-6482

Visually impaired; Goodwill Industries;
Cleveland Hearing and Speech Center

Typical grant range: $1,500 to $7,000

654
**Eva L. and Joseph M. Bruening
Foundation**
1422 Euclid Avenue, Suite 627
Cleveland, OH 44115
(216) 621-2632

Physically disabled; recreation; Cleveland
Hearing and Speech Center

Grants awarded to organizations located
in the Cleveland vicinity.

Typical grant range: $5,000 to $75,000

655
Cleveland Foundation
1422 Euclid Avenue, Suite 1400
Cleveland, OH 44115
(216) 861-3810

Mentally disabled, developmentally
disabled; mental health; Services for
Independent Living; Goodwill Industries

Grants awarded to organizations located
in the Cleveland vicinity.

Typical grant range: $1,000 to $75,000

656
Columbus Foundation
1234 E. Broad Street
Columbus, OH 43205
(614) 251-4000

Visually impaired; developmentally
disabled; mental health; independent
living programs; youth; employment
projects

Grants awarded to organizations located
in the Columbus vicinity.

657
Community Foundation of Greater Lorain County
1865 N. Ridge Road East, Suite A
Lorain, OH 44055
(216) 277-0142

Deaf; cultural organizations; Easter Seal Society; Family Alliance for the Mentally Ill; Lutheran Employment Assistance Program (physically disabled)

Grants awarded to organizations located in the Lorain County vicinity.

Typical grant range: $1,500 to $12,000

658
Coshocton Foundation
P.O. Box 15
Coshocton, OH 43812
(614) 622-0010

Board of Mental Retardation; March of Dimes; Six County Mental Health; Residential Homes for Developmentally Disabled

Grants awarded to organizations located in Coshocton County.

659
Charles H. Dater Foundation, Inc.
508 Atlas Bank Building
Cincinnati, OH 45202
(513) 241-1234

Physically disabled; youth; St. Joseph's Home (therapeutic equipment); Radio Reading Service; Telecommunications for the Deaf; Riding for the Handicapped (therapeutic riding program)

Grants awarded to organizations located in the Cincinnati vicinity.

Typical grant range: $1,000 to $11,000

660
Dayton Foundation
2100 Kettering Tower
Dayton, OH 45423
(513) 222-0410

Mental health; emotionally disabled; Disabled Consumers' Network (blind); Technology Resource Center (visually impaired)

Many grants awarded to organizations located in the Dayton vicinity.

661
Dayton Power & Light Company Foundation
Courthouse Plaza, S.W.
P.O. Box 1247
Dayton, OH 45402
(513) 259-7131

Cystic Fibrosis Foundation; Easter Seals; March of Dimes

Typical grant range: $500 to $15,000

662
1525 Foundation
1525 National City Bank Building
Cleveland, OH 44114
(216) 696-4200

Physically disabled; Recording for the Blind

Most grants awarded to organizations located in Cuyahoga County.

Typical grant range: $10,000 to $100,000

663
GAR Foundation
50 S. Main Street
P.O. Box 1500
Akron, OH 44309
(216) 376-5300

Blind; physically disabled; employment programs; accessibility projects; Goodwill Industries

Most grants awarded to organizations located in the Akron vicinity.

Typical grant range: $10,000 to $75,000

664
Greater Cincinnati Foundation
425 Walnut Street, Suite 1110
Cincinnati, OH 45202
(513) 241-2880

Mentally and physically disabled; youth;
employment programs

Grants awarded to organizations located
in the Cincinnati vicinity.

665
George Gund Foundation
1845 Guildhall Building
45 Prospect Avenue West
Cleveland, OH 44115
(216) 241-3114

Eye research; physically disabled

666
**Robert E. Hillier Family
Charitable Trust**
1365 Sharon-Copley Road
P.O. Box 70
Sharon Center, OH 44274
(216) 239-2711

Goodwill Industries; Akron Blind Center

Typical grant range: $500 to $8,000

667
Martha Holden Jennings Foundation
710 Halle Building
1228 Euclid Avenue
Cleveland, OH 44115
(216) 589-5700

Mentally disabled; visually impaired;
youth

Grants awarded to organizations located
in Ohio.

Typical grant range: $2,000 to $20,000

668
Louise Kramer Foundation
c/o Society Bank Trust Dept.
34 N. Main Street
Dayton, OH 45402
(513) 226-6076

United Cerebral Palsy; Goodwill Industries

Most grants awarded to organizations
located in Dayton.

669
Kulas Foundation
Tower City Center
610 Terminal Tower
Cleveland, OH 44113
(216) 623-4770

Physically disabled; Fairmount Theatre
of the Deaf

Grants awarded to organizations located in
the Cleveland vicinity.

Typical grant range: $5,000 to $35,000

670
Lubrizol Foundation
29400 Lakeland Blvd.
Wickliffe, OH 44092
(216) 943-4200

Cleveland Hearing and Speech Center;
Goodwill Industries; Mental Health Center

Grants awarded to organizations located in
areas of company operations.

Typical grant range: $1,000 to $11,000

671
Nord Family Foundation
347 Midway Blvd.
Elyria, OH 44035
(216) 324-2822

Mentally and physically disabled;
recreation; youth; accessibility programs;
Mental Health Services; Association for
Retarded Citizens

Grants awarded to organizations located in
Cuyahoga and Lorain Counties.

Typical grant range: $10,000 to $50,000

672
Parker-Hannifin Foundation
17325 Euclid Avenue
Cleveland, OH 44112
(216) 531-3000

Mental health; mentally and physically
disabled; recreation

Typical grant range: $500 to $3,000

673
**Elisabeth Severance Prentiss
Foundation**
c/o National City Bank
P.O. Box 5756
Cleveland, OH 44101
(216) 575-2760

Association for Retarded Citizens

Grants awarded to organizations located
in the Cleveland vicinity.

674
Reeves Foundation
232-4 W. Third Street
P.O. Box 441
Dover, OH 44622
(216) 364-4660

Physically disabled; YMCA (accessibility
project); Salvation Army (accessibility
project)

Grants awarded to organizations located
in Ohio, with an emphasis in Dover.

675
Helen Steiner Rice Foundation
221 E. Fourth Street, Suite 2100, Atrium 2
Cincinnati, OH 45202
(513) 451-9241

Mental Health Services of Lorain County;
Cincinnati Riding for the Handicapped;
Resident Home for the Mentally Retarded;
Easter Seal Society

Typical grant range: $3,000 to $9,000

676
**Richland County Foundation of
Mansfield, Ohio**
24 W. Third Street, Suite 100
Mansfield, OH 44902
(419) 525-3020

Physically disabled; education; job
training

Grants awarded to organizations located
in Richland County.

677
Josephine S. Russell Charitable Trust
PNC Bank, Ohio, N.A.
P.O. Box 1198
Cincinnati, OH 45201
(513) 651-8377

Cincinnati Riding for the Handicapped;
Home and School for the Blind; Church
of Our Savior (accessibility project for
people who are physically disabled)

Grants awarded to organizations located
in the Cincinnati vicinity.

Typical grant range: $3,000 to $12,000

678
Jacob G. Schmidlapp Trust No. 1
c/o The Fifth Third Bank
Dept. 00864, Foundation Office
Cincinnati, OH 45263
(513) 579-6034

Physically disabled; Association for the
Retarded; Radio Reading Service (for
people who are blind)

Grants awarded to organizations located
in the Cincinnati vicinity.

Typical grant range: $5,000 to $60,000

679

Kelvin and Eleanor Smith Foundation
1100 National City Bank Bldg.
Cleveland, OH 44114
(216) 566-5500

Blind; mental health; Fairmount Theater of the Deaf

Grants awarded to organizations located in the Cleveland vicinity.

Typical grant range: $5,000 to $40,000

680

Stark County Foundation
United Bank Building, Suite 350
220 Market Avenue South
Canton, OH 44702
(216) 454-3426

Developmentally disabled; recreation; deaf; Belle Stone School Classes for the Hearing Impaired

Grants awarded to organizations located in Stark County.

Typical grant range: $3,000 to $20,000

681

Toledo Community Foundation, Inc.
608 Madison Avenue, Suite 1540
Toledo, OH 43604
(419) 241-5049

Mental health; Autistic Community of Northwest Ohio; Sunshine Children's Home (mentally disabled children); Adriel School (disabled-foster program)

682

Charles Westheimer Family Fund
1126 Fort View Place
Cincinnati, OH 45202
(513) 421-3030

Cincinnati Association for the Blind; Radio Reading Service; Cerebral Palsy Service Center

Grants awarded to organizations located in Cincinnati.

Typical grant range: $100 to $2,000

683

Thomas H. White Foundation
627 Hanna Building
1422 Euclid Avenue
Cleveland, OH 44115
(216) 696-7273

United Cerebral Palsy; Association for Retarded Citizens

Grants awarded to organizations located in Cleveland.

Typical grant range: $1,000 to $35,000

684

Wodecroft Foundation
1900 Chemed Center
225 E. Fifth Street
Cincinnati, OH 45202
(513) 977-8250

Cystic Fibrosis Foundation; The David Lawrence Foundation for Mental Health

Typical grant range: $1,000 to $10,000

685

Wolfe Associates Inc.
34 S. Third Street
Columbus, OH 43215
(614) 461-5220

Physically disabled; Columbus Speech and Hearing Center

Typical grant range: $2,000 to $20,000

OKLAHOMA

686

Mervin Bovaird Foundation
800 Oneok Plaza
100 W. Fifth Street
Tulsa, OK 74103
(918) 583-1777

Physically disabled; visually impaired; Goodwill Industries

Most grants awarded to organizations located in Tulsa.

Typical grant range: $1,000 to $15,000

687
Broadhurst Foundation
401 S. Boston, Suite 100
Tulsa, OK 74103
(918) 584-0661

Visually impaired; eye research; Goodwill
Industries; Mental Health Association

Most grants awarded to organizations
located in Oklahoma.

688
Cuesta Foundation, Inc.
One Williams Center, Suite 4400
Tulsa, OK 74172
(918) 584-7266

Mentally disabled; mental health;
Goodwill Industries; Christian Blind
Mission

Grants awarded to organizations located
in Oklahoma.

Typical grant range: $1,000 to $5,000

689
J.E. and L.E. Mabee Foundation, Inc.
3000 Mid-Continent Tower
401 South Boston
Tulsa, OK 74103
(918) 584-4286

Physically and mentally disabled; deaf;
youth; employment programs

Typical grant range: $50,000 to $450,000

690
McCasland Foundation
P.O. Box 400
McCasland Building
Duncan, OK 73534
(405) 252-5580

Society to Prevent Blindness; Special
Olympics

Typical grant range: $2,000 to $65,000

691
Samuel Roberts Noble Foundation, Inc.
P.O. Box 2180
2510 State Highway 199 East
Ardmore, OK 73402
(405) 223-5810

American Paralysis Foundation;
Oklahoma Special Olympics

Most grants awarded to organizations
located in Oklahoma.

Typical grant range: $10,000 to $125,000

692
**Oklahoma City Community
Foundation, Inc.**
115 Park Avenue
Oklahoma City, OK 73103
(405) 235-5603

Physically disabled; hard-of-hearing

Grants awarded to organizations located
in the Oklahoma City vicinity.

Typical grant range: $2,000 to $15,000

693
**Oklahoma Gas and Electric Company
Foundation, Inc.**
101 N. Robinson
P.O. Box 321
Oklahoma City, OK 73101
(405) 272-3196

Special Olympics; Mental Health
Association

Grants awarded to organizations located
in Oklahoma.

Typical grant range: $3,500 to $10,000

694
Puterbaugh Foundation
215 E. Choctaw, Suite 117
P.O. Box 729
McAlester, OK 74502
(918) 426-1591

Christian Record Braille Foundation;
Oklahoma Independent Living Resource
Center (physically disabled); Oklahoma
Easter Seal Society; Eye Bank; Baptist
Medical Center Foundation (hearing
impaired research)

Grants awarded to organizations located
in Oklahoma.

695
Sarkeys Foundation
116 S. Peters, Suite 219
Norman, OK 73069
(405) 364-3703

Mental health; youth; recreation; United
Cerebral Palsy

Grants awarded to organizations located
in Oklahoma.

Typical grant range: $5,000 to $80,000

696
C.W. Titus Foundation
1801 Philtower Building
Tulsa, OK 74103
(918) 582-8095

Physically disabled; recreation

Typical grant range: $1,000 to $15,000

697
Anne and Henry Zarrow Foundation
Mid-Continent Tower
P.O. Box 1530
Tulsa, OK 74101
(918) 587-3391

Tulsa Center for the Physically Limited;
National Rehabilitation Hospital; Tulsa
Psychiatric Center

Grants awarded to organizations located
in the Tulsa vicinity.

Typical grant range: $3,000 to $20,000

OREGON

698
Collins Foundation
1618 S.W. First Avenue, Suite 305
Portland, OR 97201
(503) 227-7171

Goodwill Industries; Association for
Retarded Citizens; Easter Seal Society;
Mental Health Center

Grants awarded to organizations located
in Oregon.

Typical grant range: $5,000 to $100,000

699
Jackson Foundation
c/o U.S. Bank, Trust Dept.
P.O. Box 3168
Portland, OR 97208
(503) 275-5718

Learning disabled; Easter Seal Society;
Goodwill Industries

Grants awarded to organizations located
in Oregon.

700
Meyer Memorial Trust
1515 S.W. Fifth Avenue, Suite 500
Portland, OR 97201
(503) 228-5512

Physically disabled; emotionally
disturbed; developmentally disabled;
mental health; youth; accessibility
projects; Infant Hearing Resource;
Easter Seal Society

Most grants awarded to organizations
located in Oregon.

701
Oregon Community Foundation
621 S.W. Morrison, Suite 725
Portland, OR 97205
(503) 227-6846

Disabled (all areas); Goodwill Industries;
Easter Seal Society; Portland Center for
Hearing and Speech; Association for
Retarded Citizens; March of Dimes;
Oregon School for the Blind; Mental
Health Association

Grants awarded to organizations located
in Oregon.

Typical grant range: $1,000 to $20,000

702
Rose E. Tucker Charitable Trust
900 S.W. Fifth Avenue
Portland, OR 97204
(503) 224-3380

Mental health; Association for Retarded
Citizens; Easter Seal Society

Most grants awarded to organizations
located in the Portland vicinity.

Typical grant range: $2,000 to $11,000

PENNSYLVANIA

703
Arcadia Foundation
105 E. Logan Street
Norristown, PA 19401
(215) 275-8460

Visually impaired; physically disabled;
independent living programs; Associated
Services for the Blind

Grants awarded to organizations located
in Pennsylvania.

Typical grant range: $1,000 to $25,000

704
H.M. Bitner Charitable Trust
c/o Mellon Bank, N.A.
One Mellon Bank Center, Room 3845
Pittsburgh, PA 15258
(412) 234-4695

Eye research; Housing Options for the
Mentally Ill; Overbrook School for the
Blind; Goodwill Industries; Recording
for the Blind; Pennsylvania School for
the Deaf

Typical grant range: $500 to $4,000

705
Buhl Foundation
Four Gateway Center, Room 1522
Pittsburgh, PA 15222
(412) 566-2711

Greater Pittsburgh Guild for the Blind;
YMCA (physically disabled); The DePaul
Institute (children who are deaf); Pace
School (autism)

Most grants awarded to organizations
located in the Pittsburgh vicinity.

Typical grant range: $5,000 to $75,000

706
**Anne L. and George H. Clapp
Charitable and Educational Trust**
c/o Mellon Bank, N.A.
Three Mellon Bank Center, Suite 4000
Pittsburgh, PA 15259
(412) 234-7210

Physically disabled; Western
Pennsylvania School for Blind Children

Grants awarded to organizations located
in the Pittsburgh vicinity.

Typical grant range: $5,000 to $20,000

707
Hall Foundation
P.O. Box 1200
Camp Hill, PA 17011
(717) 236-0384

Goodwill Industries of Central
Pennsylvania; March of Dimes Fund

Grants awarded to organizations located
in Pennsylvania.

708
H.J. Heinz Company Foundation
P.O. Box 57
Pittsburgh, PA 15230
(412) 456-5772

Mentally and physically disabled;
recreation

Grants awarded to organizations located
in areas of company operations.

Typical grant range: $500 to $5,000

709
Hillman Foundation, Inc.
2000 Grant Building
Pittsburgh, PA 15219
(412) 338-3466

School for Exceptional Children; Greater
Pennsylvania Guild for the Blind

Most grants awarded to organizations
located in the Pittsburgh vicinity.

Typical grant range: $5,000 to $75,000

710
T. James Kavanagh Foundation
57 Northwood Road
Newton Square, PA 19073
(215) 356-0743

Physically disabled; elderly; Church
(accessibility project)

Most grants awarded to Catholic
organizations.

Typical grant range: $500 to $3,000

711
**Josiah W. and Bessie H. Kline
Foundation, Inc.**
42 Kline Village
Harrisburg, PA 17104
(717) 232-0266

Cystic Fibrosis Foundation; Pennsylvania
Special Olympics

Typical grant range: $2,000 to $25,000

712
McCune Foundation
1104 Commonwealth Building
316 Fourth Avenue
Pittsburgh, PA 15222
(412) 644-8779

Mentally and physically disabled; visually
impaired; youth; education; accessibility
projects

Most grants awarded to organizations
located in the Pittsburgh vicinity.

Typical grant range: $50,000 to $400,000

713
John R. McCune Charitable Trust
P.O. Box 1749
Pittsburgh, PA 15230
(412) 644-7796

Mentally and physically disabled; deaf;
education

Grants awarded to organizations located
in Pennsylvania.

Typical grant range: $15,000 to $50,000

714
Mellon Bank Foundation
c/o Mellon Bank Corp.
One Mellon Bank Center, Suite 1830
Pittsburgh, PA 15258
(412) 234-2732

Vocational Rehabilitation Center; United
Cerebral Palsy; Greater Pittsburgh Guild
for the Blind

Grants awarded to organizations located
in Southwestern Pennsylvania.

715
R.K. Mellon Family Foundation
P.O. Box 2930
Pittsburgh, PA 15230
(412) 392-2800

Deaf; Canine Companions for Independence;
Church (accessibility project)

Typical grant range: $5,000 to $35,000

716
Richard King Mellon Foundation
P.O. Box 2930
Pittsburgh, PA 15230
(412) 392-2800

Physically disabled; visually impaired;
education; youth

Most grants awarded to organizations
located in Pittsburgh.

Typical grant range: $40,000 to $250,000

717
W.I. Patterson Charitable Fund
407 Oliver Building
Pittsburgh, PA 15222
(412) 281-5580

Goodwill Industries; Pennsylvania Special
Olympics; Greater Pittsburgh Guild for the
Blind; Christian Education for the Blind;
Spina Bifida Association (camping program);
Vocational Rehabilitation Center (training
and placement center)

Grants awarded to organizations located
in Allegheny County.

Typical grant range: $1,000 to $7,500

718
Pew Charitable Trusts
One Commerce Square
2005 Market Street, Suite 1700
Philadelphia, PA 19103
(215) 575-9050

Physically disabled; visually impaired;
mental health

719
Philadelphia Foundation
1234 Market Street, Suite 1900
Philadelphia, PA 19107
(215) 563-6417

March of Dimes; St. Edmond's Home for
Crippled Children; Disabled in Action;
Associated Services for the Blind; Mental
Health Center

Most grants awarded to organizations
located in the Philadelphia vicinity.

Typical grant range: $5,000 to $30,000

720
Pittsburgh Foundation
One PPG Place, 30th Floor
Pittsburgh, PA 15222
(412) 391-5122

Disabled (all areas); mental health;
developmentally disabled; youth

Grants awarded to organizations located
in the Pittsburgh vicinity.

Typical grant range: $5,000 to $50,000

721
Harry Plankenhorn Foundation, Inc.
c/o Abram M. Snyder
R.D. 2
Cogan Station, PA 17728

Association for Retarded Citizens;
Lycoming County Crippled Children
Society; Deaf of Lycoming County;
Enterprises for the Handicapped; Multiple
Sclerosis Society; Lycoming County
Association for the Blind; Lycoming
County Association for the Deaf;
Williamsport Muscular Dystrophy

Grants awarded to organizations located
in Lycoming County.

Typical grant range: $1,000 to $20,000

722
PPG Industries Foundation
One PPG Place
Pittsburgh, PA 15272
(412) 434-2962

Mentally and physically disabled;
visually impaired

Grants awarded to organizations located
in areas of company operations, with an
emphasis in Pittsburgh.

723
Scaife Family Foundation
Three Mellon Bank Center
525 William Penn Place, Suite 3900
Pittsburgh, PA 15219
(412) 392-2900

Mentally and physically disabled;
education; youth

Typical grant range: $20,000 to $85,000

724
Ethel Sergeant Clark Smith
Memorial Fund
101 Bryn Mawr Avenue, Suite 200
Bryn Mawr, PA 19010
(215) 525-9667

Delco Blind/Sight Center; St. Edmonds
Home for Crippled Children; Recording
for the Blind

Grants awarded to organizations located
in Delaware County.

Typical grant range: $5,000 to $40,000

725
Hoxie Harrison Smith Foundation
210 Fairlamb Avenue
Havertown, PA 19083
(215) 446-4651

Physically disabled; youth; Associated
Services for the Blind

726
Staunton Farm Foundation
c/o Mellon Bank
One Mellon Bank Center, 40th Fl.
Pittsburgh, PA 15258

Visually impaired; Southwind, Inc.
(emergency psychiatric care); Mental
Health Association

Grants awarded to organizations located
in Allegheny County.

727
Harry C. Trexler Trust
33 S. Seventh Street, Suite 205
Allentown, PA 18101
(215) 434-9645

Visually impaired; physically disabled;
youth

Grants awarded to organizations located
in Lehigh County.

Typical grant range: $12,000 to $30,000

728
Union Pacific Foundation
Martin Tower
Eighth and Eaton Avenues
Bethlehem, PA 18018
(215) 861-3225

Mentally and physically disabled; youth;
employment programs

Grants awarded to organizations located
in areas of company operations.

Typical grant range: $2,000 to $20,000

729
USX Foundation, Inc.
600 Grant Street
Pittsburgh, PA 15219
(412) 433-5237

Mentally and physically disabled;
visually impaired

Grants awarded to organizations located
in areas of company operations.

Typical grant range: $3,000 to $40,000

730
Widener Memorial Foundation in Aid of Handicapped Children
665 Thomas Road
P.O. Box 178
Lafayette Hill, PA 19444
(215) 836-7500

School District of Philadelphia (physically disabled); Cabrini College (accessibility project); YMCA (accessibility project); Easter Seal Society; Zoological Society of Philadelphia (children with disabilities); Pegasus Riding Center (children with disabilities); Please Touch Museum (accessibility project)

Typical grant range: $10,000 to $75,000

PUERTO RICO

731
Puerto Rico Community Foundation
Royal Bank Center Building, Suite 1417
Hato Rey, PR 00917
(809) 751-3822

Physically disabled; youth

Grants awarded to organizations located in Puerto Rico.

Typical grant range: $5,000 to $35,000

RHODE ISLAND

732
Hasbro Charitable Trust, Inc.
c/o Hasbro, Inc.
1027 Newport Avenue
Pawtucket, RI 02861
(401) 727-5429

Physically disabled; recreation; cultural programs; National Organization on Disability; March of Dimes

Grants awarded to organizations located in areas of company operations.

733
Rhode Island Foundation/Rhode Island Community Foundation
70 Elm Street
Providence, RI 02903
(401) 274-4564

Disabled (all areas); mental health; independent living programs; Sheltered Workshop

Grants awarded to organizations located in Rhode Island.

734
Herbert E. and Daisy A. Stride Memorial Foundation
c/o Aquidneck Medical Association
Memorial Blvd.
Newport, RI 02840
(401) 847-2290

Rhode Island Society for the Blind; March of Dimes

Typical grant range: $500 to $2,500

SOUTH CAROLINA

735
Central Carolina Community Foundation
P.O. Box 11222
Columbia, SC 29211
(803) 254-5601

Physically disabled; recreation; National Multiple Sclerosis Society

Typical grant range: $1,000 to $5,000

736
Close Foundation, Inc.
104 E. Springs Street
Lancaster, SC 29721
(803) 286-2196

Foundation for the Multi-Handicapped, Blind and Deaf

Typical grant range: $2,000 to $25,000

737
Community Foundation of Greater Greenville, Inc.
655 S. Main Street
P.O. Box 6909
Greenville, SC 29606
(803) 233-5925

Mental health; mentally disabled

Grants awarded to organizations located in Greenville County.

738
Gregg-Graniteville Foundation, Inc.
P.O. Box 418
Graniteville, SC 29829
(803) 663-7552

Special Olympics; Recording for the Blind; Mental Health Association

Typical grant range: $1,000 to $12,000

739
John I. Smith Charities, Inc.
c/o NationsBank, Trust Dept.
P.O. Box 608
Greenville, SC 29608
(803) 271-5847

Physically disabled; Speech, Hearing and Learning Center

Grants awarded to organizations located in South Carolina.

Typical grant range: $100 to $22,000

740
Spartanburg County Foundation
320 E. Main Street
Spartanburg, SC 29302
(803) 582-0138

Foundation for the Multi-Handicapped; YMCA Family Center (accessibility project)

Grants awarded to organizations located in Spartanburg county.

Typical grant range: $1,000 to $12,000

SOUTH DAKOTA

741
Sioux Falls Area Foundation
141 North Main Avenue, Suite 500
Sioux Falls, SD 57102
(605) 336-7055

Crippled Children's Hospital and School

Grants awarded to organizations located in the Sioux Falls vicinity.

TENNESSEE

742
Community Foundation of Greater Memphis
5210 Poplar Avenue, Suite 150
Memphis, TN 38119
(901) 761-3806

Visually impaired; mentally disabled; mental health; physically disabled; recreation

743
East Tennessee Foundation
360 NationsBank Center
550 W. Main Street
Knoxville, TN 37902
(615) 524-1223

Visually impaired; physically disabled

744
HCA Foundation
c/o Hospital Corp. of America
One Park Plaza, P.O. Box 550
Nashville, TN 37202-0550
(615) 320-2165

Disabled (all areas); Special Olympics; League for the Hearing Impaired; March of Dimes; Center for Independent Living

Grants awarded to organizations located in areas of company operations, with an emphasis in Nashville.

Typical grant range: $1,000 to $25,000

745
Plough Foundation
6077 Primacy Parkway, Suite 230
Memphis, TN 38119
(901) 761-9180

Physically disabled; employment
programs; Alliance for the Mentally Ill

Grants awarded to organizations located
in Memphis and in Shelby county.

Typical grant range: $15,000 to $100,000

TEXAS

746
Abell-Hanger Foundation
P.O. Box 430
Midland, TX 79702
(915) 684-6655

Disabled (all areas); developmentally
disabled; eye research; Texas Society
to Prevent Blindness; Association for
Retarded Citizens; Midland Cerebral
Palsy Center

Grants awarded to organizations located
in Texas.

Typical grant range: $15,000 to $75,000

747
Amarillo Area Foundation, Inc.
700 First National Place I
801 South Fillmore
Amarillo, TX 79101
(806) 376-4521

Amarillo Regional Speech and Hearing
Center; Goodwill Industries; Regional
Education for the Deaf

Typical grant range: $5,000 to $25,000

748
Amini Foundation
8000 IH-Ten West, Suite 820
San Antonio, TX 78230

Physically disabled; recreation;
San Antonio Wheelchair Athletes

Most grants awarded to organizations
located in San Antonio.

749
M.D. Anderson Foundation
1301 Fannin Street, 21st Floor
P.O. Box 809
Houston, TX 77001
(713) 658-2316

Mentally and physically disabled;
visually impaired

Grants awarded to organizations located
in Texas, with an emphasis in the Houston
vicinity.

Typical grant range: $5,000 to $75,000

750
Effie and Wofford Cain Foundation
4131 Spicewood Springs Road, Suite A-1
Austin, TX 78759
(512) 346-7490

Mentally and physically disabled;
developmentally disabled

Grants awarded to organizations located
in Texas.

Typical grant range: $5,000 to $75,000

751
**Harry S. and Isabel C. Cameron
Foundation**
c/o NationsBank
P.O. Box 298502
Houston, TX 77298
(713) 787-4553

Physically disabled; Speech and Hearing
Center; Mental Health Association

Most grants awarded to organizations
located in Houston.

Typical grant range: $1,000 to $9,000

752
Amon G. Carter Foundation
1212 NCNB Center
P.O. Box 1036
Fort Worth, TX 76101
(817) 332-2783

Physically disabled; visually impaired;
Center for Computer Assistance to the
Disabled; Easter Seal Society

Grants awarded to organizations located
in the Fort Worth vicinity.

Typical grant range: $2,000 to $35,000

753
Cockrell Foundation
1600 Smith, Suite 4600
Houston, TX 77002
(713) 651-1271

Physically disabled; deaf; youth

Grants awarded to organizations located
in the Houston vicinity.

Typical grant range: $5,000 to $50,000

754
Community Foundation of Abilene
500 Chestnut, Suite 1509
P.O. Box 1001
Abilene, TX 79604
(915) 676-3883

Learning disabled; Goodwill Industries

Grants awarded to organizations located
in the Abilene vicinity.

Typical grant range: $1,000 to $12,000

755
Constantin Foundation
3811 Turtle Creek Blvd., Suite 320-LB 39
Dallas, TX 75219
(214) 522-9300

Visually impaired; physically disabled;
youth

Grants awarded to organizations located
in the Dallas vicinity.

Typical grant range: $10,000 to $50,000

756
Joe and Jessie Crump Fund
c/o Team Bank, N.A.
P.O. Box 2050
Ft. Worth, TX 76113
(817) 884-4151

Physically disabled; youth

Grants awarded to organizations located
in Texas.

757
**Davidson Family Charitable
Foundation**
310 West Texas, Suite 709
Midland, TX 79701
(915) 687-0995

Developmentally disabled; Association
for Retarded Citizens; Cerebral Palsy
Center

Grants awarded to organizations located
in Texas.

758
Ken W. Davis Foundation
P.O. Box 3419
Fort Worth, TX 76113
(817) 332-4081

Physically disabled; visually impaired

759
James R. Dougherty, Jr. Foundation
P.O. Box 640
Beeville, TX 78104
(512) 358-3560

Muscular Dystrophy Association;
Recording for the Blind

Grants awarded to organizations located
in Texas.

Typical grant range: $1,000 to $4,000

760
Dresser Foundation, Inc.
P.O. Box 718
Dallas, TX 75221
(214) 740-6078

Hard-of-hearing; visually impaired; Cystic Fibrosis Foundation

Grants awarded to organizations located in areas of company operations.

Typical grant range: $1,000 to $15,000

761
El Paso Community Foundation
Texas Commerce Bank Bldg., Suite 1616
El Paso, TX 79901
(915) 533-4020

Physically and mentally disabled

Grants awarded to organizations located in the El Paso vicinity.

762
Ellwood Foundation
P.O. Box 52482
Houston, TX 77052
(713) 652-0613

Mental health; visually impaired

Most grants awarded to organizations located in the Houston vicinity.

Typical grant range: $5,000 to $50,000

763
Fasken Foundation
500 W. Texas Avenue, Suite 1160
Midland, TX 79701
(915) 683-5401

March of Dimes; Multiple Sclerosis Society; Recording Library for the Blind

Grants awarded to organizations located in the Midland vicinity.

764
First Interstate Foundation of Texas
1000 Louisiana Street
P.O. Box 3326, MS No. 584
Houston, TX 77253
(713) 250-1850

Physically disabled; Shriners Hospital for Crippled Children; Foundation for the Retarded; Special Olympics

Grants awarded to organizations located in areas of company operations.

765
Fondren Foundation
7 TCT 37
P.O. Box 2558
Houston, TX 77252
(713) 236-4403

Mental health; physically disabled; hard-of-hearing

Most grants awarded to organizations located in Houston.

Typical grant range: $15,000 to $125,000

766
George Foundation
207 S. Third Street
P.O. Drawer C
Richmond, TX 77469
(713) 342-6109

Physically disabled; visually impaired; mental health

Most grants awarded to organizations located in Ft. Bend County.

Typical grant range: $10,000 to $60,000

767
G.A.C. Halff Foundation
745 E. Mulberry, Suite 400
San Antonio, TX 78212
(210) 735-3300

Physically disabled; visually impaired

Grants awarded to organizations located in San Antonio.

Typical grant range: $3,000 to $20,000

768
Ewing Halsell Foundation
711 Navarro Street, Suite 537
San Antonio, TX 78205
(210) 223-2640

Visually impaired; mental health;
physically disabled

Most grants awarded to organizations
located in San Antonio.

Typical grant range: $1,000 to $40,000

769
**George and Mary Josephine Hamman
Foundation**
910 Travis Street, Suite 1438
Houston, TX 77002
(713) 658-8345

Eye research; Goodwill Industries;
Houston School for Deaf Children;
Muscular Dystrophy Association

Grants awarded to organizations located
in Texas.

770
Hillcrest Foundation
c/o NationsBank, Trust Division
P.O. Box 830241
Dallas, TX 75283

Developmentally disabled; physically
disabled; employment programs;
Goodwill Industries; Lighthouse
for the Blind

Grants awarded to organizations located
in Texas, with an emphasis in Dallas.

Typical grant range: $5,000 to $50,000

771
Hoblitzelle Foundation
5956 Sherry Lane, Suite 901
Dallas, TX 75225
(214) 373-0462

Center for Computer Assistance to the
Disabled; Dallas Lighthouse for the Blind;
Easter Seal Society; United Cerebral
Palsy; Citizens Development Center
(accessibility project)

Grants awarded to organizations located
in Texas.

Typical grant range: $15,000 to $75,000

772
Houston Endowment, Inc.
600 Travis, Suite 6400
Houston, TX 77002
(713) 238-8100

Visually impaired; hard-of-hearing;
mentally disabled; eye research; youth;
independent living programs; Society to
Prevent Blindness

Grants awarded to organizations located
in Texas.

Typical grant range: $5,000 to $250,000

773
Harris and Eliza Kempner Fund
P.O. Box 119
Galveston, TX 77553
(409) 765-6671

Visually impaired; physically disabled;
mental health

Grants awarded to organizations located
in Galveston.

Typical grant range: $1,500 to $8,500

774
Eugene McDermott Foundation
3808 Euclid
Dallas, TX 75205
(214) 521-2924

Mental health; mentally disabled

Grants awarded to organizations located in Dallas.

Typical grant range: $2,500 to $25,000

775
Meadows Foundation, Inc.
Wilson Historic Block
3003 Swiss Avenue
Dallas, TX 75204
(214) 826-9431

Mental health; hard-of-hearing; physically disabled; developmentally disabled

Grants awarded to organizations located in Texas.

Typical grant range: $25,000 to $80,000

776
Moody Foundation
704 Moody National Bank Building
Galveston, TX 77550
(409) 763-5333

Disabled (all areas); youth; employment program

Grants awarded to organizations located in Texas.

Typical grant range: $15,000 to $200,000

777
Permian Basin Area Foundation
550 West Texas, Suite 110
P.O. Box 10424
Midland, TX 79702
(915) 682-4704

Mentally disabled; Midland Cerebral Palsy Center

778
RGK Foundation
2815 San Gabriel
Austin, TX 78705
(512) 474-9298

Mental health; Association for Retarded Citizens; Carroll Center for the Blind

779
Sid W. Richardson Foundation
309 Main Street
Fort Worth, TX 76102
(817) 336-0494

Mentally disabled; education; Association for the Blind; Center for Computer Assistance to the Disabled; Very Special Arts

Grants awarded to organizations located in Texas.

Typical grant range: $10,000 to $125,000

780
Rockwell Fund, Inc.
1360 Post Oak Blvd., Suite 780
Houston, TX 77056
(713) 629-9022

Physically disabled; mentally disabled; recreation; hard-of-hearing; Mental Health Association

Grants awarded to organizations located in the Houston vicinity.

Typical grant range: $10,000 to $25,000

781
San Antonio Area Foundation
530 McCullough, Suite 600
San Antonio, TX 78215
(210) 225-2243

Physically disabled; eye research; hard-of-hearing; learning disabilities; Goodwill Industries; Easter Seal Rehabilitation Center; Retina Research Foundation

Grants awarded to organizations located in the San Antonio vicinity.

Typical grant range: $500 to $15,000

782
W.L. & Louise E. Seymour Foundation
c/o Society National Bank
P.O. Box 99016
El Paso, TX 79999

Physically disabled; visually impaired

Grants awarded to organizations located
in El Paso.

Typical grant range: $5,000 to $25,000

783
Strake Foundation
712 Main Street, Suite 3300
Houston, TX 77002
(713) 546-2400

Visually impaired; Goodwill Industries;
Houston School for the Deaf; March of
Dimes; Mental Health Association;
Special Olympics

Grants awarded to organizations located
in Texas.

Typical grant range: $2,000 to $20,000

784
T.L.L. Temple Foundation
109 Temple Blvd.
Lufkin, TX 75901
(409) 639-5197

Mental health; physically disabled;
education

Typical grant range: $10,000 to $100,000

785
Vale-Asche Foundation
1010 River Oaks Bank Building
2001 Kirby Drive, Suite 910
Houston, TX 77019
(713) 520-7334

Physically and mentally disabled

Grants awarded to organizations located
in Houston.

Typical grant range: $2,000 to $30,000

786
Rachael & Ben Vaughan Foundation
P.O. Box 1579
Corpus Christi, TX 78403
(512) 241-2890

Goodwill Industries; Center for Hearing
Impaired Children

Typical grant range: $500 to $7,000

787
Crystelle Waggoner Charitable Trust
c/o NationsBank of Texas, N.A.
P.O. Box 1317
Ft. Worth, TX 76101
(817) 390-6114

Mental Health Association (depression
program); YWCA (physically disabled);
Goodwill Industries (expand vocational
rehabilitation program)

Typical grant range: $1,000 to $12,000

788
Lola Wright Foundation
P.O. Box 1138
Georgetown, TX 78627
(512) 869-2574

Physically and mentally disabled; mental
health; rehabilitation

Grants awarded to organizations located
in Texas.

Typical grant range: $3,000 to $30,000

UTAH

789
Castle Foundation
c/o West One Trust Co.
P.O. Box 3058
Salt Lake City, UT 84110
(801) 534-6085

Physically disabled; National Society for
the Prevention of Blindness

Grants awarded to organizations located
in Utah.

Typical grant range: $1,000 to $7,000

790

**Lawrence T. and Janet T. Dee
Foundation**
3905 Harrison Blvd., Suite W306
Ogden, UT 84403

March of Dimes; Palisade Handicapped
Children; National Society to Prevent
Blindness

Grants awarded to organizations located
in Utah.

791

**Dr. Ezekiel R. and Edna Wattis Dumke
Foundation**
448 S. 400 East, Suite 100
Salt Lake City, UT 84111
(801) 328-3531

Physically disabled; blind; recreation

Typical grant range: $3,000 to $20,000

792

Marriner S. Eccles Foundation
701 Deseret Building
79 S. Main Street
Salt Lake City, UT 84111
(801) 322-0116

Mental health; Park City Handicapped
Sports; National Society to Prevent
Blindness

Grants awarded to organizations located
in Utah.

Typical grant range: $3,000 to $30,000

793

**Willard L. Eccles Charitable
Foundation**
P.O. Box 45385
Salt Lake City, UT 84145
(801) 532-1500

National Society to Prevent Blindness;
Handicapped Sports Association;
Disabled Ski Program; Utah School for
the Blind

Grants awarded to organizations located
in Utah.

Typical grant range: $5,000 to $75,000

794

**Junior E. and Blanche B. Rich
Foundation**
c/o First Security Bank of Utah, N.A.
P.O. Box 30007
Salt Lake City, UT 84130

National Federation of the Blind; State
Library Division for the Blind

Grants awarded to organizations located
in Weber County.

Typical grant range: $100 to $2,000

VIRGINIA

795

Beazley Foundation, Inc.
3720 Brighton Street
Portsmouth, VA 23707
(804) 393-1605

Goodwill Industries; Easter Seal Society

796

**Community Foundation Serving
Richmond & Central Virginia**
9211 Forest Hill Avenue, Suite 109
Richmond, VA 23235
(804) 330-7400

Riverside School (project for students
with dyslexia); Southside Planning
Committee (home repairs for people
with disabilities)

Grants awarded to organizations located
in the Richmond vicinity and Central
Virginia.

Typical grant range: $1,000 to $11,000

797

Massey Foundation
P.O. Box 26765
Richmond, VA 23261

Mentally and physically disabled; deaf;
youth

Grants awarded to organizations located
in Virginia.

Typical grant range: $1,000 to $30,000

798
Memorial Foundation for Children
P.O. Box 8342
Richmond, VA 23226

National Society to Prevent Blindness;
Virginia Foundation for the Exceptional
Child; Virginia Special Olympics; Greater
Richmond Autism Support; Learning
Disabilities Council

Grants awarded to organizations located
in the Richmond vicinity.

Grants awarded to organizations helping
children.

Typical grant range: $5,000 to $22,000

799
Norfolk Foundation
1410 NationsBank Center
Norfolk, VA 23510
(804) 622-7951

Physically disabled; employment
programs; Goodwill Industries

Grants awarded to organizations located
in the Norfolk vicinity.

Typical grant range: $15,000 to $50,000

800
Perry Foundation
P.O. Box 558
Charlottesville, VA 22902
(804) 973-9441

Physically disabled; Recording for
the Blind

Grants awarded to organizations located
in Virginia.

801
**C.E. Richardson Benevolent
Foundation**
74 W. Main Street, Room 211
P.O. Box 1120
Pulaski, VA 24301
(703) 980-6628

National Multiple Sclerosis Society;
Easter Seal Society of Virginia (mentally
and physically disabled); New River
Valley for the Mentally Retarded
(therapeutic recreation)

Typical grant range: $1,000 to $6,000

802
**Wheat, First Securities/Butcher &
Singer Foundation**
P.O. Box 1357
Richmond, VA 23211
(804) 782-3518

Visually impaired; Special Olympics

Typical grant range: $1,000 to $15,000

WASHINGTON

803
**Norman Archibald Charitable
Foundation**
First Interstate Bank of Washington, N.A.
P.O. Box 21927
Seattle, WA 98111
(206) 292-3543

Hard-of-hearing; speech impaired; mental
health; mentally disabled; physically
disabled; recreation

Most grants awarded to organizations
located in the Puget Sound vicinity.

Typical grant range: $1,000 to $11,000

804
Bullitt Foundation, Inc.
1212 Minor Avenue
Seattle, WA 98101
(206) 343-0807

Hard-of-hearing; physically disabled;
education

Typical grant range: $10,000 to $60,000

805
Ben B. Cheney Foundation, Inc.
1201 Pacific Avenue, Suite 1600
Tacoma, WA 98402
(206) 572-2442

Learning disabled; hard-of-hearing; youth;
Resource Center for the Handicapped

Typical grant range: $2,000 to $45,000

806
Comstock Foundation
819 Washington Trust Financial Center
West 717 Sprague Avenue
Spokane, WA 99204
(509) 747-1527

Eastern Washington Center for the Deaf
and Hard of Hearing; Lilac Blind
Foundation; Goodwill Industries;

Typical grant range: $1,000 to $30,000

807
Forest Foundation
820 A Street, Suite 345
Tacoma, WA 98402
(206) 627-1634

School for Hearing Impaired Children;
Special Olympics; Resource Center for
the Handicapped

Typical grant range: $2,000 to $30,000

808
Foundation Northwest
421 W. Riverside Avenue, Suite 400
Spokane, WA 99201
(509) 624-2606

Visually impaired; Goodwill Industries

809
Glaser Foundation, Inc.
P.O. Box 6548
Bellevue, WA 98008

Physically disabled; mental health; day
care for children with disabilities; cultural
organizations ; accessibility projects;
Northwest School for the Hearing
Impaired

Grants awarded to organizations located
in the Puget Sound vicinity.

810
**Florence B. Kilworth Charitable
Foundation**
c/o Puget Sound National Bank
P.O. Box 11500, MS 8262
Tacoma, WA 98411
(206) 593-3884

Northwest School for the Hearing
Impaired; Goodwill Industries

Grants awarded to organizations located
in Tacoma and in Pierce County.

811
Laird, Norton Foundation
1300 Norton Building
Seattle, WA 98104
(206) 464-5292

Mentally disabled; physically disabled;
recreation; visually impaired; Alliance
for the Mentally Ill

812
Elizabeth A. Lynn Foundation
20016 50th Avenue West, Suite 101
Lynnwood, WA 98036
(206) 744-0888

Physically disabled; Northwest School for
the Hearing Impaired

813
Medina Foundation
1300 Norton Building
801 Second Avenue, 13th Floor
Seattle, WA 98104
(206) 464-5231

Mentally disabled; mental health;
Community Services for the Blind;
Foundation for the Handicapped;
Special Olympics

Grants awarded to organizations located
in the Seattle vicinity.

Typical grant range: $5,000 to $20,000

814
R.D. Merrill Foundation
1411 Fourth Ave. Bldg., Suite 1415
Seattle, WA 98101
(206) 682-3939

Hard-of-hearing; speech impaired;
visually impaired; March of Dimes;
Cystic Fibrosis Foundation; Lighthouse
for the Blind

Grants awarded to organizations located
in Washington.

815
Norcliffe Foundation
First Interstate Center
999 Third Avenue, Suite 1006
Seattle, WA 98104

Physically disabled; recreation;
Lighthouse for the Blind; Multiple
Sclerosis Society; Northwest School
for Hearing Impaired Children

Grants awarded to organizations located
in the Seattle vicinity.

Typical grant range: $500 to $20,000

816
Seattle Foundation
425 Pike Street, Suite 510
Seattle, WA 98101
(206) 622-2294

Visually impaired; Library for the Blind
and Physically Handicapped; Mental
Health Center; Goodwill Industries;
Hearing, Speech and Deafness Center;
Special Olympics

Grants awarded to organizations located
in Seattle.

Typical grant range: $3,000 to $20,000

817
Skinner Foundation
1326 Fifth Avenue, Suite 711
Seattle, WA 98101
(206) 623-6480

Mental health; Northwest School for
Hearing Impaired Children; Special
Olympics; March of Dimes; Deaf
Community Services; Multiple Sclerosis
Society

Grants awarded to organizations located
in areas of company operations (Skinner
Corporation).

Typical grant range: $1,000 to $11,000

818
Teachers Foundation, Inc.
325 Eastlake Avenue, East
Seattle, WA 98109

Physically disabled; Northwest School
for Hearing Impaired Children

Grants awarded to organizations located
in Washington, with an emphasis in
Seattle.

Typical grant range: $500 to $10,000

WEST VIRGINIA

819
Beckley Area Foundation, Inc.
P.O. Box 1092
Beckley, WV 25802

Physically disabled; Sheltered Workshop

Grants awarded to organizations located
in the Beckley vicinity.

Typical grant range: $500 to $6,000

820
Greater Kanawha Valley Foundation
1426 Kanawha Blvd., East
Charleston, WV 25301
(304) 346-3620

Mentally and physically disabled

Grants awarded to organizations located
in the Greater Kanawha Valley.

Typical grant range: $1,000 to $14,000

821
Bernard McDonough Foundation, Inc.
1000 Grand Central Mall
P.O. Box 1825
Parkersburg, WV 26102
(304) 485-4494

Physically disabled; visually impaired

Grants awarded to organizations located
in West Virginia.

Typical grant range: $1,000 to $20,000

822
Parkersburg Community Foundation
402 Juliana Street
P.O. Box 1762
Parkersburg, WV 26102
(304) 428-4438

Physically disabled; recreation; youth;
accessibility projects

Grants awarded to organizations located
in the Parkersburg vicinity.

823
Hugh I. Shott, Jr. Foundation
c/o First National Bank of Bluefield
500 Federal Street
Bluefield, WV 24701
(304) 325-8181

Physically disabled; Opportunity
Workshop for the Handicapped

WISCONSIN

824
Banta Company Foundation, Inc.
100 Main Street
P.O. Box 8003
Menasha, WI 54952
(414) 722-7777

Association for Retarded Citizens; United
Cerebral Palsy; Goodwill Industries;
Special Olympics; Alliance for the
Mentally Ill

Grants awarded to organizations located
in areas of company operations.

825
**Lynde and Harry Bradley
Foundation, Inc.**
777 E. Wisconsin Avenue, Suite 2285
Milwaukee, WI 53202
(414) 291-9915

Mentally and physically disabled; visually
impaired; Goodwill Industries

Typical grant range: $20,000 to $125,000

826
**Frank G. Brotz Family
Foundation, Inc.**
3518 Lakeshore Road
P.O. Box 551
Sheboygan, WI 53081
(414) 458-2121

Visually impaired; physically disabled;
recreation

Grants awarded to organizations located
in Wisconsin.

827
Community Foundation for the Fox Valley Region, Inc.
P.O. Box 563
Appleton, WI 54912
(414) 830-1290

Developmentally disabled; mentally disabled; physically disabled; recreation; youth; Waupaca High School (software and computer for students with disabilities)

Grants awarded to organizations located in the Fox Valley vicinity.

828
Patrick and Anna M. Cudahy Fund
P.O. Box 11978
Milwaukee, WI 53211
(708) 866-0760

Blind; hard-of-hearing; mentally and physically disabled; youth; recreation

Typical grant range: $3,000 to $25,000

829
Edward U. Demmer Foundation
c/o Bank One Wisconsin Trust Co., N.A.
P.O. Box 1308
Milwaukee, WI 53201
(414) 765-2800

Center for Deaf-Blind Persons; National Society to Prevent Blindness; Milwaukee Hearing Society

Grants awarded to organizations located in Wisconsin.

830
Albert J. & Flora Ellinger Foundation, Inc.
c/o Marshall & Ilsley Trust Co.
P.O. Box 2035
Milwaukee, WI 53202
(414) 287-7177

Badger Association of the Blind; Center for the Blind and Visually Impaired

Grants awarded to organizations located in Wisconsin.

Typical grant range: $500 to $1,500

831
Ralph Evinrude Foundation, Inc.
c/o Quarles and Brady
411 E. Wisconsin Avenue
Milwaukee, WI 53202
(414) 277-5000

Hearing impaired; physically disabled; mental health; Center for Blind and Visually Impaired Children

Grants awarded to organizations located in Milwaukee.

Typical grant range: $500 to $4,000

832
Johnson's Wax Fund, Inc.
1525 Howe Street
Racine, WI 53403
(414) 631-2826

Emotionally disabled; Goodwill Industries; Very Special Arts

Grants awarded to organizations located in areas of company operations, with an emphasis in Wisconsin.

Typical grant range: $2,000 to $40,000

833
La Crosse Community Foundation
P.O. Box 578
La Crosse, WI 54602
(608) 782-3223

Mental health; physically disabled

Grants awarded to organizations located in La Crosse County.

Typical grant range: $500 to $15,000

834
Madison Community Foundation
615 E. Washington Avenue
Madison, WI 53703
(608) 255-0503

Alliance for the Mentally Ill; Mental Health Center; Wisconsin Council of the Blind (independent living program)

Grants awarded to organizations located in the Madison vicinity.

Typical grant range: $1,000 to $25,000

835
Faye McBeath Foundation
1020 North Broadway
Milwaukee, WI 53202
(414) 272-2626

Disabled (all areas); youth; elderly;
Advocates for Retarded Citizens; Badger
Association of the Blind; Goodwill
Industries; Mental Health Association;
United Cerebral Palsy; Very Special Arts

Grants awarded to organizations located
in Wisconsin, with an emphasis in
Milwaukee.

Typical grant range: $10,000 to $40,000

836
Milwaukee Foundation
1020 North Broadway
Milwaukee, WI 53202
(414) 272-5805

Disabled (all areas); speech impaired;
developmentally disabled; special
education; youth; cultural programs;
employment program; Mental Health
Association; Center for Blind and
Visually Impaired Children; Advocates
for Retarded Citizens

Grants awarded to organizations located
in the Milwaukee vicinity.

Typical grant range: $5,000 to $50,000

837
**Northwestern National Insurance
Foundation**
18650 W. Corporate Drive
Brookfield, WI 53005
(414) 792-3100

Cystic Fibrosis Foundation; Easter Seal
Society

Grants awarded to organizations located
in areas of company operations.

838
Louis L. Phillips Charities, Inc.
P.O. Box 202
Eau Claire, WI 54702
(715) 832-3431

United Cerebral Palsy; Eye Bank

Grants awarded to organizations located
in Wisconsin.

Typical grant range: $2,000 to $15,000

839
Walter Schroeder Foundation, Inc.
1000 N. Water Street, 13th Floor
Milwaukee, WI 53202
(414) 287-7177

Hard-of-hearing; Easter Seal Society;
Volunteer Service of Visually
Handicapped

Grants awarded to organizations located
in Milwaukee County.

840
A.O. Smith Foundation, Inc.
P.O. Box 23965
Milwaukee, WI 53223
(414) 359-4100

Physically disabled; learning disabled;
youth; employment project; Advocates for
Retarded Citizens; Mental Health Center;
Goodwill Industries

Grants awarded to organizations located
in areas of company operations (A.O.
Smith Corporation).

841
**Wausau Area Community
Foundation, Inc.**
500 Third Street, Suite 316
Wausau, WI 54403
(715) 845-9555

Physically disabled; Alliance for the
Mentally Ill; Marathon County Special
Education (employment program)

Grants awarded to organizations located
in the Wausau vicinity.

Typical grant range: $300 to $3,000

842
Wisconsin Energy Corporation Foundation
231 W. Michigan Street
Milwaukee, WI 53201

Mentally disabled; visually impaired

Grants awarded to organizations located in areas of company operations.

Typical grant range: $500 to $15,000

843
Ziemann Foundation, Inc.
P.O. Box 86
Waukesha, WI 53187

Physically and mentally disabled; developmentally disabled

Grants awarded to organizations located in Wisconsin.

Typical grant range: $1,000 to $9,000

WYOMING

844
Mary and Doc Robertson Handicapped Children's Trust
c/o Norwest Bank Wyoming
P.O. Box 2799
Casper, WY 82602

Association for Retarded Citizens

845
Newell B. Sargent Foundation
P.O. Box 18
Worland, WY 82401

Guide Dogs for the Blind; Muscular Dystrophy; Library Foundation (accessibility project); Christian Record Services (project for people who are blind); Fishing Wyoming Project (physically disabled)

Grants awarded to organizations located in Wyoming.

Typical grant range: $300 to $3,500

846
Tom and Helen Tonkin Foundation
c/o Norwest Bank Wyoming, Casper, N.A.
P.O. Box 2799
Casper, WY 82602
(307) 266-1100

Physically disabled; youth

Grants awarded to organizations located in Wyoming.

Typical grant range: $1,000 to $8,000

847
Wyoming Community Foundation
P.O. Box 4008
Laramie, WY 82071
(307) 766-6810

Mentally disabled; Mental Health Center

Grants awarded to organizations located in Wyoming.

Federal Programs

42.001 BOOKS FOR THE BLIND AND PHYSICALLY HANDICAPPED

FEDERAL AGENCY: LIBRARY OF CONGRESS

AUTHORIZATION: Public Laws 71-787, 87-765, and 89-522, 2 U.S.C. 35a, 135a-1, 135b.

OBJECTIVES: To provide library service to the blind and physically handicapped residents of the United States and its Territories, and to American citizens living abroad.

TYPES OF ASSISTANCE: Use of Property, Facilities, and Equipment.

USES AND USE RESTRICTIONS: The program provides books on cassette, disc, in braille, talking book, and recorded cassette machines. There are 56 regional libraries and 87 subregional libraries in the United States with a collection of approximately 67,000 titles in recorded and braille formats and 30,000 music scores, textbooks, and instructional materials in braille, large type and recorded formats.

ELIGIBILITY REQUIREMENTS:

Applicant Eligibility: An applicant must provide a certificate of his inability to read or manipulate standard printed material from a competent authority, defined in cases of blindness, visual disability, or physical limitations, as doctors of medicine, doctors of osteopathy, ophthalmologists, optometrists, registered nurses, therapists, professional staff of hospitals, institutions, and public or welfare agencies. In the absence of any of these, certification may be made by professional librarians or by any person whose competence under specific circumstances is acceptable to the Library of Congress. In the case of reading disability from organic dysfunction, competent authority is defined as doctors of medicine and doctors of osteopathy who may consult with colleagues in associated disciplines.

Beneficiary Eligibility: Blind and physically handicapped residents of the United States and its Territories, and American citizens living abroad will benefit.

Credentials/Documentation: An applicant must provide a certificate of his inability to read or manipulate standard printed material from a competent authority, defined in cases of blindness, visual disability, or physical limitations, as doctors of medicine, doctors of osteopathy, ophthalmologists, optometrists, registered nurses, therapists, professional staff of hospitals, institutions and public or welfare agencies. In the absence of any of these, certification may be made by professional librarians or by any person whose competence under specific circumstances is acceptable to the Library of Congress. In the case of reading disability from organic dysfunction, competent authority is defined as doctors of medicine and doctors of osteopathy who may consult with colleagues in associated disciplines. This program is excluded from coverage under OMB Circular No. A-87.

APPLICATION AND AWARD PROCESS:

Preapplication Coordination: This program is excluded from coverage under OMB Circular No. A-102. This program is excluded from coverage under E.O. 12372.

Application Procedure: Applications can be made to the National Library Service for the Blind and Physically Handicapped in Washington, or the 56 regional libraries, or 87 subregional libraries. This program is excluded from coverage under OMB Circular No. A-110.

Award Procedure: Not applicable.

Deadlines: Not applicable.

Range of Approval/Disapproval Time: Not applicable.

Appeals: Not applicable.

Renewals: Not applicable.

ASSISTANCE CONSIDERATIONS:

Formula and Matching Requirements: Not applicable.

Length and Time Phasing of Assistance: Not applicable.

POST ASSISTANCE REQUIREMENTS:

Reports: None.

Audits: None.

Records: None.

FINANCIAL INFORMATION:

Account Identification: 03-0141-0-1-503.

Obligations: (13 percent salaries and expenses; 87 percent equipment and support) FY 93 $40,215,000; FY 94 est $42,713,000; and FY 95 est $50,155,000.

Range and Average of Financial Assistance: Not applicable.

PROGRAM ACCOMPLISHMENTS: In fiscal year 1993, 764,800 blind and physically handicapped readers were served by regional and subregional libraries throughout the United States with a collection of 67,000 titles in recorded and braille formats. Circulation of volumes and containers was 21,826,000. Estimated readership: fiscal year 1994, 769,000; fiscal year 1995, 773,000. Estimated circulation: fiscal year 1994, 22,100,000; fiscal year 1995, 22,400,000.

REGULATIONS, GUIDELINES, AND LITERATURE: "Reading is for Everyone." Application form, list of regional and subregional libraries, 36 CFR (Chapter VII).

INFORMATION CONTACTS:

Regional or Local Office: Fifty-six regional and 87 subregional libraries in the United States. Each State has an agency distributing talking book machines. Local public libraries have information available. Otherwise contact the headquarters office listed in this program.

Headquarters Office: Frank Kurt Cylke, Director, National Library Service for the Blind and Physically Handicapped, Library of Congress, 1291 Taylor Street, NW., Washington DC 20542. Telephone: (202) 707-5100.

EXAMPLES OF FUNDED PROJECTS: Not applicable.

CRITERIA FOR SELECTING PROPOSALS: Not applicable.

64.007 BLIND VETERANS REHABILITATION CENTERS AND CLINICS

FEDERAL AGENCY: VETERANS HEALTH ADMINISTRATION, DEPARTMENT OF VETERANS AFFAIRS

AUTHORIZATION: 38 U.S.C. 610.

OBJECTIVES: To provide personal and social adjustment programs and medical or health-related services for eligible blind veterans at selected VA Medical Centers maintaining blind rehabilitation centers.

TYPES OF ASSISTANCE: Provision of Specialized Services.

USES AND USE RESTRICTIONS: To assist in the rehabilitation of blind veterans.

ELIGIBILITY REQUIREMENTS:

Applicant Eligibility: Any blind veteran who meets one of the following requirements for admission to a VA Medical Center: (1) requires treatment for a service-connected disability or disease incurred or aggravated in military service; (2) has a service-connected, compensable disability or is in receipt of retirement pay for a service-incurred disability when in need of hospital care for a nonservice-connected condition; (3) has been discharged under other than dishonorable conditions: (a) from war-time service, (b) after January 31, 1955, or (c) was awarded the Medal of Honor in peacetime, and is unable to pay the cost of necessary care and so states under oath; or (4) is: (a) in receipt of a VA pension or (b) 65 years of age or older and has had either war-time or peace-time active military service. Active duty personnel of the armed forces may be transferred to a center.

Beneficiary Eligibility: All blind veterans.

Credentials/Documentation: Military discharge papers.

APPLICATION AND AWARD PROCESS:

Preapplication Coordination: None.

Application Procedure: Application may be made through any VA hospital or outpatient clinic, by completing VA Form 10-10. Also transfer of active duty personnel of armed forces.

Award Procedure: VA ward physician determines, with recourse to Hospital Director.

Deadlines: None.

Range of Approval/Disapproval Time: Immediately.

Appeals: Not applicable.

Renewals: Not applicable.

ASSISTANCE CONSIDERATIONS:

Formula and Matching Requirements: Not applicable.

Length and Time Phasing of Assistance: Following admission, veteran is provided approximately 4 months of specialized rehabilitation in a VA Blind Center or Clinic plus any necessary medical or health related services.

POST ASSISTANCE REQUIREMENTS:

Reports: Not applicable.

Audits: Not applicable.

Records: Not applicable.

FINANCIAL INFORMATION:

Account Identification: 36-0160-0-1-703.

Obligations: (Salaries and expenses) FY 94 $20,884,000; and FY 95 est $22,884,000.

Range and Average of Financial Assistance: Not applicable.

PROGRAM ACCOMPLISHMENTS: In 1993, 941 veterans and servicepersons received the personal and social reorganization program at the six Blind Rehabilitation Centers and three clinics. Data unavailable for fiscal year 1994.

REGULATIONS, GUIDELINES, AND LITERATURE: "Federal Benefits for Veterans and Dependents," VA Fact Sheet IS-1, $2.00, available from Superintendent of Documents, Government Printing Office, Washington, DC 20402. Coordinated Services for Blinded Veterans, IB 11-59, available from Director, Blind Rehabilitation Service (117D), Department of Veterans Affairs, Central Office, Washington, DC 20420.

INFORMATION CONTACTS:

Headquarters Office: Associate Deputy Chief Medical Director for Clinical Programs (117D), Department of Veterans Affairs, Washington, DC 20420. Telephone: (202) 535-7637.

EXAMPLES OF FUNDED PROJECTS: Not applicable.

CRITERIA FOR SELECTING PROPOSALS: Not applicable.

64.013 VETERANS PROSTHETIC APPLIANCES

FEDERAL AGENCY: VETERANS HEALTH ADMINISTRATION, DEPARTMENT OF VETERANS AFFAIRS

AUTHORIZATION: 38 U.S.C. Sections 1162, 1701, 1710, 1712, 1713, 1714, 1717, 1719, 1723, 1724, 3104, 3901, 3902, 3903, and 8123.

OBJECTIVES: To provide, through purchase and/or fabrication, prosthetic and related appliances, equipment and services to disabled veterans so that they may live and work as productive citizens.

TYPES OF ASSISTANCE: Sale, Exchange, or Donation of Property and Goods.

USES AND USE RESTRICTIONS: Appliances and services are provided only for the use and benefit of the disabled veteran to whom they are furnished. The program also includes the replacement and repair of appliances and training in the use of artificial limbs, artificial eyes, wheelchairs, aids for blind, hearing aids, braces, orthopedic shoes, eyeglasses, crutches and canes, medical equipment, implants, and medical supplies, and automotive adaptive equipment.

ELIGIBILITY REQUIREMENTS:

Applicant Eligibility: Any disabled veteran or authorized representative on his behalf meeting the criteria below may apply for prosthetic appliances or services.

Beneficiary Eligibility: Disabled veterans eligible for VA outpatient treatment for service-connected or nonservice-connected conditions requiring prosthetic services; veterans receiving hospital care in VA facilities or at VA expense, or receiving domiciliary, or nursing home care in VA facilities; veterans in receipt of 50 percent compensation for service-connected disabilities or special monthly compensation or increased pension based on being housebound or the need for regular aid and attendance; veterans in receipt of compensation for disabilities resulting from hospitalization, medical or surgical treatment, or the pursuit of a cause of vocational rehabilitation; veterans of the World War I; or former prisoner of war. Ineligible veterans are those not eligible for outpatient care or nonservice-connected veterans residing or sojourning in foreign lands.

Credentials/Documentation: None.

APPLICATION AND AWARD PROCESS:

Preapplication Coordination: None.

Application Procedure: Eligible veteran may request prosthetic services by reporting in person at any VA Medical Center as well as by correspondence, telephone, or community physician prescription.

Award Procedure: Not applicable.

Deadlines: None.

Range of Approval/Disapproval Time: Usually immediately, although delays of 30 to 60 days have occurred in unusual cases.

Appeals: A veteran who is administratively refused prosthetics services by a local VA health care facility may appeal to the Secretary of Veterans Affairs. Determinations of the Veterans Health Administration involving the need or nature of medical treatment as distinguished from legal or basic eligibility for medical services, are not appealable.

Renewals: None.

ASSISTANCE CONSIDERATIONS:

Formula and Matching Requirements: Not applicable.

Length and Time Phasing of Assistance: For veterans eligible for outpatient medical treatment and those in receipt of special monthly compensation or increased pension based on the need for regular aid and attendance, assistance is maintained for as long as eligibility continues (usually for life). Veterans in receipt of compensation for disabilities resulting from hospitalization, medical or surgical treatment, or the pursuit of a course of vocational rehabilitation. Veterans receiving hospital, domiciliary, or nursing home care, assistance is available until discharge from such care.

POST ASSISTANCE REQUIREMENTS:

Audits: Not applicable.

Records: Not applicable.

FINANCIAL INFORMATION:

Account Identification: 36-0160-0-1-703.

Obligations: (Value and repair of prosthetic appliances) FY 94 $236,326,000; FY 95 est $249,700,000; and FY 96 est $257,191,000.

Range and Average of Financial Assistance: $10 to $25,000; $118.

PROGRAM ACCOMPLISHMENTS: The program has provided 1,500,000 prosthetic item/services in the form of prosthetic appliances, sensory aids, medical equipment, medical supplies, implants, therapeutic devices and repair services during fiscal year 1994. Approximately the same prosthetic item/services will be provided in fiscal year 1995.

REGULATIONS, GUIDELINES, AND LITERATURE: 38 CFR 17.115, 17.115a, 17.115b, 17.115c, 17.115d, 17.116, 17.118, 17.119, 17.119a, 17.119b, 17.119c, 17.119d.

INFORMATION CONTACTS:

Regional or Local Office: Initial contact should be made with the Prosthetic Representatives in 140 VA field stations, any VA hospital or outpatient clinic, or any veterans' service organization representative.

Headquarters Office: Director, Prosthetic and Sensory Aids (117C), Department of Veterans Affairs, Washington, DC 20420. Telephone: (202) 535-7293.

EXAMPLES OF FUNDED PROJECTS: Not applicable.

CRITERIA FOR SELECTING PROPOSALS: Not applicable.

84.023 SPECIAL EDUCATION-INNOVATION AND DEVELOPMENT

FEDERAL AGENCY: OFFICE OF SPECIAL EDUCATION AND REHABILITATIVE SERVICES, DEPARTMENT OF EDUCATION

AUTHORIZATION: Individuals with Disabilities Education Act, Part E, as amended, Public Laws 91-230, 95-49, 98-199, 99-457, 100-630, and 101-476, 20 U.S.C. 1441-1442.

OBJECTIVES: To advance and improve the knowledge base and improve the practice of professionals, parents, and others providing early intervention, special education, and related services, including professionals in regular education environments, to provide children with disabilities effective instruction and enable them to successfully learn.

TYPES OF ASSISTANCE: Project Grants; Project Grants (Contracts); Project Grants (Cooperative Agreements).

USES AND USE RESTRICTIONS: To support research and related activities including model programs designed to improve the education of children with disabilities.

ELIGIBILITY REQUIREMENTS:

Applicant Eligibility: State or local educational agencies, institutions of higher education, and other public or private agencies and organizations may apply. Only nonprofit organizations are eligible for awards except under 20 U.S.C. 1442.

Beneficiary Eligibility: Infants, toddlers, children, and youth with disabilities will benefit.

Credentials/Documentation: Costs will be determined in accordance with OMB Circular No. A-87 for State and local governments. OMB Circular No. A-21 for Educational Institutions applies.

APPLICATION AND AWARD PROCESS:

Preapplication Coordination: The standard application forms as furnished by the Federal agency and required by OMB Circular No. A-102 must be used for this program. This program is excluded from coverage under E.O. 12372.

Application Procedure: Applications, if hand carried, should be delivered to: Department of Education, Application Control Center, Room 3633, ROB No. 3, 7th and D Streets, SW., Washington, DC 20202. Mailing address: Department of Education Application Control Center, 400 Maryland Ave., SW., Washington, DC 20202. Applications are reviewed by field readers. Their recommendations are the basis for approval or disapproval. This program is subject to the provisions of OMB Circular No. A-110.

Award Procedure: The standard application forms as furnished by the Federal agency and required by OMB Circular No. A-102 must be used for this program. Awards are made directly to successful applicants with no additional redistribution to other parties unless proposed by the applicant.

Deadlines: Contact the headquarters office for application deadlines.

Range of Approval/Disapproval Time: Approximately 90 to 180 days.

Appeals: Contract proposals can be revised on the basis of recommendations made during the review and negotiation process. This appeal process does not apply to grants or cooperative agreements.

Renewals: Funding is generally for a one-year period. Multi-year projects may receive continuation funding based on staff review, satisfactory performance, and availability of funds.

ASSISTANCE CONSIDERATIONS:

Formula and Matching Requirements: None.

Length and Time Phasing of Assistance: Funding is generally for one year periods for a maximum of five years. Multi-year projects are subject to satisfactory progress, and a continuation application must be submitted for approval for each subsequent year of the project.

POST ASSISTANCE REQUIREMENTS:

Reports: Program and final reports as required by award document. A final report is submitted to the Grants Officer in the Department of Education at completion of project.

Audits: In accordance with the provisions of OMB Circular No. A-128, "Audits of State and Local Governments," State and local governments that receive financial assistance of $100,000 or more within the State's fiscal year shall have an audit made for that year. State and local governments that receive between $25,000 and $100,000 within the State's fiscal year shall have an audit made in accordance with Circular No. A-128, or in accordance with Federal laws and regulations governing the programs in which they participate.

Records: All recipients of grants or contracts are required to retain all records relative to the grant or contract for a period of three years from the termination date of the grant or contract.

FINANCIAL INFORMATION:

Account Identification: 91-0300-0-1-501.

Obligations: (Grants and contracts) FY 93 $20,606,000; FY 94 est $20,635,000; and FY 95 est $19,885,000.

Range and Average of Financial Assistance: $4,000 to $700,000; $154,000.

PROGRAM ACCOMPLISHMENTS: In fiscal year 1993, 84 new awards were made. In fiscal year 1994, 54 new awards are planned.

REGULATIONS, GUIDELINES, AND LITERATURE: Regulations published in the Federal Register November 12, 1987, pp. 43482; amended October 22, 1991 and June 29, 1991, 34 CFR 324.

INFORMATION CONTACTS:

Regional or Local Office: Not applicable.

Headquarters Office: Division of Innovation and Development, Office of Assistant Secretary for Special Education and Rehabilitative Services, Department of Education, 400 Maryland Avenue, SW., Washington, DC 20202. Contact: Dores Andres. Telephone: (202) 205-8125.

EXAMPLES OF FUNDED PROJECTS: Investigation of family-focused early intervention services; academic and social interventions to promote mainstreaming and integration for students with autism in public school settings; and utility of alternative assessment models for identification of the mildly-disabled.

CRITERIA FOR SELECTING PROPOSALS: Research projects: The Secretary evaluates new applications for research projects under the following weighted criteria (maximum possible score: 100 points): (a) Plan of operation (10 points); (b) quality of key personnel (10 points); (c) budget and cost-effectiveness (10 points); (d) evaluation plan (5 points); (e) adequacy of resources (5 point); (f) potential importance (15 points); (g) probable impact (15 points); and (h) technical soundness of research and development plan (30 points); (20 U.S.C. 1441 1442).

84.024 EARLY EDUCATION FOR CHILDREN WITH DISABILITIES

FEDERAL AGENCY: OFFICE OF SPECIAL EDUCATION AND REHABILITATIVE SERVICES, DEPARTMENT OF EDUCATION

AUTHORIZATION: Individuals with Disabilities Education Act, Part C, Section 623, as amended, Public Laws 91-230, 98-199, 99-457, 100-630, 101-476, and 102-119, 20 U.S.C. 1423.

OBJECTIVES: To support demonstration, dissemination, and implementation of effective approaches to preschool and early childhood education for children with disabilities.

TYPES OF ASSISTANCE: Project Grants; Project Grants (Cooperative Agreements); Project Grants (Contracts).

USES AND USE RESTRICTIONS: Awards are made for research, demonstration, training, and other activities that focus on services to children with disabilities from birth through eight years of age. Parent participation, dissemination of information to the professional community and general public, and evaluation of the effectiveness of each project are required.

ELIGIBILITY REQUIREMENTS:

Applicant Eligibility: Public agencies and private nonprofit organizations. Profit makers are eligible for research projects and training projects.

Beneficiary Eligibility: Infants, toddlers, and children with disabilities, aged eight and under benefit.

Credentials/Documentation: Costs will be determined in accordance with OMB Circular No. A-87 for State and local governments. OMB Circular No. A-21 for educational institutions applies.

APPLICATION AND AWARD PROCESS:

Preapplication Coordination: Coordination with public schools is required and encouraged with State departments of education. This program is eligible for coverage under E.O. 12372, "Intergovernmental Review of Federal Programs." An applicant should consult the office or official designated as the single point of contact in his or her State for more information on the process the State requires to be followed in applying for assistance, if the State has selected the program for review.

Application Procedure: The standard application forms as furnished by the Federal agency and required by OMB Circular No. A-102 must be used for this program. Application should be sent to: Department of Education Application Control Center, Room 5673, ROB No. 3, 7th and D Streets, SW., Washington, DC. Mailing address: Department of Education Application Control Center, 400 Maryland Ave., SW., Washington, DC 20202-3561. This program is subject to the provisions of OMB Circular No. A-110.

Award Procedure: Applications are reviewed by outside experts on the basis of their recommendations and those of the Office. Award is made by the Secretary of Education.

Deadlines: Contact the headquarters office for application deadlines.

Range of Approval/Disapproval Time: Eight to ten weeks. Applicants notified approximately 20 weeks after submission.

Appeals: Not applicable.

Renewals: Grants are generally awarded for three year periods with second and third year funding contingent upon successful performance and availability of funds. Research Institutes and demonstration projects may be awarded for five years with years 2 through 5 contingent upon successful performance and availability of funds.

ASSISTANCE CONSIDERATIONS:

Formula and Matching Requirements: For demonstration, outreach, and experimental projects, 10 percent of the total cost of the project must be provided by the grant recipient. This may be in-kind or cash.

Length and Time Phasing of Assistance: One year with renewal possible; total of three years or five years for demonstration projects.

POST ASSISTANCE REQUIREMENTS:

Reports: Progress reports and final reports as required by award document.

Audits: In accordance with the provisions of OMB Circular No. A-128, "Audits of State and Local Governments," State and local governments that receive financial assistance of $100,000 or more within the State's fiscal year shall have an audit made for that year. State and local governments that receive between $25,000 and $100,000 within the State's fiscal year shall have an audit made in accordance with Circular No. A-128, or in accordance with Federal laws and regulations governing the programs in which they participate.

Records: Records are to be retained as required by award document.

FINANCIAL INFORMATION:

Account Identification: 91-0300-0-1-501.

Obligations: (Grants and contracts) FY 93 $25,163,000; FY 94 est $25,167,000; and FY 95 est $25,167,000.

Range and Average of Financial Assistance: $100,000 to $4,686,000; $206,000.

PROGRAM ACCOMPLISHMENTS: In fiscal year 1993, 42 new awards were made and in fiscal year 1994, 33 new awards were planned. In fiscal year 1995, approximately 33 new awards are planned.

REGULATIONS, GUIDELINES, AND LITERATURE: Regulations published in the Federal Register August 11, 1987, Vol. 52, No. 154, pp. 29816-29819 34 CFR 309, amended October 22, 1991 and June 29, 1992.

INFORMATION CONTACTS:

Regional or Local Office: Not applicable.

Headquarters Office: Division of Educational Services, Special Education Programs, Office of Assistant Secretary for Special Education and Rehabilitative Services, Department of Education, 400 Maryland Avenue, SW., Washington, DC 20202. Contact: Gail Houle. Telephone: (202) 205-9045. Use the same number for FTS.

EXAMPLES OF FUNDED PROJECTS: Programs for integrating preschool, children with disabilities with non-disabled children; an intervention model for autistic children; a project for chronically ill infants in an intensive care unit.

CRITERIA FOR SELECTING PROPOSALS: The funding criteria for the Department of Education apply (e.g., staff, budget) and the revised Part 309 regulations require the following criteria to be used to evaluated applications: (1) Geographic distribution; (2) the significance of the problem or issue to be addressed based on previous research findings related to the problem or issue; the number of individuals that will benefit; (3) the probable impact of the proposed project in meeting the needs of children with disabilities, birth through age eight, and their families; (4) the contribution that the project will make to current knowledge and practice; (5) the methods used for dissemination of the project; (6) the proposed sample or target population, including the numbers of participants involved and the methods to be used to implement the design; (7) the anticipated outcomes; (8) the extent to which the management plan will ensure proper and efficient administration of the project; (9) the clarity in the goals and objectives; (10) the adequacy of proposed timeliness for accomplishing those activities; (11) effective use of resources and personnel; (12) methods of evaluation; (13) qualifications of key personnel and the amount of time each person will commit to the project; and (14) the adequacy of resources and the adequacy of the budget and the reasonableness of costs in relation to the objectives of the project.

84.025 SERVICES FOR CHILDREN
WITH DEAF-BLINDNESS

FEDERAL AGENCY: OFFICE OF SPECIAL EDUCATION AND REHABILITATIVE SERVICES, DEPARTMENT OF EDUCATION

AUTHORIZATION: Individuals with Disabilities Education Act, Part C, Section 622, as amended, Public Laws 91-230, 98-199, 99-457, 100-630, 101-476, and 102-119, 20 U.S.C. 1422.

OBJECTIVES: To provide technical assistance, under Part H, to State education agencies, local education agencies, designated lead agencies, and others that are involved in the early intervention or education of children with deaf-blindness.

TYPES OF ASSISTANCE: Project Grants; Project Grants (Contracts); Project Grants (Cooperative Agreements).

USES AND USE RESTRICTIONS: Awards support activities designed to ensure that States have the necessary capacity to serve children who are deaf-blind and are responsible for providing services to children who are deaf-blind and the State is not obligated to make available a free appropriate public education under Part B of the IDEA.

ELIGIBILITY REQUIREMENTS:

Applicant Eligibility: Public or private nonprofit agencies, organizations, or institutions may apply.

Beneficiary Eligibility: Infants, toddlers, children, youth and young adults with disabilities benefit.

Credentials/Documentation: Costs will be determined in accordance with OMB Circular No. A-87 for State and local governments.

APPLICATION AND AWARD PROCESS:

Preapplication Coordination: This program is eligible for coverage under E.O. 12372, "Intergovernmental Review of Federal Programs." An applicant should consult the office or official designated as the single point of contact in his or her State for more information on the process the State requires to be followed in applying for assistance, if the State has selected the program for review.

Application Procedure: The standard application forms as furnished by the Federal agency and required by OMB Circular No. A-102 must be used for this program.

Award Procedure: Applications will be read by a field reader panel; notification of awards will be made through the contracts or grants office.

Deadlines: Contact headquarters office for application deadlines.

Range of Approval/Disapproval Time: Approximately three to four months.

Appeals: Not applicable.

Renewals: Funding is on a one year basis for a project period of up to three years in most cases.

ASSISTANCE CONSIDERATIONS:

Formula and Matching Requirements: None.

Length and Time Phasing of Assistance: Approximately 12 month periods.

POST ASSISTANCE REQUIREMENTS:

Reports: Progress reports shall be made on a annual basis. Final reports shall be submitted at the end of the project period.

Audits: In accordance with the provision of OMB Circular No. A-128, "Audits of State and Local Governments," State and local governments that receive financial assistance of $100,000 or more within the State's fiscal year shall have an audit made for that year. State and local governments that receive between $25,000 and $100,000 within the State's fiscal year shall have an audit made in accordance with Circular No. A-128, or in accordance with Federal laws and regulations governing the programs in which they participate.

Records: As stated in grant or contract terms and conditions, the awardee shall maintain accounts, records, and other evidence pertaining to all costs incurred, revenues or other applicable credits acquired under this grant.

FINANCIAL INFORMATION:

Account Identification: 91-0300-0-1-501.

Obligations: (Grants and contracts) FY 93 $12,832,000; FY 94 est $12,832,000; and FY 95 est $12,832,000.

Range and Average of Financial Assistance: $28,000 to $979,000; $200,000.

PROGRAM ACCOMPLISHMENTS: The program provides technical assistance to teachers, professionals, and other staff working with children and youth who are deaf-blind. Projects reported nearly 8,000 children and youth being served. In fiscal year 1993, seven new and 59 continuation awards were made. In fiscal year 1994, approximately 5 new and 60 continuation awards are planned. In fiscal year 1995, approximately 51 new and 14 continuation awards are planned.

REGULATIONS, GUIDELINES, AND LITERATURE: Final regulations published October 11, 1991, 34 CFR 307, as amended, June 29, 1992.

INFORMATION CONTACTS:

Regional or Local Office: None.

Headquarters Office: Division of Educational Services, Office of Special Education Programs, Assistant Secretary for the Office of Special Education and Rehabilitative Services, Department of Education, 400 Maryland Avenue, SW., Washington, DC 20202. Contact: Charles Freeman. Telephone: (202) 205-8165. Use the same number for FTS.

EXAMPLES OF FUNDED PROJECTS: Training and technical assistance are provided to State education agencies to improve services to deaf-blind children and youth.

CRITERIA FOR SELECTING PROPOSALS: Applications will be evaluated on the basis of the criteria and weighing factors cited in the RFP or Program regulations. Applications will be reviewed for completeness and conformity to the requirements of the RFP or Program regulations. A panel of qualified evaluators will review and rank the applications.

84.026 MEDIA AND CAPTIONING SERVICES FOR INDIVIDUALS WITH DISABILITIES

FEDERAL AGENCY: OFFICE OF SPECIAL EDUCATION AND REHABILITATIVE SERVICES, DEPARTMENT OF EDUCATION

AUTHORIZATION: Individuals with Disabilities Education Act, Part F, as amended, Public Laws 91-230, 93-380, 94-482, 99-457, 100-630, and 101-479, 20 U.S.C. 1451 and 1452.

OBJECTIVES: To maintain a free loan service of captioned films for individuals who are deaf or hard of hearing and instructional media for the educational, cultural, and vocational enrichment of individuals who are disabled. Provide for acquisition and distribution of media materials and equipment; provide contracts and grants for research into the use of media and technology, train teachers, parents, and others in media and technology utilization.

TYPES OF ASSISTANCE: Project Grants; Project Grants (Cooperative Agreements); Project Grants (Contracts).

USES AND USE RESTRICTIONS: Awards support research in the use of educational and training films and videos and other educational media and technology for the disabled individuals; training teachers, parents, and others who work with disabled persons in the use of the educational media and acquire, produce, and distribute films/videos and other related media, technology and materials. The captioned feature films and videos are limited to registered deaf and hard of hearing users.

ELIGIBILITY REQUIREMENTS:

Applicant Eligibility: Profit and nonprofit, public and private agencies, organizations, or institutions may apply.

Beneficiary Eligibility: Individuals with disabilities benefit.

Credentials/Documentation: Cost will be determined in accordance with OMB Circular No. A-87 for State and local governments.

APPLICATION AND AWARD PROCESS:

Preapplication Coordination: This program is eligible for coverage under E.O.12372, "Intergovernmental Review of Federal Programs." An applicant should consult the office or official designated as the single point of contact in his or her State for more information on the process the State requires to be followed in applying for assistance, if the State has selected the program for review.

Application Procedure: The standard application forms as furnished by the Federal agency and required by OMB Circular No. A-102 must be used for this program. Offerers submit proposals in response to the RFP. This program is subject to the provisions of OMB Circular No. A-110.

Award Procedure: The Secretary of Education makes final decisions to approve, defer, or reject individual proposals and applications based on objective reviews by outside experts and staffs.

Deadlines: Contact the headquarters office for application deadlines.

Range of Approval/Disapproval Time: About 90 to 150 days.

Appeals: Contract proposals can be revised on the basis of recommendations made during the review and negotiation process.

Renewals: Projects can be renewed on the basis of satisfactory completion of objectives, and recommended for an additional period of support.

ASSISTANCE CONSIDERATIONS:

Formula and Matching Requirements: None.

Length and Time Phasing of Assistance: Not applicable.

POST ASSISTANCE REQUIREMENTS:

Reports: On captioned films and video usage, report cards are mailed to distribution centers to show usage. On projects, administrative reports and annual reports are required to be sent to the Project Officer.

Audits: In accordance with the provisions of OMB Circular No. A-128, "Audits of State and Local Governments," State and local governments that receive financial assistance of $100,000 or more within the State's fiscal year shall have an audit made for that year. State and local governments that receive between $25,000 and $100,000 within the State's fiscal year shall have an audit made in accordance with Circular No. A-128, or in accordance with Federal laws and regulations governing the programs in which they participate.

Records: Required to be maintained during a project, and retained for a period of three years after the project is terminated.

FINANCIAL INFORMATION:

Account Identification: 91-0300-0-1-501.

Obligations: (Grants and contracts) FY 93 $17,891,712; FY 94 est $18,642,000; and FY 95 est $17,642,000.

Range and Average of Financial Assistance: $7,500 to $3,000,000; $300,000.

PROGRAM ACCOMPLISHMENTS: In fiscal year 1993, 83 new awards are planned. In fiscal year 1994, 70 new awards are planned. In fiscal year 1995, 61 new awards are anticipated.

REGULATIONS, GUIDELINES, AND LITERATURE: Final regulations were published in the Federal Register October 19, 1988, 34 CFR 330, 331, 332; as amended, October 22, 1991.

INFORMATION CONTACTS:

Regional or Local Office: Not applicable.

Headquarters Office: Division of Educational Services, Office of Special Education

Programs, Office of Assistant Secretary for Special Education and Rehabilitative Services, Department of Education, Washington, DC 20202. Contact: Ernest Hairston. Telephone: (202) 205-9172; 205-8170 (TDD). Use the same number for FTS.

EXAMPLES OF FUNDED PROJECTS: A captioned films/videos distribution center recording textbooks for the blind and print disabled; individual closed captioned sports programs; descriptive videos; national theatre of the deaf closed-captioned; primetime movies, mini-series and specials; syndicated to programming, symposium on educational technology; closed captioned national news and public information; special research, development and evaluation project; closed captioned daytime programming; cultural project for deaf and hard of hearing individuals; close captioned children's programs; captioned videos; and a captioned video selection project.

CRITERIA FOR SELECTING PROPOSALS: As presented in each Request for Proposal and Application for Grants.

84.027 SPECIAL EDUCATION-GRANTS TO STATES
(Part B, Individuals with Disabilities Education Act)

FEDERAL AGENCY: OFFICE OF ASSISTANT SECRETARY FOR SPECIAL EDUCATION AND REHABILITATIVE SERVICES, DEPARTMENT OF EDUCATION

AUTHORIZATION: Individuals with Disabilities Education Act, Part B, Sections 611-620, as amended, Public Laws 91-230, 93-380, 94-142, 98-199, 99-457, 100-630, and 101-476, 20 U.S.C. 1411-1420.

OBJECTIVES: To provide grants to States to assist them in providing a free appropriate public education to all children with disabilities.

TYPES OF ASSISTANCE: Formula Grants.

USES AND USE RESTRICTIONS: Funds are used by State and local educational agencies, in accordance with the priorities in the Act, to help provide the special education and related services needed to make a free appropriate public education available to all eligible children with one or more of thirteen specified disabilities.

ELIGIBILITY REQUIREMENTS:

Applicant Eligibility: State educational agencies in the 50 States, District of Columbia, Puerto Rico, American Samoa, Commonwealth of the Northern Mariana Islands, Guam, Virgin Islands, the Republic of the Marshall Islands, Palau, and the Federated States of Micronesia may apply to the Department of Education for participation in the Part B, IDEA program. The Department of the Interior, Bureau of Indian Affairs receives 1.25 percent of the total amount available to States. Local educational agencies apply to their State educational agency for funds.

Beneficiary Eligibility: Children with mental retardation, hearing impairments, deafness, speech, or language impairments, visual impairments including blindness, serious emotional disturbance, orthopedic impairments, autism, traumatic brain injury, other health impairments, specific learning disabilities, deaf-blindness, or multiple disabilities that need special education and related services benefit.

Credentials/Documentation: The designated plan review agencies must be given an opportunity to review the State Plan. Costs will be determined in accordance with OMB Circular No. A-87 State and local governments.

APPLICATION AND AWARD PROCESS:

Preapplication Coordination: All public and private institutions and institutions of higher education, professional associations, other organizations interested in personnel preparation should be given an opportunity to participate in the development of a State's comprehensive system of personnel development. Representatives of private schools must have an opportunity to participate in the development of State standards. Children in private elementary and secondary schools to the extent consistent with their number and location in the State must have an opportunity to participate in the program assisted or carried out under this grant by providing them with special educational related services, unless prohibited by State law in force on December 2, 1983. Public hearings must be held in order to provide general comment on the triennial program plan. This program is eligible for coverage under E.O. 12372, "Intergovernmental Review of Federal Programs." An applicant should consult the office or official designated as the single point of contact in his or her State for more information on the process the State requires to be followed in applying for assistance, if the State has selected the program for review. The standard application forms as furnished by the Federal agency and required by OMB Circular No. A-102 must be used for this program.

Application Procedure: States must submit a three-year State plan which: 1) Meets the conditions in Section 612 and Section 613 of Part B of the Individuals with Disabilities Education Act and 2) describes the purposes and activities for which funds under this Act will be expended during each of the three fiscal years covered by the State plan. Local education agencies submit their applications for subgrants to their State educational agency for approval. This program is excluded from coverage under OMB Circular No. A-110.

Award Procedure: Once the State plan is submitted and approved, a grant award document representing the total grant amount for that fiscal year, or portion thereof, if under a continuing resolution, is forwarded to the State department of education. During the three-year cycle, amendments may be required in order to maintain a fully approved State plan. Notification of the award is made to the designated State Central Information Reception Agency.

Deadlines: Varies within each State. Submission date is set for March 1 to expedite funding, but plans or amendments are accepted throughout the fiscal year.

Range of Approval/Disapproval Time: Not applicable.

Appeals: The Secretary of Education must give a State educational agency an opportunity for a hearing before taking any action involving the proposed disapproval of a State plan and the withholding of payments. If a State disagrees with a final action, it may, within 60 days after notice of such action, file a petition for review of that action with the U.S. Circuit Court of Appeals. A State may also engage in a hearing with the Secretary of Education if the State disagrees with the action taken regarding a request for a waiver of the Part B supplementing and supplanting requirements.

Renewals: None.

ASSISTANCE CONSIDERATIONS:

Formula and Matching Requirements: Funds for the 50 States, the District of Columbia, and Puerto Rico, are allotted on the basis of a certified count of the number of children with disabilities aged 3 through 21 years, receiving special education and related services on December 1 of the fiscal year that the grant is made. Funds to the outlying areas are allotted proportionately among them on the basis of their respective need, not to exceed one percent of the aggregate amounts available to the States in a fiscal year, as determined by the Secretary of Education. The Department of the Interior receives 1.25 percent of the total amount available to States. There are non-supplanting and excess cost requirements. The statistical factors used are: 1) The total number of children with disabilities receiving special education (3 through 21 years old) by State: the sources are the unpublished reports from the State educational agencies; 2) the average national per pupil expenditure; and 3) "Revenues and Expenditures," CES. Statistical factors used for eligibility do not apply to this program. This program has maintenance of effort (MOE) requirements. See funding agency for further details.

Length and Time Phasing of Assistance: Grants are issued each fiscal year. Obligation period is a 15 month period from July 1 through September 30 plus a one-year carryover provision.

POST ASSISTANCE REQUIREMENTS:

Reports: Annual data report and performance reports are submitted to the Department of Education from the State departments of education.

Audits: In accordance with the provisions of OMB Circular No. A-128, "Audits of State and Local Governments," State and local governments that receive $100,000 or more a year in Federal financial assistance shall have an audit made for that year. State and local governments that receive between $25,000 and $100,000 a year shall have an audit made in accordance with Circular No. A-128, or in accordance with Federal laws and regulations governing the programs in which they participate.

Records: All records supporting claims for Federal funds or relating to the accountability of the grantee for the expenditure of such funds must be accessible for administrative review.

FINANCIAL INFORMATION:

Account Identification: 91-0300-0-1-501.

Obligations: (Grants) FY 93 $1,719,893,000; FY 94 est $2,149,686,000; and FY 95 est $2,353,032,000.

Range and Average of Financial Assistance: The range is $644,245 to $152,398,865; $26,596,724.

PROGRAM ACCOMPLISHMENTS: In fiscal year 1994, all eligible State agencies are expected to receive funding.

REGULATIONS, GUIDELINES, AND LITERATURE: Regulations were published on August 23, 1977, 34 CFR 300, as amended, September 29, 1992.

INFORMATION CONTACTS:

Regional or Local Office: State Educational Agency, Part B Coordinator or Director of Special Education.

Headquarters Office: Division of Assistance to States, Office of the Assistant Secretary for Special Education and Rehabilitative Services, Department of Education, 400 Maryland Avenue, SW., Washington, DC 20202. Contact: Thomas Irvin. Telephone: (202) 205-8825. Use the same number for FTS.

CRITERIA FOR SELECTING PROPOSALS: The applicants eligible to participate in the program qualify for funding based upon an approved State plan. The criteria for approving a State plan appear in the regulations for implementation of Part B of the Individuals with Disabilities Education Act, formerly the Education of the Handicapped Act. See 34 CFR 300.

84.029 SPECIAL EDUCATION-PERSONNEL DEVELOPMENT AND PARENT TRAINING
(Training Personnel for the Education of Individuals with Disabilities)

FEDERAL AGENCY: OFFICE OF SPECIAL EDUCATION AND REHABILITATIVE SERVICES, DEPARTMENT OF EDUCATION

AUTHORIZATION: Individuals with Disabilities Education Act, Part D, Sections 631, 632, 634, and 635, as amended, Public Laws 91-230, 98-199, 99-457, 100-630, and 101-476, 20 U.S.C. 1431, 1432, 1434, and 1435.

OBJECTIVES: (1) To address identified shortages of special education teachers and related service personnel; (2) to improve the quality and increase the supply of teachers, supervisors, administrators, researchers, teacher educators, speech pathologists, educational interpreters for the hearing impaired, and other special personnel such as specialists in physical education and recreation, paraprofessionals, vocational/career education, volunteers; and (3) to provide parent training and information services.

TYPES OF ASSISTANCE: Project Grants; Project Grants (Cooperative Agreements); Project Grants (Contracts).

USES AND USE RESTRICTIONS: Awards may be used for undergraduate, graduate, and summer traineeships, special study institutes, and special projects. Funds may be obligated for student stipends, dependency allowances, or institutional support.

ELIGIBILITY REQUIREMENTS:

Applicant Eligibility: Eligibility varies with activity: Institutions of higher education and other appropriate nonprofit agencies are eligible for preservice training awards of special education, related services, and early intervention personnel. Institutions of higher education; State agencies, and other appropriate nonprofit agencies are eligible for special projects. Parent organizations are eligible for parent projects. State agencies and, where State agencies do not apply, institutions of higher education are eligible for State grants.

Beneficiary Eligibility: Infants, toddlers, children, and youth with disabilities are beneficiaries of this program.

Credentials/Documentation: Costs will be determined in accordance with OMB Circular No. A-87 for State and local governments.

APPLICATION AND AWARD PROCESS:

Preapplication Coordination: The standard application forms as furnished by the Federal agency and required by OMB Circular No. A-102 must be used for this program. The standard application form to be used is ED Form 9037. This program is eligible for coverage under E.O. 12372, "Intergovernmental Review of Federal Programs." An applicant should consult the office or official designated as the single point of contact in his or her State for more information on the process the State requires to be followed in applying for assistance, if the State has selected the program for review.

Application Procedure: Applications should be sent to the Department of Education, Application Control Center, Room 3633, ROB No. 3, 7th and D Streets, SW., Washington,

DC. Mailing address: the Department of Education, Application Control Center, 400 Maryland Ave., SW., Washington, DC 20202. This program is subject to the provisions of OMB Circular No. A-110.

Award Procedure: Upon receipt of new applications they are processed and assigned to field review for evaluation. A funding recommendation is made by the staff to the Secretary of Education for approval or disapproval. Official grant documents are prepared and sent to the certifying representative in the applicant's agency.

Deadlines: Contact the headquarters office for application deadlines.

Range of Approval/Disapproval Time: Approximately 120 to 200 days.

Appeals: Not applicable.

Renewals: Renewals are made only through reapplication on an annual basis.

ASSISTANCE CONSIDERATIONS:

Formula and Matching Requirements: There are no matching requirements.

Length and Time Phasing of Assistance: The budget period is usually for 12 months. Multi-year grants for project periods of 24 to 60 months are often awarded subject to submission of satisfactory annual applications and appropriations. Payment of funds is made in accordance with Department of Education policy and procedures.

POST ASSISTANCE REQUIREMENTS:

Reports: A financial status report and a performance report are required annually. A final performance report is required within 90 days after termination of the project period.

Audits: In accordance with the provisions of OMB Circular No. A-128, "Audits of State and Local Governments," State and local governments that receive financial assistance of $100,000 or more within the State's fiscal year shall have an audit made for that year. State and local governments that receive between $25,000 and $100,000 within the State's fiscal year shall have an audit made in accordance with Circular No. A-128, or in accordance with Federal laws and regulations governing the programs in which they participate.

Records: Grantee must maintain appropriate records applicable to pertinent credits acquired under the grant for a period of five years after the close of the award period or until audited, whichever is earlier.

FINANCIAL INFORMATION:

Account Identification: 91-0300-0-1-501.

Obligations: (Grants) FY 93 $102,520,000; FY 94 est $104,074,000; and FY 95 est $103,124,000.

Range and Average of Financial Assistance: $30,000 to $1,376,000; $100,000.

PROGRAM ACCOMPLISHMENTS: In fiscal year 1993, 235 new awards were made. In fiscal year 1994, 270 new awards are planned.

REGULATIONS, GUIDELINES, AND LITERATURE: Final regulations were published in the Federal Register on November 10, 1988; amended October 22, 1991 and July 24, 1992; 34 CFR 316, 318, and 319.

INFORMATION CONTACTS:

Regional or Local Office: Not applicable.

Headquarters Office: Division of Personnel Preparation, Special Education Programs, Office of Assistant Secretary for Special Education and Rehabilitative Services, Department of Education, Washington, DC 20202. Contact: Max Mueller. Telephone: (202) 205-9554. Use the same number for FTS.

EXAMPLES OF FUNDED PROJECTS: 1) A State education agency is funded to prepare regular education teachers, principals and administrators to work with handicapped children in the regular school setting; 2) a university is funded to train masters and post-masters students in broad spectrum special education so that they may teach and provide other services to all types of handicapped children; 3) a nonprofit educational agency is funded for the training of paraprofessionals, special education teachers, and regular educators in an interface so that a child can advance easily and readily from a special education to regular education placement with the assistance of a paraprofessional who is known to both the special education and regular education teacher; and 4) Native American teachers are being trained by a university with direct on-site (on reservation) experience so the teachers trained will work directly with handicapped Native American children in an appropriate bilingual and bicultural setting.

CRITERIA FOR SELECTING PROPOSALS: Selection is based on need, priority and quality. For preservice training of special education teachers and related services personnel, need is established through identification of critical personnel shortages by the applicant and the Department. Priority is noted by funding areas within the printed budget included within the application package. These areas are generally limited to training. Quality is judged by peer review by field reviewers. Priorities are described in 34 CFR 318.10 and 318.11. They are not ranked but funding amounts may vary from fiscal year to fiscal year contingent on Congressional appropriations. The budget is included in the Application Guidelines package.

84.086 SPECIAL EDUCATION-PROGRAM FOR SEVERELY DISABLED CHILDREN

FEDERAL AGENCY: OFFICE OF SPECIAL EDUCATION AND REHABILITATIVE SERVICES, DEPARTMENT OF EDUCATION

AUTHORIZATION: Individuals with Disabilities Education Act, Part C, Section 624, as amended, Public Laws 91-230, 98-199, 99-457, 100-630, 101-476 and 102-119, 20 U.S.C. 1424.

OBJECTIVES: To address the special education, related services, and early intervention needs of children and youth with severe disabilities.

TYPES OF ASSISTANCE: Project Grants; Project Grants (Cooperative Agreements); Project Grants (Contracts).

USES AND USE RESTRICTIONS: Awards are authorized for research, development, demonstration, training, dissemination and other activities. Recipients of awards are required to coordinate their activities with similar activities assisted under other sections of the Individuals with Disabilities Education Act.

ELIGIBILITY REQUIREMENTS:

Applicant Eligibility: Public and private, nonprofit organizations, and institutions may apply.

Beneficiary Eligibility: Infants, toddlers, children, and youth with severe disabilities benefit.

Credentials/Documentation: Costs will be determined in accordance with OMB Circular No. A-87 for State and local governments.

APPLICATION AND AWARD PROCESS:

Preapplication Coordination: This program is eligible for coverage under E.O. 12372, "Intergovernmental Review of Federal Programs." An applicant should consult the office or official designated as the single point of contact in his or her State for more information on the process the State requires to be followed in applying for assistance, if the State has selected the program for review.

Application Procedure: The standard application forms as furnished by the Federal agency and required by OMB Circular No. A-102 must be used for this program. This program is subject to the provisions of OMB Circular No. A-110.

Award Procedure: Applications will be read by field reader panel. Notification of awards will be made through the contract (grant) office.

Deadlines: Contact the headquarters office for application deadlines.

Range of Approval/Disapproval Time: From three to four months.

Appeals: Not applicable.

Renewals: Funding is generally incremental for three year projects.

ASSISTANCE CONSIDERATIONS:

Formula and Matching Requirements: None.

Length and Time Phasing of Assistance: From 12 to 60 months.

POST ASSISTANCE REQUIREMENTS:

Reports: Progress reports should be made on an annual basis. Final reports should be submitted at the end of the project period.

Audits: In accordance with the provisions of OMB Circular No. A-128, "Audits of State and Local Governments," State and local governments that receive financial assistance of $100,000 or more within the State's fiscal year shall have an audit made for that year. State and local governments that receive between $25,000 and $100,000 within the State's fiscal year shall have an audit made in accordance with Circular No. A-128, or in accordance with Federal laws and regulations governing the programs in which they participate.

Records: Accounts, records, and other evidence pertaining to all costs incurred.

FINANCIAL INFORMATION:

Account Identification: 91-0300-0-1-501.

Obligations: (Grants and contracts) FY 93 $9,325,000; FY 94 est $9,330,000; and FY 95 est $10,030,000.

Range and Average of Financial Assistance: $135,000 to $700,000; $190,000.

PROGRAM ACCOMPLISHMENTS: Forty-six awards were made in fiscal year 1993, 10 new awards were made in fiscal year 1994. In fiscal year 1995, approximately 12 new awards are planned.

REGULATIONS, GUIDELINES, AND LITERATURE: Title 34 CFR 315. Final regulations published August 24, 1987, Vol. 52; amended October 22, 1991, June 29, 1992.

INFORMATION CONTACTS:

Regional or Local Office: Not applicable.

Headquarters Office: Division of Educational Services, Office of Special Education Programs, Assistant Secretary, for the Office of Special Education and Rehabilitative Services, Department of Education, 400 Maryland Ave., SW., Switzer Bldg., Room 4620, Washington, DC 20202. Contact: Dawn Hunter. Telephone: (202) 205-5809. Use the same number for FTS.

EXAMPLES OF FUNDED PROJECTS: Projects include developing innovative ways to educate children with severe disabilities full-time in general education classrooms, statewide systems change, model inservice training projects, outreach projects serving students with severe disabilities in integrated environments, and social relationships research institute are examples.

CRITERIA FOR SELECTING PROPOSALS: Applications will be evaluated on the basis of the criteria and weighing factors cited in the RFP or program regulations. Applications will be reviewed for completeness and conformity to the requirements of the RFP or program regulations. A panel of qualified evaluators will review and rank the applications.

84.125 CLEARINGHOUSE ON DISABILITY INFORMATION

FEDERAL AGENCY: OFFICE OF ASSISTANT SECRETARY FOR SPECIAL EDUCATION AND REHABILITATIVE SERVICES, DEPARTMENT OF EDUCATION

AUTHORIZATION: Rehabilitation Act of 1973, Section 15, as amended, Public Law 93-112 and Public Law 102-569, 29 U.S.C 714.

OBJECTIVES: Provide information and data regarding the location, provision, and availability of services and programs for persons with disabilities.

TYPES OF ASSISTANCE: Dissemination of Technical Information.

USES AND USE RESTRICTIONS: Not applicable.

ELIGIBILITY REQUIREMENTS:

Applicant Eligibility: Information is available to all interested persons and organizations upon request.

Beneficiary Eligibility: All interested persons and organizations upon request.

Credentials/Documentation: This program is excluded from coverage under OMB Circular No. A-87.

APPLICATION AND AWARD PROCESS:

Preapplication Coordination: This program is excluded from coverage under E.O. 12372. This program is excluded from coverage under OMB Circular No. A-102.

Application Procedure: This program is excluded from coverage under OMB Circular No. A-110.

Award Procedure: Not applicable.

Deadlines: Not applicable.

Range of Approval/Disapproval Time: Not applicable.

Appeals: Not applicable.

Renewals: Not applicable.

ASSISTANCE CONSIDERATIONS:

Formula and Matching Requirements: None.

Length and Time Phasing of Assistance: Not applicable.

POST ASSISTANCE REQUIREMENTS:

Reports: Not applicable.

Audits: Not applicable.

Records: Not applicable.

FINANCIAL INFORMATION:

Account Identification: 91-0301-0-1-506.

Obligations: Not identifiable.

Range and Average of Financial Assistance: Not applicable.

PROGRAM ACCOMPLISHMENTS: The Clearinghouse serves as a resource to individuals and organizations that supply information relating to various disabling conditions and its primary function is to direct inquiries to appropriate Federal and national private resources. Special emphasis is placed on national information resources serving people with disabilities and service providers, Federal assistance to programs serving individuals with disabilities, Federal legislation and regulations affecting individuals with disabilities. In fiscal year 1993, the Clearinghouse responded to 9,199 written requests for information, and 1,562 telephone requests. Four issues of the publication OSERS News in Print were distributed; 22,000 copies of each issue were disseminated to regular mailing lists, and in response to special requests. Disseminated through the clearinghouse were 25,000 Pocket Guides to Federal Help for Individuals with Disabilities; 5,000 Summary of Existing Legislations Affecting People with Disabilities; 3,000 OSERS News Updates; and 5,000 information packets.

REGULATIONS, GUIDELINES, AND LITERATURE: Publications are made available to the public on request. Single copies are free. Some of the publications are also for sale by the Superintendent of Documents, Government Printing Office, Washington, DC 20402.

INFORMATION CONTACTS:

Regional or Local Office: Not applicable.

Headquarters Office: Office of Assistant Secretary for Special Education and Rehabilitative Services, Department of Education. Contact: Clearinghouse on Disability Information, Carolyn Corlett. Telephone: (202) 205-8241. Use the same number for FTS.

EXAMPLES OF FUNDED PROJECTS: Not applicable.

CRITERIA FOR SELECTING PROPOSALS: Not applicable.

84.129 REHABILITATION LONG-TERM TRAINING

FEDERAL AGENCY: OFFICE OF ASSISTANT SECRETARY FOR SPECIAL EDUCATION AND REHABILITATIVE SERVICES, DEPARTMENT OF EDUCATION

AUTHORIZATION: Rehabilitation Act of 1973, Title III, Part A, Section 302, and Title

VIII, Section 803, as amended, Public Law 93-112; Public Law 99-506, and Public Law 102-569, 29 U.S.C. 774.

OBJECTIVES: To support projects to increase the numbers and improve the skills of personnel trained in providing vocational rehabilitation services to individuals with disabilities in areas targeted as having personnel shortages.

TYPES OF ASSISTANCE: Project Grants (Contracts).

USES AND USE RESTRICTIONS: Training grants are provided in fields directly related to the vocational and independent living rehabilitation of individuals with disabilities, such as rehabilitation counseling, independent living, rehabilitation medicine, physical and occupational therapy, prosthetics-orthotics, speech-language, pathology and audiology, rehabilitation of individuals who are blind and individuals who are deaf, and rehabilitation technology.

ELIGIBILITY REQUIREMENTS:

Applicant Eligibility: State vocational rehabilitation agencies (including territories/possessions), and other public or nonprofit agencies and organizations, including institutions of higher education may apply.

Beneficiary Eligibility: Individuals preparing for employment in the rehabilitation of individuals with disabilities will benefit.

Credentials/Documentation: An application should show evidence of current accreditation by or seeking of accreditation from the designated accreditation agency in the respective professional field. Costs will be determined in accordance with OMB Circular No. A-87 for State and local governments. Costs will be determined in accordance with OMB Circular No. A-21 for educational institutions.

APPLICATION AND AWARD PROCESS:

Preapplication Coordination: The standard application forms as furnished by the Federal agency and required by OMB Circular No. A-102 must be used for this program. This program is eligible for coverage under E.O. 12372, "Intergovernmental Review of Federal Programs." An applicant should consult the office or official designated as the single point of contact in his or her State for more information on the process the State requires to be followed in applying for assistance, if the State has selected the program for review.

Application Procedure: Most new applications are made to Department of Education, Application Control Center, 400 Maryland Ave., SW., Washington, DC 20202-4725. Attention: 84.129. Most continuation applications are submitted to the appropriate Regional Office. This program is subject to the provisions of OMB Circular No. A-110.

Award Procedure: Most new and continuation grants are awarded by the Rehabilitation Services Administration through its Regional Offices. All new applications are reviewed by a panel of at least three individuals. Each panel will generally include two or more nonfederal consultants with experience and training in the related field.

Deadlines: Contact the headquarters or regional offices for application deadlines.

Range of Approval/Disapproval Time: From 120 to 160 days.

Appeals: None.

Renewals: Renewals are available only through the new application process. Projects with an approved multi-year project period may be continued based on the availability of adequate funds and an annual review of accomplishments to determine satisfactory performance.

ASSISTANCE CONSIDERATIONS:

Formula and Matching Requirements: Grantees are required to share in the costs of projects with the proportion subject to individual negotiation.

Length and Time Phasing of Assistance: Projects may generally be supported for a maximum of three years, funds are granted on a twelve month basis.

POST ASSISTANCE REQUIREMENTS:

Reports: Annual financial and progress reports must be submitted as required by grant award terms and conditions.

Audits: Audits must be conducted on a continuing basis or at scheduled intervals, usually once a year, but at least once every two years. In accordance with the provisions of OMB Circular No. A-128, "Audits of State and Local Governments," State and local governments that receive financial assistance of $100,000 or more within the State's fiscal year shall have an audit made for that year. State and local governments that receive between $25,000 and $100,000 within the State's fiscal year shall have an audit in accordance with Circular No. A-128, or in accordance with Federal laws and regulations governing the programs in which they participate.

Records: Proper records must be maintained for three years after project completion or until all audit questions are resolved.

FINANCIAL INFORMATION:

Account Identification: 91-0301-0-1-506.

Obligations: (Grants and contracts) FY 93 $24,408,864; FY 94 est $23,968,208; and FY 95 est $20,585,654.

Range and Average of Financial Assistance: $36,000 to $300,000; $100,577.

PROGRAM ACCOMPLISHMENTS: Approximately 13,650 persons were trained under the program during the 1992-93 academic year. Approximately 243 projects (89 new and 154 continuations) were funded in fiscal year 1994. For fiscal year 1995, approximately 201 projects are planned (58 new and 143 continuations).

REGULATIONS, GUIDELINES, AND LITERATURE: Regulations can be found in 34 CFR 385-390.

INFORMATION CONTACTS:

Headquarters Office: Rehabilitation Services Administration, Office of Special Education and Rehabilitative Services, Department of Education, Washington, DC 20202-2649. Contact: Richard Melia. Telephone: (202) 205-9400. Use the same number for FTS.

EXAMPLES OF FUNDED PROJECTS: 1) Residency scholarships in physical medicine and rehabilitation; 2) teaching and graduate scholarships in rehabilitation counseling; 3) teaching and non-academic training awards in rehabilitation facility administration; and 4) teaching grants for training rehabilitation personnel in physical and occupational therapy.

CRITERIA FOR SELECTING PROPOSALS: The relevance of the purpose of the content and the training project to the administratively established mission of the public rehabilitation program and the objectives of the Rehabilitation Services Administration. The methodology to be employed in implementing the project and its feasibility for the achievement of the established educational objectives. The existence of a working relationship with the State vocational rehabilitation agency and other agencies and rehabilitation facilities providing vocational rehabilitation services. Criteria for evaluating applications are published in program regulations 34 CFR 385-390.

84.132 CENTERS FOR INDEPENDENT LIVING

FEDERAL AGENCY: OFFICE OF ASSISTANT SECRETARY FOR SPECIAL EDUCATION AND REHABILITATIVE SERVICES, DEPARTMENT OF EDUCATION

AUTHORIZATION: Rehabilitation Act of 1973, Title VII, Chapter 1, Part C, as amended, Public Law 93-112; Public Law 99-506, Public Law 102-569, 29 U.S.C. 796e.

OBJECTIVES: To provide independent living services to individuals with significant disabilities to assist them to function more independently in family and community settings, by developing and supporting a statewide network of centers for independent living.

TYPES OF ASSISTANCE: Project Grants.

USES AND USE RESTRICTIONS: Federal funds are used for the establishment and operation of centers for independent living which offer a combination of services. Services must include independent living core services which mean information and referral services, training in independent living skills, peer counseling, individual and systems advocacy, and as appropriate, a combination of any other independent living services specified in Section 7 (30)(B) of the Act. Each center must have a governing board composed of a majority of persons with severe disabilities. The majority of the staff and individuals in decision making positions must be individuals with disabilities. Not less than 1.8 percent and not more than two percent of Federal funds appropriated for the program must be reserved to provide training and technical assistance under contracts with entities experienced in the operation of centers for independent living.

ELIGIBILITY REQUIREMENTS:

Applicant Eligibility: The principal eligible applicants are the private nonprofit agencies that received funding directly or through subgrants or contracts under the Centers for Independent Living program in fiscal year 1992. If funds remain available after all principal eligible applicants have been funded, other centers for independent living, as defined in Section 702 of the Act, and State agencies may receive funding based on satisfactory applications (including territories/possessions).

Beneficiary Eligibility: Individuals with significant physical or mental impairments whose abilities to function independently in the families or communities or whose abilities to obtain, maintain, or advance in employment is substantially limited. Eligibility shall not be based on the presence of any one or more specific severe disabilities.

Credentials/Documentation: Costs will be determined in accordance with OMB Circular No. A-87 for State and local governments. Costs will be determined in accordance with OMB Circular No. A-21 for educational institutions.

APPLICATION AND AWARD PROCESS:

Preapplication Coordination: This program is eligible for coverage under E.O. 12372, "Intergovernmental Review of Federal Programs." An applicant should consult the office or official designated as the single point of contact in his or her State for more information on the process the State requires to be followed in applying for assistance, if the State has selected the program for review. The standard application forms, as furnished by the Federal agency and required by OMB Circular No. A-102, must be used for this program.

Application Procedure: This program is subject to the provisions of OMB Circular No. A-110. Applications for new awards from eligible agencies should be submitted to the Department of Education, Application Control Center, 400 Maryland Ave., SW., Washington, DC 20202-4725, unless otherwise directed in the Federal Register Announcement.

Award Procedure: New awards are made on approval of the Commissioner of Rehabilitation Services Administration, and the Assistant Secretary, OSERS, based on the findings of Federal and nonfederal reviews of applications to ensure the applicants satisfactorily demonstrate that as of October 1, 1993, they will meet the standards described in Section 725 (b) of the Act and provide assurances described in Section 725 (c) of the Act.

Deadlines: Contact headquarters or regional offices for application deadlines.

Range of Approval/Disapproval Time: From 60 to 90 days.

Appeals: None.

Renewals: Projects may be continued based on a self-evaluation report and accomplishments as described in the Center's self-evaluation and annual report requirements under Section 725 (c)(8) of the Act, submittal of a continuation application, and the availability of funds. Renewals are available through the regular continuation application process and are processed through the headquarter and the regional offices.

ASSISTANCE CONSIDERATIONS:

Formula and Matching Requirements: No minimum share is required, but each applicant is encouraged to furnish as large a part of the total cost as possible.

Length and Time Phasing of Assistance: Existing projects are approved on an annual basis with funding on a twelve month basis. New projects are funded for five years with funding approved on a twelve month basis.

POST ASSISTANCE REQUIREMENTS:

Reports: Annual and fiscal progress reports and self-evaluations (A-F Reports) must be submitted as prescribed by Section 725 (c)(8) and grant award terms and conditions.

Audits: Audits must be conducted on a continuing basis or at scheduled intervals. In accordance with the provisions of OMB Circular No. A-128, "Audits of State and Local Governments," State and local governments that receive financial assistance of $100,000 or more within the State's fiscal year shall have an audit made for that year. State and local governments that receive between $25,000 and $100,000 within the State's fiscal year shall have an audit made in accordance with Circular No. A-128, or in accordance with Federal laws and regulations governing the programs in which they participate. The Centers must practice sound fiscal management, including making arrangements for an annual independent fiscal audit.

Records: Fiscal records must be maintained for three years after the grant ends and the final financial report is submitted or until all audit questions are resolved.

FINANCIAL INFORMATION:

Account Identification: 91-0301-0-1-506.

Obligations: (Grants) FY 93 $31,446,000; FY 94 est $36,818,000; and FY 95 est $39,068,000.

Range and Average of Financial Assistance: $26,566 to $640,467; $192,465.

PROGRAM ACCOMPLISHMENTS: In fiscal year 1993, 179 continuation grants were funded for the operation of 212 centers. Fiscal year 1993 is a transition year and significant changes are expected to be made in the funding pattern of Centers for Independent Living.

REGULATIONS, GUIDELINES, AND LITERATURE: Section 721 of the Rehabilitation Act, as amended, Program Regulations at 34 CFR 364 and 366.

INFORMATION CONTACTS:

Headquarters Office: Office of Developmental Programs, Rehabilitation Services Administration, OSERS, Department of Education, 330 C Street, SW., Washington, DC 20202-2575. Contact: Don Thayer. Telephone: (202) 205-9315 (Voice) or (202) 205-8352 (TT). Use the same number for FTS.

EXAMPLES OF FUNDED PROJECTS: Provided services will vary from one center to another. Centers provide a combination of services, including: information and referral; independent living skills training; individual and systems advocacy; counseling services; housing; rehabilitation technology; mobility training; life skills training; interpreter and reader services; personal assistance services; accessible transportation; supported living; therapeutic treatment; provision of prostheses and other devices; and other services described in Section 7 (30)(B) of the Act.

CRITERIA FOR SELECTING PROPOSALS: Selection criteria for this program include evidence of need, past performance, the plan for satisfying or demonstrating success in the standards and assurances set forth in Section 725, quality of key personnel, budget, and cost-effectiveness, evaluation plan, involvement of persons with severe disabilities and the ability of applicant to carry out the plans. Criteria for evaluating applications are published in program regulations 34 CFR 366.

84.133 NATIONAL INSTITUTE ON DISABILITY AND REHABILITATION RESEARCH

FEDERAL AGENCY: OFFICE OF ASSISTANT SECRETARY FOR SPECIAL EDUCATION AND REHABILITATIVE SERVICES, DEPARTMENT OF EDUCATION

AUTHORIZATION: Rehabilitation Act of 1973, Title II, as amended, Public Law 93-112; Public Laws 95-602, 98-221, 99-506, 100-630, and 102-569.

OBJECTIVES: To support and coordinate research and its utilization to improve the lives of people of all ages with physical and mental disabilities, especially persons with severe disabilities through: (1) Identifying and eliminating causes and consequences of disability; (2) maximizing the health, physical, and emotional status of persons with disabilities and their functional ability, self-sufficiency, self-development and personal autonomy; (3) preventing or minimizing personal and family, physical, mental, social, educational, vocational, and economic effects of disability; and (4) reducing and eliminating physical, social, educational, vocational, and environmental barriers to permit access to services and assistance and to use their abilities in daily life.

TYPES OF ASSISTANCE: Project Grants; Project Grants (Contracts); Project Grants (Cooperative Agreements); Project Grants (Fellowships).

USES AND USE RESTRICTIONS: Grants, cooperative agreements, and contracts are awarded for research, demonstrations, dissemination/utilization projects of national significance, and career training projects. All applications must meet standards of excellence in research and evaluation design. Fellowships support individual investigators in pursuing research in rehabilitation.

ELIGIBILITY REQUIREMENTS:

Applicant Eligibility: Grants and cooperative agreements may be made to and contracts with States, public, private, or nonprofit agencies and organizations, institutions of higher education, and Indian tribes and tribal organizations for research projects and specialized research activities related to the rehabilitation of individuals with disabilities; fellowships may be awarded to individuals.

Beneficiary Eligibility: Persons of all ages with disabilities will benefit.

Credentials/Documentation: Applicants should present written evidence of other agencies' willingness to cooperate when the project involves their acceptance or the utilization of their facilities or services. Costs will be determined in accordance with OMB Circular No. A-87 for State and local governments. Nonprofit organizations must show proof of such status.

APPLICATION AND AWARD PROCESS:

Preapplication Coordination: The NIDRR long-range research plan as required by Congress is the basis for program announcements that are published in the Federal Register and Requests for Proposals that are published in the Commerce Business Daily. The standard application forms as furnished by the Federal agency or published in the Federal Register and required by OMB Circular No. A-102 must be used for this program. This program is excluded from coverage under E.O. 12372.

Application Procedure: Application forms are submitted to: Application Control Center, Department of Education, 400 Maryland Ave., SW., Washington, DC 20202. This program is subject to the provisions of OMB Circular No. A-110.

Award Procedure: Official notice of approved applications is made through issuance of a Notice of Grant Award or an official letter of fellowship award. Grants and fellowships are awarded by the Secretary, Department of Education.

Deadlines: Established when grants and contracts are solicited by Program Announcements and Requests for Proposals are solicited. Announcements may be published throughout the year.

Range of Approval/Disapproval Time: Ranges from 30 to 365 days. Generally, solicited grants, fellowships, and contracts will be acted upon within 120 days.

Appeals: No formal appeal procedures. If an application is disapproved, the reasons for disapproval will be fully stated. Applicants will be sent copies of the reviewers' comments appraising their applications.

Renewals: Grant and contract extensions and renewals may be available, if formally applied for and approved. The Secretary may elect to extend the period of a fellowship. Renewals must compete with new applications on the basis of program relevance as well as standard requirements for excellence in design. If an application is recommended for approval for two or more years, the grantee or contractor must submit a formal request each year for continuation with a progress report that will be evaluated prior to a recommendation of continuation.

ASSISTANCE CONSIDERATIONS:

Formula and Matching Requirements: Grantees funded under 204(a) and 202(k) (Public Law 93-112, as amended) are required to share in the cost of projects. The amount of cost-sharing is negotiable. Cost-sharing for other grantees is at the Secretary's option.

Length and Time Phasing of Assistance: Funds are granted on a 12 month basis with support beyond the first year contingent upon acceptable evidence of satisfactory progress, continuing program relevance, and availability of funds. Awards may be made for a maximum of five years.

POST ASSISTANCE REQUIREMENTS:

Reports: Annual reports of progress and annual expenditures are required on all projects. Comprehensive final reports are due 90 days after the end of the project.

Audits: All fiscal transactions identifiable to Federal financial assistance are subject to audit by ED Audit Agency.

Records: Proper accounting records, identifiable by grant or contract number including all receipts and expenditures, must be maintained for three years. Subsequent to audit, they must be maintained until all questions are resolved.

FINANCIAL INFORMATION:

Account Identification: 91-0301-0-1-506.

Obligations: (Grants) FY 93 $67,229,000; FY 94 est $68,146,000; and FY 95 est $66,031,000.

Range and Average of Financial Assistance: Grants and contracts range from $10,000 to $750,000. Individual project grants average about $150,000 a year. However, these figures vary with type of program.

PROGRAM ACCOMPLISHMENTS: In fiscal year 1993, four fellowships were awarded; 41 continuations and 19 new field-initiated grants were supported; 15 rehabilitation research and training centers were maintained and 29 new ones were funded; five rehabilitation engineering centers were maintained and 10 new grants were funded; 13 spinal cord model systems projects were continued; 15 research and demonstration projects were continued and 14 new projects were funded; 25 utilization projects were continued and three new projects were funded; nine research training grants were continued and three new grants were funded.

REGULATIONS, GUIDELINES, AND LITERATURE: Grant administrative policies for programs and fellowships may be obtained from the National Institute on Disability and Rehabilitation Research, Department of Education, 400 Maryland Avenue, SW., Washington, DC 20202.

INFORMATION CONTACTS:

Regional or Local Office: Contact headquarters office.

Headquarters Office: Director, National Institute on Disability and Rehabilitation Research, Office of Assistant Secretary for Special Education and Rehabilitative Services, Department of Education, 600 Independence Avenue, SW., Washington, DC 20202-2572. For grants and contracts contact: Dianne Villines. Telephone: (202) 205-5450; for fellowships contact: Joseph Fenton. Telephone: (202) 205-9143. Use the same number for FTS.

EXAMPLES OF FUNDED PROJECTS: (1) Research and Training Centers with emphasis on vocational rehabilitation, medical rehabilitation, rehabilitation of persons with mental retardation, deafness rehabilitation, rehabilitation of persons with mental illness, and rehabilitation of those with severe visual disabilities; (2) Rehabilitation Engineering Centers with the application of engineering advances as applied to rehabilitation of persons with physical disabilities; special activities in prosthetics, orthotics, and rehabilitation aids and devices for various handicapping conditions; (3) specific research and demonstration projects concerned with medical, psychosocial, sensory, psychiatric, and vocational rehabilitation; (4) research utilization and dissemination of research findings; (5) field initiated projects in rehabilitation research; (6) innovation grants for conferences, testing of devices and curriculum development; and (7) grants for advanced training in research related to disability.

CRITERIA FOR SELECTING PROPOSALS: Objectives of projects and programs must be in consonance with and should contribute to achievement of the goals and objectives of the Institute and the policies established by the National Council on Disability. Adequate facilities must be available or planned to carry out the specific project or program. Personnel must be trained and qualified to carry out the proposed programs, and staffing patterns must be appropriate. Demonstrations of adequate plans and procedures for insuring the relevance to current needs in rehabilitation and the potential for project results must be effectively utilized. Commitment of available resources on the part of the applicant and evidence that the applicant has knowledge of rehabilitation issues as well as knowledge of past and present related research activities. A statement showing that the estimated cost to the government is reasonable in relation to anticipated project results (cost-effectiveness). Demonstrate the ability and capacity in long-range planning to achieve stated goals. Demonstrate, coordinate and cooperate with regional programs, State agency programs, and private rehabilitation facilities. Specific weighted selection criteria are contained in program regulations. For fellowships, criteria are specified in program regulations, 34 CFR 356. These criteria include the education and experience of the individual and the quality of the fellowship proposal.

84.158 SECONDARY EDUCATION AND TRANSITIONAL SERVICES FOR YOUTH WITH DISABILITIES

FEDERAL AGENCY: OFFICE OF SPECIAL EDUCATION AND REHABILITATIVE SERVICES, DEPARTMENT OF EDUCATION

AUTHORIZATION: Individuals with Disabilities Education Act, Part C, Section 626, as amended, Public Laws 91-230, 93-380, 98-199, 99-457, 100-630, and 101-476, 20 U.S.C. 1425; 29 U.S.C. 1501 et seq.

OBJECTIVES: (1) Strengthen and coordinate special education and related services for youth with disabilities currently in school or who recently left school to assist them in the transition to postsecondary education, vocational training, competitive employment (including supported employment), continuing education, independent and community living, or adult services; (2) stimulate the improvement and development of programs for secondary special education; and (3) stimulate the improvement of the vocational and life skills of students with disabilities to enable them to be better prepared for transition to adult life and services.

TYPES OF ASSISTANCE: Project Grants; Project Grants (Cooperative Agreements); Project Grants (Contracts).

USES AND USE RESTRICTIONS: Awards may include research, development, demonstrations, training, dissemination, and other activities addressing program objectives.

ELIGIBILITY REQUIREMENTS:

Applicant Eligibility: Institutions of higher education, State educational agencies, local educational agencies and other appropriate public and private nonprofit institutions or agencies, including the State job training coordinating councils and service delivery area administrative entities established under the Job Training Partnership Act, 29 U.S.C. 1501 et seq.

Beneficiary Eligibility: Youth with disabilities benefit.

Credentials/Documentation: Costs will be determined in accordance with OMB Circular No. A-87 for State and local governments. OMB Circular No. A-21 for educational institutions also applies.

APPLICATION AND AWARD PROCESS:

Preapplication Coordination: The standard application forms as furnished by the Federal agency and required by OMB Circular No. A-102 must be used for this program. This program is eligible for coverage under E.O. 12372, "Intergovernmental Review of Federal Programs." An applicant should consult the office or official designated as the single point of contact in his or her State for more information on the process the State requires to be followed in applying for assistance, if the State has selected the program for review.

Application Procedure: Applications must be sent to the Department of Education Application Control Center, Attention: CFDA 84.158, 400 Maryland Ave., SW., Washington, DC 20202-4725. Applications are reviewed by field readers and selection is made according to published criteria. This program is subject to the provisions of OMB Circular No. A-110.

Award Procedure: Following review of applications by field readers, the Assistant Secretary of Special Education and Related Services determines the successful applicants. Initial contact is made with the successful grantees by telephone. Unsuccessful applicants will receive written notification of rejection.

Deadlines: Contact the headquarters office for applications deadlines.

Range of Approval/Disapproval Time: The approval time is eight weeks.

Appeals: Not applicable.

Renewals: Funding is generally for a one year period for a maximum of three years.

ASSISTANCE CONSIDERATIONS:

Formula and Matching Requirements: This program has no statutory formula or matching requirements.

Length and Time Phasing of Assistance: Three year grant periods with yearly renewals may be funded.

POST ASSISTANCE REQUIREMENTS:

Reports: Progress reports and final reports shall be submitted as required by the award document.

Audits: In accordance with the provisions of OMB Circular No. A-128, "Audits of State and Local Governments," State and local governments that receive $100,000 or more a year in Federal financial assistance shall have an audit made for that year. State and local governments that receive between $25,000 and $100,000 a year shall have an audit made in accordance with Circular No. A-128, or in accordance with Federal laws and regulations governing the programs in which they participate.

Records: As stated in the grant or contract terms and conditions, the awardee shall maintain accounts, records, and other evidence pertaining to all costs incurred, revenues, or other applicable acquired under this grant.

FINANCIAL INFORMATION:

Account Identification: 91-0300-0-1-501.

Obligations: (Grants and contracts) FY 93 $21,965,856; FY 94 est $21,966,000; and FY 95 est $23,966,000.

Range and Average of Financial Assistance: Awards range from $100,000 to $1,500,000; $151,000.

PROGRAM ACCOMPLISHMENTS: In fiscal year 1993, 27 new awards were made and in fiscal year 1994, 16 new awards are planned. In fiscal year 1995, 24 new awards are planned.

REGULATIONS, GUIDELINES, AND LITERATURE: Regulations were published July 11, 1984 (34 CFR 326). Amendments were published in the Federal Register on September 10, 1987, October 22, 1991 and December 20, 1991, 34 CFR 325.

INFORMATION CONTACTS:

Regional or Local Office: Not applicable.

Headquarters Office: Division of Educational Services, Office of Special Education Programs, 600 Independence Ave., SW., Washington, DC 20202. Contact: Michael Ward. Telephone: (202) 205-8163. Use the same number for FTS.

EXAMPLES OF FUNDED PROJECTS: Model Demonstration: (1) Development of criteria for entry into various worksettings and living arrangements; (2) development of strategies to increase job retention through extended year and evening programs; (3) development of strategies and materials to enhance the development of transitional programs in rural areas; (4) model development to assist autistic adolescents and adults in securing competitive employment; (5) cooperative models to assist youth to participate in adult services; (6) development of job training strategies to assist youth in entering competitive employment; and (7) identify/develop alternatives for youth with disabilities who have dropped out of school.

CRITERIA FOR SELECTING PROPOSALS: The criteria to evaluate applications for model projects include: (a) Plan of operation (10 points); (b) quality of key personnel (10 points); (c) budget and cost-effectiveness (10 points); and (d) evaluation plan (10 points); (e) adequacy of resources (5 points); (f) importance (10 points); (g) impact (10 points); and (h) technical soundness (25 points). The criteria for selection of research and evaluation projects include: (a) Plan of operation (10 points); (b) quality of key personnel (10 points); (c) budget and cost-effectiveness (10 points); (d) evaluation plan (5 points); (e) adequacy of resources (5 points); (f) importance (10 points); (g) impact (10 points); and (h) technical soundness (40 points).

84.180 TECHNOLOGY, EDUCATIONAL MEDIA AND MATERIALS FOR INDIVIDUALS WITH DISABILITIES

FEDERAL AGENCY: OFFICE OF SPECIAL EDUCATION AND REHABILITATIVE SERVICES, DEPARTMENT OF EDUCATION

AUTHORIZATION: Individuals with Disabilities Education Act, Part G, as amended, Public Laws 99-457, 100-630, and 101-476, 20 U.S.C. 1461.

OBJECTIVES: To advance the availability, quality, use effectiveness of technology, educational media, and materials in the education of children and youth with disabilities and the provision of related services and early intervention services to infants and toddlers with disabilities.

TYPES OF ASSISTANCE: Project Grants; Project Grants (Cooperative Agreements); Project Grants (Contracts).

USES AND USE RESTRICTIONS: Contracts, grants or cooperative agreements may support projects or centers for the purpose of advancing and improving technology, educational media, and materials in the education of the disabled; and how they can be used more effectively to design and adapt new technology, educational media, and materials in developing and marketing new technology, and to disseminate information on their availability and use.

ELIGIBILITY REQUIREMENTS:

Applicant Eligibility: Institutions of higher education, State and local educational agencies, public agencies, and private nonprofit or profit agencies or organizations may apply.

Beneficiary Eligibility: Infants, toddlers, children, and youth with disabilities benefit.

Credentials/Documentation: Costs will be determined in accordance with OMB Circular No. A-87 for State and local governments. OMB Circular No. A-21 for educational institutions applies.

APPLICATION AND AWARD PROCESS:

Preapplication Coordination: The standard application forms as furnished by the Federal agency and required by OMB Circular No. A-102 must be used for this program. This program is eligible for coverage under E.O. 12372, "Intergovernmental Review of Federal Programs." An applicant should consult the office or official designated as the single point of contact in his or her State for more information on the process the State requires to be followed in applying for assistance, if the State has selected the program for review.

Application Procedure: Announcements for grants and cooperative agreements are published in the Federal Register. Contracts are announced through publication in the Commerce Business Daily (CBD). Officials submit proposals in response to the announcement. Applications, if hand carried, should be delivered to: Department of Education Application Control Center, Room 3633, ROB No. 3, 7th and D Streets, SW., Washington, DC 20202. Mailing Address: Department of Education Application Control Center, 400 Maryland Avenue, SW., Washington, DC 20202. Applications are reviewed by field readers. Their recommendations are the basis for approval or disapproval. This program is subject to the provisions of OMB Circular No. A-110.

Award Procedure: The Secretary of Education makes final decisions to approve, defer or reject individual proposals based on objective reviews by outside experts and staff. Negotiations are conducted by telephone. Unsuccessful applicants will receive written notification.

Deadlines: Contact the headquarters office for application deadlines.

Range of Approval/Disapproval Time: Approximately 90 to 180 days.

Appeals: Contract proposals can be revised on the basis of recommendations made during the review and negotiation process. This appeal process does not apply to grants or cooperative agreements.

Renewals: Funding is generally for a one year period. Multi-year projects may received continuation funding based on staff review, satisfactory performance, and availability of funds.

ASSISTANCE CONSIDERATIONS:

Formula and Matching Requirements: None.

Length and Time Phasing of Assistance: One to five years depending on announcement. Multi-year awards are subject to satisfactory progress, and a continuation application must be submitted for approval for each subsequent year of the project.

POST ASSISTANCE REQUIREMENTS:

Reports: Program reports and final reports as required by award documents.

Audits: In accordance with the provisions of OMB Circular No. A-128, "Audits of State and Local Governments," State and local governments that receive financial assistance of $100,000 or more within the State's fiscal year shall have an audit made for that year. State and local governments that receive between $25,000 and $100,000 within the State's fiscal year shall have an audit made in accordance with Circular No. A-128, or in accordance with Federal laws and regulations governing the programs in which they participate.

Records: All recipients are required to maintain all records during the project period and for three years after the project is terminated.

FINANCIAL INFORMATION:

Account Identification: 91-0300-0-1-501.

Obligations: (Grants and contracts) FY 93 $10,820,000; FY 94 est $10,862,000; and FY 95 est $10,862,000.

Range and Average of Financial Assistance: $100,000 to $500,000; $250,000.

PROGRAM ACCOMPLISHMENTS: In fiscal year 1993, 21 new awards were made. In fiscal year 1994, 17 new awards are planned.

REGULATIONS, GUIDELINES, AND LITERATURE: Final regulations were published in the Federal Register on March 3, 1988, amended October 22, 1991; 34 CFR 333.

INFORMATION CONTACTS:

Regional or Local Office: Not applicable.

Headquarters Office: Division of Innovation and Development, Office of Assistant Secretary for Special Education and Rehabilitative Services, Department of Education, 600 Independence Avenue, SW., Washington, DC 20202. Contact: Ellen Schiller. Telephone: (202) 205-8123. Use the same number for FTS.

EXAMPLES OF FUNDED PROJECTS: No examples are currently available.

CRITERIA FOR SELECTING PROPOSALS: As presented in each Request for Proposal and Application for grants or cooperative agreements.

84.235 SPECIAL PROJECTS AND DEMONSTRATIONS FOR PROVIDING VOCATIONAL REHABILITATION SERVICES TO INDIVIDUALS WITH SEVERE DISABILITIES

FEDERAL AGENCY: OFFICE OF ASSISTANT SECRETARY FOR SPECIAL EDUCATION AND REHABILITATIVE SERVICES, DEPARTMENT OF EDUCATION

AUTHORIZATION: Rehabilitation Act of 1973, Title III, Section 311(a), (b), and (e), Title VIII, Section 802, as amended, Public Law 99-506; Public Law 102-569.

OBJECTIVES: To provide financial assistance to projects for expanding and otherwise improving vocational rehabilitation services and other rehabilitation services for individuals with severe disabilities.

TYPES OF ASSISTANCE: Project Grants.

USES AND USE RESTRICTIONS: Authorized activities under this program include carrying out special projects concerned with establishing programs for expanding or otherwise improving vocational rehabilitation services and other rehabilitation services to individual with disabilities, especially those that are the most severely disabled. Projects may also be conducted to meet the special needs of individuals that are unserved or underserved. Applying new types or patterns of services or devices for individuals with disabilities (including programs for providing opportunities for new careers and career advancement); operating programs to demonstrate methods of making recreation activities fully accessible to individuals with disabilities; operating programs to meet the special needs of isolated populations of individuals with disabilities, particularly among American Indians residing on or outside of reservations; research and evaluation for youths who are individuals with disabilities to provide job training to prepare them for entry into the labor force.

ELIGIBILITY REQUIREMENTS:

Applicant Eligibility: Eligible applicants are States, public, and other nonprofit organizations, as stated in 34 CFR 373.2, and 376.2. Grants cannot be made directly to individuals.

Beneficiary Eligibility: Benefitting are individuals with physical, mental, learning or emotional problems. Persons who may be served include, but are not limited to, those who are deaf, blind, mobility impaired, etc.

Credentials/Documentation: Costs will be determined in accordance with OMB Circular No. A-87 for State and local Governments. Costs will also be determined in accordance with OMB Circular No. A-21 for educational institutions.

APPLICATION AND AWARD PROCESS:

Preapplication Coordination: This program is subject to the provisions of OMB Circular No. A-102. This program is eligible for coverage under E.O. 12372, "Intergovernmental Review of Federal Programs." An applicant should consult the office or official designated as the single point of contact in his or her State for more information on the process the State requires to be followed in applying for assistance, if the State has selected the program for review.

Application Procedure: Applications should be submitted to the Department of Education, Application Control Center. Attention: (CFDA 84-235), 400 Maryland Avenue, SW., Washington, DC 20202-4725. The standard application kit as furnished by the Federal agency and required by OMB Circular No. A-102 must be used for this program. ED No. 80-0013 must also be submitted.

Award Procedure: Awards are made on approval of the Commissioner, RSA and the Assistant Secretary, OSERS, for new projects and the Commissioner, RSA, for continuation projects.

Deadlines: Contact the headquarters office, RSA, for application deadlines.

Range of Approval/Disapproval Time: The range is approximately 150 to 180 days.

Appeals: None.

Renewals: Projects with multi-year periods may be continued based on annual review of accomplishments and availability of adequate funds. Renewals are available through the continuation application process.

ASSISTANCE CONSIDERATIONS:

Formula and Matching Requirements: This program has no statutory formula or matching requirements.

Length and Time Phasing of Assistance: Grants are awarded for up to 36 months.

POST ASSISTANCE REQUIREMENTS:

Reports: Annual financial reports and reports of progress must be submitted as prescribed by grant award terms and conditions. Final financial and programmatic reports are required at the end of the final project year.

Audits: None.

Records: Fiscal records must be maintained for the periods of time specified in the grant award.

FINANCIAL INFORMATION:

Account Identification: 91-0301-0-1-506.

Obligations: (Grants) FY 93 $19,942,000; FY 94 est $19,942,000; and FY 95 est $21,942,000.

Range and Average of Financial Assistance: Range: $50,000 to $287,880; $140,000 per year.

PROGRAM ACCOMPLISHMENTS: In fiscal year 1993, 36 continuations and 59 new grants were funded. In fiscal year 1994, 87 continuations and 11 grants were awarded.

REGULATIONS, GUIDELINES, AND LITERATURE: Regulations: (A) The Education Department General Administrative Regulations (EDGAR) in 34 CFR 74, 75, 77, 79, 80, 81, 82, 85, and 86; and (B) the regulations for this program in 34 CFR 369 and 373 apply.

INFORMATION CONTACTS:

Headquarters Office: Rehabilitation Services Administration, Office of the Assistant Secretary for Special Education and Rehabilitative Services, Department of Education, Washington, DC 20202. Contact: Thomas E. Finch. Telephone: (202) 205-9796. Use the same number for FTS.

EXAMPLES OF FUNDED PROJECTS: Funded projects include: 1) Transportation services; 2) projects to increase client choice; 3) services to people with traumatic brain injury; 4) long-term services to people with mental illness; 5) services to low-functioning adults who are deaf or hard of hearing; 6) functional assessment of cognitive disorders; and 7) training and placement of individuals who abuse drugs other than alcohol.

CRITERIA FOR SELECTING PROPOSALS: Funding priorities are published in the Federal Register. Applications for discretionary grants are subject to peer review procedures leading to recommendations for approval or disapproval by Federal and nonfederal experts. Criteria for evaluating applications are published in program and department regulations (34 CFR 369 and 373).

88.001 ARCHITECTURAL AND TRANSPORTATION BARRIERS COMPLIANCE BOARD

FEDERAL AGENCY: ARCHITECTURAL AND TRANSPORTATION BARRIERS COMPLIANCE BOARD

AUTHORIZATION: Rehabilitation Act of 1973, Section 502, as amended, Public Law 93-112, 29 U.S.C. 792; Architectural Barriers Act of 1968, as amended, Public Law 90-480; Public Law 94-541, 42 U.S.C. 4151 et seq; Americans with Disabilities Act of 1990, Public Law 101-336.

OBJECTIVES: To enforce Federal laws requiring accessibility for persons with disabilities in certain federally funded buildings and facilities throughout the Nation; set guidelines and requirements for accessibility standards prescribed by Federal agencies under the Americans with Disabilities Act and the Architectural Barriers Act; provide technical assistance to organizations and agencies, and individuals requesting help in explaining the guidelines and requirements and in solving accessible design and construction problems; conduct research to determine appropriate specifications for accessibility.

TYPES OF ASSISTANCE: Dissemination of Technical Information.

USES AND USE RESTRICTIONS: Technical information and assistance on creating a barrier free environment is available to Federal, State and local government agencies and to private organizations and individuals.

ELIGIBILITY REQUIREMENTS:

Applicant Eligibility: Requests for information may be made by the general public as well as all agencies of Federal, State, and local government.

Beneficiary Eligibility: General public, all levels of government, and private organizations will benefit.

Credentials/Documentation: This program is excluded from coverage under OMB Circular No. A-87.

APPLICATION AND AWARD PROCESS:

Preapplication Coordination: This program is excluded from coverage under E.O. 12372.

Application Procedure: Requests for information and assistance should be sent to Director, Office of Technical and Information Services, Architectural and Transportation Barriers Compliance Board, Suite 1000, 1331 F Street, NW., Washington, DC 20004-1111. Telephone: (202) 272-5434 (voice); (202) 272-5449 (TTY); Toll-free 1-800-USA-ABLE (voice and TTY) technical assistance: 1-800-USA-ABLE. This program is excluded from coverage under OMB Circular No. A-110.

Award Procedure: Not applicable.

Deadlines: Not applicable.

Range of Approval/Disapproval Time: Not applicable.

Appeals: Not applicable.

Renewals: Not applicable.

ASSISTANCE CONSIDERATIONS:

Formula and Matching Requirements: Not applicable.

Length and Time Phasing of Assistance: Not applicable.

POST ASSISTANCE REQUIREMENTS:

Reports: Not applicable.

Audits: Not applicable.

Records: Not applicable.

FINANCIAL INFORMATION:

Account Identification: 95-3200-0-1-751.

Obligations: (Salaries and expenses) FY 93 $3,303,000; FY 94 est $3,258,000; and FY 95 $3,244,000.

Range and Average of Financial Assistance: Not applicable.

PROGRAM ACCOMPLISHMENTS: Distributed over 13,000 packets of technical information and over 17,000 copies of the ADA Accessibility Guidelines; published ADA Accessibility Guidelines Checklist; mailed nearly 60,000 copies of 32 Access Board publications. In addition, two Access America newsletters were published and distributed to nearly 17,000 individuals, businesses, and organizations; developed technical bulletins on text telephones, surfaces, and using ADAAG; trained over 7,000 people in ADA or Uniform Federal Accessibility Standards. Closed 127 Architectural Barriers Act complaints between October 1, 1992, and September 30, 1993. Received 101 new cases during the year.

REGULATIONS, GUIDELINES, AND LITERATURE: General information publications, "Uniform Federal Accessibility Standards," technical assistance papers, Americans with Disabilities Act accessibility guidelines, pamphlets, technical assistance bulletins and the agency's annual report to the President and Congress are available.

INFORMATION CONTACTS:

Regional or Local Office: Not applicable.

Headquarters Office: Director, Office of Technical and Information Services, Architectural and Transportation Barriers Compliance Board, Suite 1000, 1331 F Street, NW., Washington, DC 20004-1111. Telephone: (202) 272-5434 (voice); (202) 272-5449 (TTY); Toll-free 1-800-USA-ABLE (voice and TTY); Technical assistance: 1-800- USA-ABLE (voice and TTY); 1-800-993-2822 (TTY).

EXAMPLES OF FUNDED PROJECTS: Not applicable.

CRITERIA FOR SELECTING PROPOSALS: Not applicable.

93.125 MENTAL HEALTH PLANNING AND DEMONSTRATION PROJECTS

FEDERAL AGENCY: SUBSTANCE ABUSE AND MENTAL HEALTH SERVICES ADMINISTRATION, PUBLIC HEALTH SERVICE, DEPARTMENT OF HEALTH AND HUMAN SERVICES

AUTHORIZATION: Public Health Service Act, Title V, Section 5204A; Alcohol, Drug Abuse and Mental Health Reorganization Act, Public Law 102-321, 42 U.S.C. 290bb-32.

OBJECTIVES: To promote the development of community support systems for the long-term mentally ill, including inappropriately institutionalized individuals, mentally disturbed children and youth,and homeless individuals in communities; and to assist States in plans for measurable goals and objectives to improve the delivery of mental health services, especially for chronically mentally ill individuals, seriously emotionally disturbed children, and elderly individuals.

TYPES OF ASSISTANCE: Project Grants.

USES AND USE RESTRICTIONS: Grant resources are to be used to encourage States and communities to give greater priority to the needs of individuals with the most severe disorders, including homeless individuals, to make the necessary administrative and programmatic arrangements to improve opportunities and services, to reduce fragmentation of services, integrate families and consumers into all aspects of services planning, provision, monitoring and evaluation, and to test alternative approaches to providing treatment, support, and rehabilitation services.

ELIGIBILITY REQUIREMENTS:

Applicant Eligibility: States, political subdivisions of States, nonprofit private agencies, and Indian Tribes and tribal organizations.

Beneficiary Eligibility: State and local governments, local communities, and academic institutions.

Credentials/Documentation: Costs will be determined in accordance with OMB Circular No. A-87 for State and local governments.

APPLICATION AND AWARD PROCESS:

Preapplication Coordination: Preapplication coordination is not required. This program is eligible for coverage under E.O. 12372, "Intergovernmental Review of Federal Programs". An applicant should consult the office or official designated as the single point of contact in his or her State for more information on the process the State requires to be followed in applying for assistance, if the State has selected this program for review.

Application Procedure: Standard application forms, as furnished by the Public Health Service (PHS-5161-1, Revised July 1992) and required by 45 CFR, Part 92 for State and local governments, must be used by this program. This program is subject to the provisions of 45 CFR, Part 92.

Award Procedure: Applications for grants are reviewed by a committee of nonfederal experts and by the Center for Mental Health Services National Advisory Council. Final finding decisions are made by the Center Director.

Deadlines: Contact Headquarters Office for application deadlines.

Range of Approval/Disapproval Time: Approximately 6 months.

Renewals: Type II renewals (competitive continuation grants) are available for grantees who have received less than 5 years of research demonstration funding.

ASSISTANCE CONSIDERATIONS:

Formula and Matching Requirements: Matching requirements pertain in specific instances (Part E of Title V of the Public Health, Services Act as amended by 42 USC 290ff.)

Length and Time Phasing of Assistance: Projects will be funded for up to 5 years. Payments will be made under an Electronic Transfer System.

POST ASSISTANCE REQUIREMENTS:

Reports: Progress and financial status reports must be submitted within 90 days after termination of a grant period.

Audits: In accordance with the provisions of OMB Circular No. A-128, "Audits of State and Local Governments," State and local governments that receive financial assistance of $100,000 or more within the State's fiscal year shall have an audit made for that year. State and local governments that receive between $25,000 and $100,000 within the State's fiscal year shall have an audit made in accordance with Circular No. A-128, or in accordance with Federal laws and regulations governing the programs in which they participate. In addition, grants and cooperative agreements are subject to inspection and audits by DHHS and other Federal officials.

Records: Records must be retained for at least 3 years after the date of submission of required financial status reports.

FINANCIAL INFORMATION:

Account Identification: 75-1362-0-1-550.

Obligations: (Grants) FY 93 $38,723,691; FY 94 $39,400,000; and FY 95 est $38,700,000.

Range and Average of Financial Assistance: $1,572 to $2,514,706; $242,554.

PROGRAM ACCOMPLISHMENTS: Funding was provided for 120 projects in fiscal year 1993, and 110 projects in fiscal year 1994. In fiscal 1995, an estimated 110 projects will be funded.

REGULATIONS, GUIDELINES, AND LITERATURE: Guidelines are provided along with instructions in application kits. PHS Grants Policy Statement, DHHS Publication No. (OASH) 94-50,000, (Rev.) April 1, 1994.

INFORMATION CONTACTS:

Regional or Local Office: Not applicable.

Headquarters Office: Program Contacts: For Adult Community Support Program Grants: Anne Mathews-Younes, Acting Chief, Community Support Program Section, Division of Demonstration Programs, Center for Mental Health Services, Substance Abuse and Mental Health Services Administration, Public Health Service, Department of Health and Human Services, Parklawn Building, Room 11C-22, 5600 Fishers Lane, Rockville, MD 20857. Telephone: (301) 443-3653. For Child and Adolescent Service System Program Grants and Comprehensive Community Mental Health Service Family Branch, contact: Gary DeCarolis, Chief, Child Adolescent and Development Program, Division of Demonstration Programs, Center for Mental Health Services, SAMHSA, Room 11C-17, 5600 Fishers Lane, Rockville, Maryland 20857. Telephone: (301) 443-1333. For Research Demonstration Grants, contact: Diane L. Sondheimer, Director, Child and Adolescent Studies Program, Child, Adolescent and Family Branch, DDP, CMHS (address and phone same as above). For ACCESS grants for homeless mentally ill individuals: Frances Randolph, Dr. P.H., Acting Director, ACCESS Program, Homeless Program Section, Division of Demonstration Programs, Center for Mental Health Services, Substance Abuse and Mental Health Services Administration, Public Health Service, Department of Health and Human Services, Parklawn Building, Room 11C-05, 5600 Fishers Lane, Rockville, MD 20857. Telephone: (301) 443-3653. Grants Management Contact: Ms. Carole Edison, Grants Management Officer, Center for Mental Health Services, Substance Abuse and Mental Health Services Administration, Public Health Service, Department of Health and Human Services, Parklawn Building, Room 15C-05, 5600 Fishers Lane, Rockville, MD 20857. Telephone: (301) 443-4456. Use the same numbers for FTS.

EXAMPLES OF FUNDED PROJECTS: (1) Service system improvement strategies involving families and consumers; (2) service and research demonstration projects on supported housing, comprehensive systems, consumer-operated alternatives, case management services, psychosocial rehabilitation, and crisis response services; and (3) research demonstration on services for homeless mentally ill persons.

CRITERIA FOR SELECTING PROPOSALS: (1) Significance of the proposed project to national goals and objectives; (2) quality of the proposed project; (3) geographical distribution; and (4) availability of funds.

93.173 RESEARCH RELATED TO DEAFNESS AND COMMUNICATION DISORDERS

FEDERAL AGENCY: NATIONAL INSTITUTE ON DEAFNESS AND OTHER COMMUNICATION DISORDERS, NATIONAL INSTITUTES OF HEALTH, PUBLIC HEALTH SERVICE, DEPARTMENT OF HEALTH AND HUMAN SERVICES

AUTHORIZATION: Public Health Service Act, Sections 301, 464 A-F, and 487, as amended; 42 U.S.C. 241, 285m, 285m-3, and 288; Public Law 100-553; 102 Stat. 2769; Small Business Research and Development Enhancement Act of 1992, Public Law 102-564.

OBJECTIVES: To investigate solutions to problems directly relevant to patients with deafness or disorders of human communication, such as hearing, balance, smell, taste, voice, speech, and language. The National Institute on Deafness and Other Communication Disorders (NIDCD) supports research including investigation into the etiology, pathology, detection, treatment, and prevention of all forms of disorders of hearing and other communication processes, primarily through the support of basic research in anatomy, audiology, biochemistry, bioengineering, epidemiology, genetics, immunology, microbiology, molecular biology, the neurosciences, otolaryngology, psychology, pharmacology, physiology, speech and language pathology, and other scientific disciplines. Multipurpose Deafness and Other Communication Disorders Centers Program: To provide funding for the development, modernization and operation of new and existing centers for studies of disorders of hearing and other communication processes. Small Business Innovation Research (SBIR) program: To expand and improve the SBIR program; to increase private sector commercialization of innovations derived from Federal research and development; to increase small business participation in Federal research and development; and to foster and encourage participation of socially and economically disadvantaged small business concerns and women-owned small business concerns in technological innovation. Small Business Technology Transfer (STTR) program: To stimulate and foster scientific and technological innovation through cooperative research and development carried out between small business concerns and research institutions and to increase private sector commercialization of innovations derived from Federal research and development. Small Instrumentation Program: To support the purchase of relatively low-cost pieces of research equipment that generally are not funded in research project grants and that also do not qualify for support under the National Institutes of Health's larger shared instrumentation.

TYPES OF ASSISTANCE: Project Grants.

USES AND USE RESTRICTIONS: Research Grants and Centers Grants may be used to provide salaries, equipment, supplies, travel, and other expenses for research. Some National Research Service Awards (NRSAs) are made directly to individuals for research training in specified biomedical shortage areas. In addition, other training grants may be made to institutions to enable them to make NRSAs to individuals selected by them. Research Career Development Awards and Clinical Investigator Development Awards are made to enhance independent research capability of selected individuals during the formative stages of their careers. Multipurpose Deafness and Other Communication Disorders Centers Grants provide for the development, modernization, and operation of new and existing centers for training investigators and for studies of disorders of hearing and other communication processes for the purposes stated above. Small Business Innovation Research (SBIR) Program: Phase I grants (of approximately 6 months' duration) are to establish the technical merit and feasibility of a proposed research effort that may lead to a commercial product or process. SBIR Phase II grants are for the continuation of the research efforts initiated in Phase I and that are likely to result in commercial products or processes. Only Phase I awardees are eligible to apply for Phase II support. STTR Phase I grant (normally of 1-year duration) are to determine the scientific, technical, and commercial merit and feasibility of the proposed cooperative effort that has potential for commercial application. Phase II funding is based on result of research initiated in Phase I and scientific and technical merit and commercial potential of Phase II application. Grant funds may be expended only for the purpose stated in the application and award document. Each individual who receives a NRSA is obligated upon termination of the award to comply with certain service and payback provisions. Small Instrumentation Program: Funds are awarded as institutional formula grants for the purchase of research equipment costing not less than $5,000 or more than $60,000 per piece. Indirect costs are not provided.

ELIGIBILITY REQUIREMENTS:

Applicant Eligibility: Research Grants and Centers Grants: Any public, private, nonprofit, or for-profit institution is eligible to apply. For-profit institutions are not eligible for National Research Service Awards. All proposals are reviewed for scientific merit, for evaluation of the qualifications of the investigators, for adequacy of the research environment and for significance of the problem. Approved proposals compete for available funds. All Career Program awardees must be citizens or have been admitted to the United States for permanent residence. Candidates must be nominated for the program by a nonfederal public or private nonprofit institution located in the United States, its possessions or Territories. To be eligible, postdoctoral NRSA trainees and fellows must have a professional or scientific degree (M.D., Ph.D., D.D.S., D.O., D.V.M., Sc.D., D.Eng., or equivalent domestic or foreign degree). SBIR grants can be awarded only to domestic small businesses (entities that are independently owned and operated for profit, are not dominant in the field in which research is proposed, and have no more than 500 employees). Primary employment (more than one-half time) of the principal investigator must be with the small business at the time of award and during the conduct of the proposed project. In both Phase I and Phase II, the research must be performed in the United States or its possessions. To be eligible for funding, an SBIR grant application must be approved for scientific merit and program relevance by a scientific review group and a national advisory council. STTR grants can be awarded only to domestic small business concerns which "partner" with a research institution in cooperative research and development. At least 40 percent of the project is to be performed by the small business concern and at least 30 percent by the research institution. In both Phase I and Phase II, the research must be performed in the U.S. and its possessions. To be eligible for funding, a grant application must be approved for scientific merit and program relevance by a scientific review group and a national advisory council. Small Instrumentation Grants Program: Eligible institutions or institutional components are those domestic, nonprofit organizations that: (1) received at least three NIH research grants totaling at least $200,000 but not exceeding $2,924,000 in the previous fiscal year, and (2) have active NIH research grant support. Only those organizations or organizational components receiving a letter of invitation to apply from the NIH are eligible for this program. Only one application may be submitted by each eligible organization or organizational component.

Beneficiary Eligibility: Health professionals, graduate students, health professional students, scientists, physicians, and other health and allied health professionals.

Credentials/Documentation: Research grants are awarded to an institution in the name of an individual investigator. Centers Grants are awarded to an institution in the name of an institution. Persons qualified to carry out research related to the NIDCD grant programs described above may apply for funds to support their investigations. Career Program training must be conducted under the direction of a competent sponsor. A candidate for a career award must have an earned M.D., Ph.D. or equivalent degree and must generally have had at least 3 years of pertinent postdoctoral training or research experience. National Research Service Awards: (1) Individual NRSA Fellowship Awards for postdoctoral training: The candidate's academic record, research experience, citizenship, institutional sponsorship, and the proposed area and plan of training must be included in the application. (2) Institutional Training Grants for predoctoral and postdoctoral training: The applicant institution must show the objectives, methodology and resources for the research training program; the qualifications and experience of directing staff; the criteria to be used in selecting individuals for stipend support; and a detailed budget and justification for the amount of grant funds requested. Costs will be determined in accordance with OMB Circular No. A-87 for State and local governments. For-profit organizations' costs are determined in accordance with 48 CFR, Subpart 31.2 of the Federal Acquisition Regulation. For other grantees, costs will be determined in accordance with HHS Regulations 45 CFR, Part 74, Subpart Q. For SBIR and STTR grants, applicant organization (small business concern) must present in a research plan an idea that has potential for commercialization and furnish evidence that scientific competence, experimental methods, facilities, equipment, and funds requested are appropriate to carry out the plan. Grant forms PHS 6246-1 and 6246-2 are used to apply for Phase I and Phase II awards, respectively, of SBIR and STTR programs.

APPLICATION AND AWARD PROCESS:

Preapplication Coordination: Not applicable. This program is excluded from coverage under E.O. 12372.

Application Procedure: Request regular grant application form PHS-398 (Rev. September 1991) from the Division of Research Grants, National Institutes of Health, Bethesda, MD 20892. Complete application forms and return to the same address. The standard application forms as furnished by PHS and required by 45 CFR, Part 92 for State and local government must be used for this program. Research Fellowships: Prior to formal application, a candidate must be accepted at an institution and have a sponsor who will supervise the training. Fellows may be sponsored by a (domestic or foreign) nonprofit institution. Application forms and information concerning current areas being supported under the Research Fellowship Award Program should be obtained from the Office of Research Manpower, National Institutes of Health, Bethesda, MD 20892. Application forms for Individual or Institutional NRSAs and information concerning the areas of science being supported may be obtained from the Office of Research Manpower, Division of Research Grants, National Institutes of Health, Bethesda, MD 20892, and should be submitted to the same address. This program is subject to the provisions of 45 CFR, Part 92 for State and local governments, and OMB Circular No. A-110 for nonprofit organizations. The Omnibus Solicitation of the Public Health Service for Small Business Innovation Research (SBIR) Grant and Cooperative Agreement Applications may be obtained by contacting the NIH SBIR support services contractor by telephone on (301) 206-9385 or fax on (301) 206-9722. The Solicitation includes application forms, which, upon completion, should be submitted to the Division of Research Grants, National Institutes of Health, Bethesda, MD 20892. Small Business Technology Transfer (STTR) program uses same procedure as SBIR immediately above. Small Instrumentation Grants Program: Those invited to apply should prepare and submit applications on Form PHS 398 (revised September 1991). Only the face page, the budget page, and the checklist page are to be completed. Additional information required includes the number and dollar amount of the grant(s) that would benefit from the requested equipment, a brief description of each beneficiary project, and an explanation of how the equipment would benefit the project.

Award Procedure: Research Grant, Centers Grant, and training program applications are reviewed initially by technical panels, composed of nongovernment scientific authorities, and by the NIDCD Advisory Council composed of leading medical and public affairs experts. Approved applications will compete on a merit basis for available funds. Formal award notices are transmitted to the grantee or awardee. All accepted SBIR/STTR applications are evaluated for scientific and technical merit by an appropriate scientific peer review panel and by a national advisory council or board. All applications receiving a priority score ranging from the best (100) to worst (500) compete for the available SBIR/STTR set-aside funds on the basis of scientific and technical merit (which includes the potential of the proposed research for commercial application), program relevance, and program balance among the areas of research.

Deadlines: All new research grant applications, program project and centers competitive renewal and supplemental grant applications, and career program applications: February 1, June 1, and October 1. Individual research competing renewal and supplemental grant applications: March 1, July 1, and November 1. Individual NRSA applications: April 5, August 5, and December 5. Institutional NRSA applications: May 10. SBIR: April 15, August 15, and December 15. STTR: December 1, only. Small Instrumentation Program: Contact Headquarters Office listed below for application deadlines.

Range of Approval/Disapproval Time: Research Grants and Centers Grants: Approximately 6 to 9 months. Career Program: From 6 to 9 months. SBIR/STTR applications: About 7-1/2 months. Institutional training grants: From 6 to 12 months. Small Instrumentation Program: From 5 to 6 months.

Appeals: A principal investigator (P.I.) may question the substantive or procedural aspects of the review of his/her application by communicating with the staff of the Institute, and subsequently, the P.I. or applicant institution may formally appeal to the Deputy Director for Extramural Research, Office of the Director, NIH.

Renewals: By application and review in the same manner as new applications. Research career awards are not renewable.

ASSISTANCE CONSIDERATIONS:

Formula and Matching Requirements: This program has no statutory formula or matching requirements.

Length and Time Phasing of Assistance: Research Grant awards are made for a 12-month period with recommendation of up to 4 years of additional support. Centers Grant awards support may be for a period not to exceed 7 years. The Director, NIDCD, may extend support for one or more additional periods of not more than 5 years. Career Program awards provide support for 3 to 5 years. Training program awards are usually for a 12-month period with recommendation of additional support of up to a total of 5 years for predoctoral training and no more than 3 years for individual postdoctoral training. Short-term research training support for health professional students may be awarded for multiple 3-month periods. An award must be expended within the grant period. SBIR Phase I awards are generally for 6 months; Phase II awards normally may not exceed 2 years. STTR Phase I awards are generally for 1 year; Phase II awards normally may not exceed 2 years. Small Instrumentation Program: Grants are made for 1 year with no future year commitments.

POST ASSISTANCE REQUIREMENTS:

Reports: Research Grants and Centers Grants: Annual and final progress reports, including a description of results, positive and negative, and a list of any publications. Career

Program: Awardee submits annual progress report. Termination notice, Form PHS 416-7, must be submitted upon completion of training. Reports are required after termination of National Research Service Awards to ascertain compliance with the service and payback provisions. A financial status report must be submitted within 90 days after the close of each budget/project period for which an award has been issued.

Audits: In accordance with the provisions of OMB Circular No. A-128, "Audits of State and Local Governments." State and local governments that receive financial assistance of $100,000 or more within the State's fiscal year shall have an audit made for that year. State and local governments that receive between $25,000 and $100,000 within the State's fiscal year shall have an audit made in accordance with Circular No. A-128, or in accordance with Federal laws and regulations governing the programs in which they participate. For nongovernmental grant recipients, audits are to be carried out in accordance with the provisions set forth in OMB Circular No. A-133. In addition, grants and cooperative agreements are subject to inspection and audits by DHHS and other Federal officials.

Records: Expenditures and other financial records must be retained for 3 years from the day on which the grantee submits the last financial status report for the report period.

FINANCIAL INFORMATION:

Account Identification: 75-0890-0-1-550.

Obligations: (Grants) FY 93 $129,503,000; FY 94 $135,391,000; and FY 95 est $140,394,000.

Range and Average of Financial Assistance: $72,486 to $458,342; $186,000.

PROGRAM ACCOMPLISHMENTS: In fiscal year 1993, of 993 research grant applications received, 605 were funded. In fiscal year 1994, an estimated 1,134 research grant applications were received and, of those, 646 were funded. For fiscal year 1995, 1,131 applications are expected to be submitted and an estimated 615 are expected to be funded.

REGULATIONS, GUIDELINES, AND LITERATURE: Research Grants and Centers Grants: 42 CFR 52 or 52a; 42 CFR 66; 42 CFR 74; 45 CFR 92; Grants will be available under the authority of and administered in accordance with the PHS Grants Policy Statement and Federal regulations at 42 CFR 52 and 42 USC 241; Omnibus Solicitation of the Public Health Service for Small Business Innovation Research (SBIR) Grant and Cooperative Agreement Applications. Omnibus Solicitation of the National Institutes of Health for Small Business Technology Transfer (STTR) Grant Applications.

INFORMATION CONTACTS:

Regional or Local Office: Not applicable.

Headquarters Office: Program Contact: Dr. Ralph F. Naunton, National Institute on Deafness and Other Communication Disorders, National Institutes of Health, Public Health Service, Department of Health and Human Services, Executive Plaza South, Room 400-B, Bethesda, MD 20892. Telephone: (301) 496-1804. Grants Management Contact: Ms. Sharon Hunt, National Institute on Deafness and Other Communication Disorders, National Institutes of Health, Public Health Service, Department of Health and Human Services, Executive Plaza South, Room 400-B, Bethesda, MD 20892. Telephone: (301) 402-0909. Use the same numbers for FTS.

EXAMPLES OF FUNDED PROJECTS: Spatial processing in auditory cortex; electrophysiology of olfactory discrimination; threshold determination with auditory brainstem response; encoding of vocal signals in the auditory system; physicochemical investigation of taste; and physiology of vestibular system.

CRITERIA FOR SELECTING PROPOSALS: The major elements in evaluating proposals include assessments of: (1) the scientific merit and general significance of the proposed study and its objectives; (2) the technical adequacy of the experimental design and approach; (3) the competency of the proposed investigator or group to successfully pursue the project; (4) the adequacy of the available and proposed project; (5) the necessity of budget components requested in relation to the proposed project; and (6) the relevance and importance to announced program objectives. The following criteria will be used in considering the scientific and technical merit of SBIR/STTR Phase I grant applications: (1) the soundness and technical merit of the proposed approach; (2) the qualifications of the proposed principal investigator, supporting staff, and consultants; (3) the technological innovation of the proposed research; (4) the potential of the proposed research for commercial application; (5) the appropriateness of the budget requested; (6) the adequacy and suitability of the facilities and research environment; and (7) where applicable, the adequacy of assurances detailing the proposed means for (a) safeguarding human or animal subjects, and/or (b) protecting against or minimizing any adverse effect on the environment. Phase II grant applications will be reviewed based upon the following criteria: (1) the degree to which the Phase I objectives were met and feasibility demonstrated; (2) the scientific and technical merit of the proposed approach for achieving the Phase II objectives; (3) the qualifications of the proposed principal investigator, supporting staff, and consultants; (4) the technological innovation, originality, or societal importance of the proposed research; (5) the potential of the proposed research for commercial application; (6) the reasonableness of the budget requested for the work proposed; (7) the adequacy and suitability of the facilities and research environment; and (8) where applicable, the adequacy of assurances detailing the proposed means for (a) safeguarding human or animal subjects, and/or (b) protecting against or minimizing any adverse effect on the environment.

93.242 MENTAL HEALTH RESEARCH GRANTS

FEDERAL AGENCY: NATIONAL INSTITUTES OF HEALTH, PUBLIC HEALTH SERVICE, DEPARTMENT OF HEALTH AND HUMAN SERVICES

AUTHORIZATION: Public Health Service Act, Title III, Section 301, Public Law 78-410, 42 U.S.C. 241, as amended; Small Business Research and Development Enhancement Act of 1992, Public Law 102-564.

OBJECTIVES: To increase knowledge and improve research methods on mental and behavioral disorders; to generate information regarding basic biological and behavioral disorders; to generate information regarding basic biological and behavioral processes underlying these disorders and the maintenance of mental health; and to improve mental health services. Research supported by the National Institute of Mental Health may employ theoretical, laboratory, clinical, methodological and field studies, any of which may involve clinical, subclinical and normal subjects and populations of all age ranges, as well as animal, computational and mathematical models appropriate to the system being investigated and the state of the field. Areas eligible for support are: AIDS behavior, neurosciences, behavioral sciences, epidemiology, clinical assessment and etiological studies, treatment, prevention, and services research. Minority Institutions Research Development Program provides awards to institutions with a substantial enrollment of racial ethnic minority students, for research projects and faculty training. Small Business Innovation Research (SBIR) program: To expand and improve the SBIR program; to increase private sector commercialization of innovations derived from Federal research and development to increase small business participation in Federal research and development; and to foster and encourage participation of socially and economically disadvantaged small business concerns and women-owned small business in technological innovation. Small Business Technology Transfer (STTR) program: To stimulate and foster scientific and technological innovation through cooperative research and development carried out between small business concerns and research institutions; to increase private sector commercialization of innovations derived from Federal research and development; and to foster and encourage participation of socially and economically disadvantaged small business concerns and women-owned small business concerns in technological innovation. Small Instrumentation Grants Program: To support the purchase of relatively low-cost pieces of research equipment that generally are not funded in research project grants and that do not qualify for support under the National Institutes of Health's (NIH) larger shared instrumentation program.

TYPES OF ASSISTANCE: Project Grants (Cooperative Agreements).

USES AND USE RESTRICTIONS: (1) Research project grants provide support for clearly defined projects or a small group of related research activities, and when appropriate, support of research conferences; (2) Program Project and Center grants support large-scale, broad-based programs of research, usually interdisciplinary consisting of several projects with a common focus; and (3) Small grants support small-scale exploratory and pilot studies or exploration of an unusual research opportunity. Small grants are limited to $50,000 direct costs for a period of 2 years or less. SBIR Phase I grants (of approximately 6-month's duration) are to establish the technical merit and feasibility of a proposed research or research and development effort that may lead to a commercial product or process. Phase II grants are for the continuation of the research or research and development initiated in Phase I and that are likely to result in commercial products or processes. Only Phase I awardees are eligible to apply for Phase II support. STTR Phase I grants (normally of 1-year duration) are to determine the scientific and technical merit and feasibility of the proposed cooperative effort that has potential for commercial application. Phase II funding is based on results of research initiated in Phase I and scientific and technical merit and commercial potential of Phase II application. Small Instrumentation Grants Program: Funds are awarded as institutional formula grants for the purchase of research equipment costing not less than $5,000 or more than $60,000 per piece.

ELIGIBILITY REQUIREMENTS:

Applicant Eligibility: Public, private, profit, or nonprofit agencies (including State and local government agencies), eligible Federal agencies, universities, colleges, hospitals, and academic or research institutions may apply for research grants. SBIR grants can be awarded only to domestic small businesses (entities that are independently owned and operated for profit, are not dominant in the field in which research is proposed, and have no more than 500 employees). Primary employment (more than one-half time) of the principal investigator must be with the small business at the time of award and during the conduct of the proposed project. In both Phase I and Phase II, the research and/or development must be performed in the U.S. and its possessions. To be eligible for funding, an SBIR grant application must be approved for scientific merit and program relevance by a scientific review group and a national advisory council. STTR grants can be awarded only to domestic small business concerns (entities that are independently owned and operated for profit, are not dominant in the field in which research is proposed and have no more than 500 employees) which "partner" (as defined in the Stevenson-Wilder Technology Innovation Act of 1980) with a research institution in cooperative research and development. At least 40 percent of the project is to be performed by the small business concern and at least 30 percent by the research institution. In both Phase I and Phase II, the research must be performed in the U.S. and its possessions. To be eligible for funding, an STTR grant application must be approved for scientific merit and program relevance by a scientific review group and a national advisory council. Small Instrumentation Grants Program: Eligible institutions or institutional components are those domestic, nonprofit organizations that: (1) received at least three NIH research grants totaling at least $200,000 but not exceeding $2,924,000 in the previous fiscal year, and (2) have active NIH research grant support. Only those organizations or organizational components receiving a letter of invitation to apply from the NIH are eligible for this program. Only one application may be submitted by each eligible organization or organizational component.

Beneficiary Eligibility: Public, private, profit or nonprofit organizations.

Credentials/Documentation: Costs will be determined in accordance with OMB Circular No. A-87 for State and local governments. For-profit organizations' costs will be determined in accordance with 48 CFR, Subpart 31.2 of the Federal Acquisition Regulations. For all other grantees, costs will be determined in accordance with HHS Regulations 45 CFR, Part 74, Subpart Q. For SBIR and STTR grants, applicant organization (small business concern) must present in a research plan an idea that has potential for commercialization and furnish evidence that scientific competence, experimental methods, facilities, equipment, and funds requested are appropriate to carry out the plan. Grant forms PHS 6246-1 and 6246-2 are used to apply for Phase I and Phase II awards, respectively, of SBIR and STTR programs.

APPLICATION AND AWARD PROCESS:

Preapplication Coordination: Not applicable. This program is excluded from coverage under E.O. 12372.

Application Procedure: The standard application forms, as furnished by PHS and required by 45 CFR, Part 92 (PHS 5161-1), must be used for applicants that are State and local governments. Application kits, containing the necessary forms (PHS 5161-1 or PHS 398, Rev. September 1991) and instructions, if not available at applicant institution, may be obtained from Office of Grants Information, Division of Grants, NIH. Telephone: (301) 594-7248. Consultation on a proposed project may be obtained from the NIMH branch responsible for the research area of interest. Applications are reviewed by principally nonfederal consultants recruited nationwide from the mental health field. The amounts of the award and period of support are determined on the basis of merit of the project. This program is subject to the provisions of 45 CFR, Part 92 for State and local governments and OMB Circular No. A-110 for nonprofit organizations. The Omnibus Solicitation of the Public Health Service for Small Business Innovation Research (SBIR) Grant and Cooperative Agreement Applications may be obtained by contacting the NIH SBIR support services contractor by telephone on (301) 206-9385 or fax on (301) 206-9722. The Solicitation includes application forms, which, upon completion, should be submitted to the Division of Research Grants, National Institutes of Health, Bethesda, MD 20892. Small Business Technology Transfer (STTR) program uses same procedure as SBIR immediately above. Small Instrumentation Grants Program: Those invited to apply should prepare and submit applications on Form PHS 398 (revised September 1991). Only the face page, the budget page, and the checklist page are to be completed. Additional information required includes the number and dollar amount of the grant(s) that would benefit from the requested equipment, a brief description of each beneficiary project, and an explanation of how the equipment would benefit the project.

Award Procedure: Research grants and cooperative agreements in support of projects recommended for approval by the National Advisory Mental Health Council (except for small grants) and approved for payment are awarded directly by the NIMH to the applicant institution. All accepted SBIR/STTR applications are evaluated for scientific and technical merit by an appropriate scientific peer review panel and by a national advisory council or board. All applications receiving a priority score ranging from the best (100) to worst (500) compete for the available SBIR/STTR set-aside funds on the basis of scientific and technical merit (which includes the potential of the proposed research for commercial application), program relevance, and program balance among the areas of research.

Deadlines: New Grants and Centers Renewals: February 1, June 1, and October 1. Other Renewals: March 1, July 1, and November 1. AIDS Grants: January 2, May 1, and September 1. SBIR: April 15, August 15, and December 15. STTR: December 1, only. Small Instrumentation Grants Program: Contact Headquarters Office listed below for deadline dates.

Range of Approval/Disapproval Time: Grants: From 240 to 270 days from submission of application. SBIR/STTR applications: About 7-1/2 months; Small Instrumentation Program and Small Grants: From 5 to 6 months. Review of AIDS-related research is expedited.

Appeals: A principal investigator (P.I.) may question the substantive or procedural aspects of the review of his/her application with the staff of the Institute, and subsequently, the P.I. and applicant institution may formally appeal to the Deputy Director for Extramural Research, Office of the Director, NIH.

Renewals: Support is recommended for a specified project period, not in excess of 5 years. Prior to termination of a project period, the grantee may apply for renewal of support for a new project period. An application for renewal is processed as a new competing request. Small grants are not renewable.

ASSISTANCE CONSIDERATIONS:

Formula and Matching Requirements: This program has no statutory formula or matching requirements.

Length and Time Phasing of Assistance: Varies, but a project period is generally limited to 5 years or less. Grantee may apply for renewal of support on a competing basis. Within the project period, continuation applications must be submitted on a non-competing basis for each year of approved support. Small Grant support is limited to 2 years and is not renewable. SBIR Phase I awards are generally for 6 months; Phase II awards normally may not exceed 2 years. STTR Phase I awards are generally for 1 year; Phase II awards normally may not exceed 2 years. Payments will be made either on a Monthly Cash Request System or under an Electronic Transfer System. Necessary instructions for the appropriate type of payment will be issued shortly after an award is made.

POST ASSISTANCE REQUIREMENTS:

Reports: Reports must be submitted as follows: (1) interim progress reports annually as part of a non-competing application for previously recommended support; (2) terminal progress report within 90 days after end of project support; (3) annual financial status report within 90 days after termination of annual grant. In addition, immediate and full reporting of any inventions is required.

Audits: In accordance with the provisions of OMB Circular No. A-128, "Audits of State and Local Governments," State and local governments that receive financial assistance of $100,000 or more within the State's fiscal year shall have an audit made for that year. State and local governments that receive between $25,000 and $100,000 within the State's fiscal year shall have an audit made in accordance with Circular No. A-128, or in accordance with Federal laws and regulations governing the programs in which they participate. For nongovernmental grant recipients, audits are to be carried out in accordance with the provisions set forth in OMB Circular No. A-133. In addition, grants and cooperative agreements are subject to inspection and audits by DHHS and other Federal officials.

Records: Records must be retained at least 3 years; records shall be retained beyond the 3-year period if audit findings have not been resolved.

FINANCIAL INFORMATION:

Account Identification: 75-0892-0-1-552.

Obligations: (Grants) FY 93 $380,252,889; FY 94 $410,194,000; and FY 95 est $431,414,000.

Range and Average of Financial Assistance: $6,196 to $4,298,139; $258,324.

PROGRAM ACCOMPLISHMENTS: NIMH funded 1,472 grants in fiscal year 1993; an estimated 1,598 grants will be funded in fiscal year 1994. An estimated 1,645 grants will be funded in fiscal year 1995. In fiscal year 1993, NIMH made 41 SBIR awards totaling $5,292,126 and 17 instrumentation awards for $222,194 (included in above figures).

REGULATIONS, GUIDELINES, AND LITERATURE: 42 CFR 52. PHS Grant Policy Statement, DHHS Publication No. (OASH) 94-50,000, (Rev.) April 1, 1994. Grants will be available under the authority of and administered in accordance with the PHS Grants Policy Statement and Federal regulations at 42 CFR 52 and 42 USC 241; Omnibus Solicitation of the Public Health Service for Small Business Innovation Research (SBIR) Grant and Cooperative Agreement Applications. Omnibus Solicitation of the National Institutes of Health for Small Business Technology Transfer (STTR) Grant Applications.

INFORMATION CONTACTS:

Regional or Local Office: Not applicable.

Headquarters Office: Dr. Stephen H. Koslow, Director, Division of Neuroscience and Behavioral Science (Behavioral, Cognitive, and Social Processes/Cognitive and Behavioral and Integrative Neurosciences; Molecular and Cellular Neuroscience; Scientific Technology and Resources). Telephone: (301) 443-3563. Dr. Jane A. Steinberg, Acting Director, Division of Clinical and Treatment Research (Schizophrenia; Mood, Anxiety, and Personality Disorders; Mental Disorders of the Aging; Child and Adolescent Disorders; Clinical Treatment; Research Publication and Operations). Telephone: (301) 443-5047. Dr. Darrel A. Regier, Director, Division of Epidemiology and Services Research (Basic Prevention and Behavioral Medicine; Prevention; Services; Epidemiology and Psychopathology; Violence and Traumatic Stress). Telephone: (301) 443-3648. Human Brain Project, SBIR/STTR, and Small Instrumentation: Dr. Michael Huerta. Telephone: (301) 443-4885: Dr. Ellen Stover, Director, Office of AIDs. Telephone: (301) 443-7281. Dr. Delores L. Parron, Associate Director for Special Populations (Minority Institutions Research Development Programs). Telephone: (301) 443-2847. Grants Management Contact: Mr. Bruce Ringler, Grants Management Officer, National Institute of Mental Health, NIH, Public Health Service, Department of Health and Human Services, Room 7C-15, Parklawn Building, 5600 Fishers Lane, Rockville, MD 20857. Telephone: (301) 443-3065. Use the same numbers for FTS.

EXAMPLES OF FUNDED PROJECTS: (1) Genetic studies of depressive disorders; (2) prospective study of children of schizophrenic parents; (3) neurological basis of major psychiatric disorders; (4) genomic control of CNS development; (5) basic social psychological interventions in senile dementia; (6) legal impact on mental health practice; (7) processes in learning and behavioral change; (8) prevention of high-risk AIDs behavior; and (9) antibodies to rationally modulate specific neurotransmitter receptors.

CRITERIA FOR SELECTING PROPOSALS: The following considerations will be used in determining projects to be funded: (1) scientific and technical merit; (2) the feasibility of the research; and (3) mental health implications and relevance to NIMH priorities and public health issues. The following criteria will be used in considering the scientific and technical merit of SBIR/STTR Phase I grant applications: (1) the soundness and technical merit of the proposed approach; (2) the qualifications of the proposed principal investigator, supporting staff, and consultants; (3) the technological innovation of the proposed research; (4) the potential of the proposed research for commercial application; (5) the appropriateness of the budget requested; (6) the adequacy and suitability of the facilities and research environment; and (7) where applicable, the adequacy of assurances detail in the proposed means for (a) safeguarding human or animal subjects, and/or (b) protecting against or minimizing any adverse effect on the environment. Phase II SBIR/STTR grant applications will be reviewed based upon the following criteria: (1) the degree to which the Phase I objectives were met and feasibility demonstrated; (2) the scientific and technical merit of the proposed approach for achieving the Phase II objectives; (3) the qualifications of the proposed principal investigator, supporting staff, and consultants; (4) the technological innovation, originality, or societal importance of the proposed research; (5) the potential of the proposed research for commercial application; (6) the reasonableness of the budget requested for the work proposed; (7) the adequacy and suitability of the facilities and research environment; and (8) where applicable, the adequacy of assurances detailing the proposed means for (a) safeguarding human or animal subjects, and/or (b) protecting against or minimizing any adverse effect on the environment.

93.632 DEVELOPMENTAL DISABILITIES UNIVERSITY AFFILIATED PROGRAMS

FEDERAL AGENCY: ADMINISTRATION FOR CHILDREN AND FAMILIES, DEPARTMENT OF HEALTH AND HUMAN SERVICES

AUTHORIZATION: Mental Retardation Facilities and Construction Act of 1963, Title I, Part B, Public Law 88-164, as amended, Public Laws 91-517, 94-103, 95-602; Omnibus Budget Reconciliation Act of 1981, as amended, Public Law 97-35; Developmental Disabilities Act of 1984; Developmental Disabilities Assistance and Bill of Rights Act, as amended, Title I, Section 100, Public Law 98-527; Developmental Disabilities Assistance and Bill of Rights Act Amendments of 1987, Public Law 100-146, Developmental Disabilities Assistance and Bill of Rights Act of 1990, Public Law 101-496; Developmental Disabilities Assistance and Bill of Right Act of 1994, Public Law 103-230, 42 U.S.C. 6061 - 6066.

OBJECTIVES: To defray the cost of administration and operation of programs that: (1) provide interdisciplinary training for personnel concerned with developmental disabilities; (2) demonstrate community service activities which include training and technical assistance and may include direct services, e.g., family support, individual support, personal assistance services, educational, vocational, clinical, health and prevention; (3) disseminate findings related to the provision of services to researchers and government agencies; and (4) generate information on the need for further service-related research.

TYPES OF ASSISTANCE: Project Grants.

USES AND USE RESTRICTIONS: Salaries for administrators, coordinators, and others needed to operate a training facility, maintenance and housekeeping personnel, overhead expenses, and expenses required to start up new programs, and faculty for training programs who will meet critical manpower shortages and are not eligible for support from other sources.

ELIGIBILITY REQUIREMENTS:

Applicant Eligibility: A public or nonprofit entity which is associated with, or is an integral part of a college or university and which provides at least: interdisciplinary training; demonstration of exemplary services, technical assistance, and dissemination of findings.

Beneficiary Eligibility: Individuals of all ages with developmental disabilities attributable to a mental and/or physical impairment, their families, and personnel and trainees providing services to them.

Credentials/Documentation: Assurance of maintenance of effort; statement of financial resources, especially other federally-assisted programs; identification of personnel needs and resources as found in developmental disabilities State Plans for the applicant's service area; evaluation of present training programs and utilization of space in the facility; and capability of informing researchers and others in development of services related research.

APPLICATION AND AWARD PROCESS:

Preapplication Coordination: No preapplication form is required. Consultation and assistance in preparing application is available at the DHHS Central Office. This program is excluded from coverage under E.O. 12372.

Application Procedure: Application forms are available from the DHHS Central Office. Completed application forms and narrative should be sent to the State Developmental Disabilities Council, Designated State Agency and Protection and Advocacy office for review and comment. The standard application forms, as furnished by DHHS must be used for this program.

Award Procedure: Applications are evaluated by outside peer reviews and grants are awarded at the DHHS ADD Central Office. Recommendations for funding are made by the Headquarters Office.

Deadlines: Contact DHHS Central Office for future deadline information.

Range of Approval/Disapproval Time: From 45 to 90 days.

Appeals: Appeals are processed in accordance with regulations in 45 CFR, Part 16.

Renewals: Same as Application Procedure.

ASSISTANCE CONSIDERATIONS:

Formula and Matching Requirements: This program has no statutory formula. Federal share of project grant awarded may not exceed 75 percent of the necessary cost of project, except that if project activities or products target individuals with developmental disabilities who live in an urban or rural area, the Federal share may not exceed 90 percent of the project's necessary costs.

Length and Time Phasing of Assistance: UAP core and training projects initiative awards are made for a 12-month budget period; feasibility study awards are made for a 6-month period.

POST ASSISTANCE REQUIREMENTS:

Reports: Semi-annual progress reports are required. Fiscal reports are required as prescribed by grant specifications. Final progress report is required upon project completion.

Audits: Audits are conducted in accordance with the requirements in 45 CFR, Parts 74 and 92.

Records: Records must be maintained for 3 years.

FINANCIAL INFORMATION:

Account Identification: 75-1536-0-1-506.

Obligations: (Grants) FY 93 $16,125,000; FY 94 $18,271,616; and FY 95 est $17,231,000.

Range and Average of Financial Assistance: $200,000 to $350,000; $200,000. Core support grants: $200,000 to $350,000; $200,000. Training Initiative Projects: $90,000.

PROGRAM ACCOMPLISHMENTS: In fiscal 1994, core support grants were awarded to 60 University Affiliated Programs. A total of 53 training initiative projects were awarded. In fiscal year 1993, core support grants were awarded to 57 University Affiliated Programs and one Satellite Center, and 38 training initiative projects were awarded to UAPS to train personnel to address the needs of individuals with developmental disabilities.

REGULATIONS, GUIDELINES, AND LITERATURE: Regulations are published in Chapter XIII of Title 45 of the Code of Federal Regulations, Part 1388.

INFORMATION CONTACTS:

Regional or Local Office: None.

Headquarters Office: Division of Program Development, Administration on Developmental Disabilities, Administration for Children and Families, Department of Health and Human Services, Washington, DC 20201. Telephone: (202) 690-5911. Contact: Gail Evans. FTS is not available.

EXAMPLES OF FUNDED PROJECTS: Grants were funded to assist in the operation of public or nonprofit facilities which are associated with a college or university and provide training programs and delivery of services for persons with developmental disabilities. In addition, training grants in the areas of early intervention programs, elderly people with developmental disabilities, community-based service programs, positive behavior management programs, assistive technology, Americans with Disabilities Act, community transition and projects of special concern to the University Affiliated Programs which are developed in consultation with the State Developmental Disabilities Council were supported.

CRITERIA FOR SELECTING PROPOSALS: A University Affiliated Program must provide and be in compliance with performance standards that reflect the special needs of all individuals with developmental disabilities who are of various ages and address the objectives of the program.

Organizations Publishing Information for People with Disabilities

Accreditation Council on Services for
People with Developmental Disabilities
8100 Professional Place, Suite 204
Landover, MD 20785

Adventures in Movement for
the Handicapped
945 Danbury Road
Dayton, OH 45420

Alexander Graham Bell Association
for the Deaf
3417 Volta Place, N.W.
Washington, DC 20007

American Alliance for Health, Physical
Education, Recreation and Dance
1900 Association Drive
Reston, VA 22091

American Association on Mental
Retardation
1719 Kalorama Road, N.W.
Washington, DC 20009

American Council of the Blind
1155 15th Street NW, Suite 720
Washington, DC 20005

American Foundation for the Blind
15 West 16th Street
New York, NY 10011

American Paralysis Association
500 Morris Avenue
Springfield, NJ 07081

American Printing House for the Blind
1839 Frankfort Avenue
P.O. Box 6085
Louisville, KY 40206

American Psychiatric Association
1400 K Street, N.W.
Washington, DC 20005

American Speech-Language-Hearing
Association
10801 Rockville Pike
Rockville, MD 20852

Architectural and Transportation
Barriers Compliance Board
1331 F Street, N.W., Suite 1000
Washington, DC 20004

Association for Education and Rehab.
of the Blind and Visually Impaired
206 N. Washington Street, Suite 320
Alexandria, VA 22314

Association for Persons with
Severe Handicaps
11201 Greenwood Avenue N.
Seattle, WA 98133

Association for Retarded Citizens
500 E. Border Street, Suite 300
Arlington, TX 76010

Autism Society of America
7910 Woodmont Avenue, Suite 650
Bethesda, MD 20814

Council for Exceptional Children
1920 Association Drive
Reston, VA 22091

Council for Learning Disabilities
P.O. Box 40303
Overland Park, KS 66204

Council of State Administrators of
Vocational Rehabilitation
P.O. Box 3776
Washington, DC 20007

Federation for Children with
Special Needs
95 Berkley Street, Suite 104
Boston, MA 02116

National Center for
Learning Disabilities
381 Park Avenue S., Suite 1420
New York, NY 10016

Guide Dog Users, Inc.
57 Grandview Avenue
Watertown, MA 02172

Helen Keller International
90 Washington Street
New York, NY 10006

Helen Keller National Center for
Deaf-Blind Youths and Adults
111 Middle Neck Road
Sands Point, NY 11050

House Ear Institute
2100 W. 3rd Street
Los Angeles, CA 90057

International Foundation for Stutterers
P.O. Box 462
Belle Mead, NJ 08502

Learning Disabilities Association
of America
4156 Library Road
Pittsburgh, PA 15234

National Library Service for the Blind
and Physically Handicapped
Library of Congress
1291 Taylor Street, N.W.
Washington, DC 20542

Lupus Foundation of America
4 Research Place, Suite 180
Rockville, MD 20850

March of Dimes Birth Defects
Foundation
1275 Mamaroneck Avenue
White Plains, NY 10605

Muscular Dystrophy Association
3300 E. Sunrise Drive
Tucson, AZ 85718

National Advisory Committee on
Scouting with Special Needs
1325 W. Walnut Hill Lane
P.O. Box 152079
Irving, TX 75015

National Association of the Deaf
814 Thayer Avenue
Silver Spring, MD 20910

National Association for Hearing
and Speech Action
10801 Rockville Pike
Rockville, MD 20852

National Association for Parents of
the Visually Impaired
P.O. Box 317
Watertown, MA 02272

National Association of the
Physically Handicapped
440 Lafayette Avenue
Cincinnati, OH 45220

National Association of State
Directors of Special Education
1800 Diagonal Road, Suite 320
Alexandria, VA 22314

National Association for
Visually Handicapped
22 W. 21st Street
New York, NY 10010

National Braille Press
88 St. Stephen Street
Boston, MA 02115

National Center for
Learning Disabilities
381 Park Avenue S., Suite 1420
New York, NY 10016

National Center for Stuttering
200 East 33rd Street
New York, NY 10016

National Community Mental
Healthcare Council
12300 Twinbrook Parkway, Suite 320
Rockville, MD 20852

National Down Syndrome Congress
1605 Chantilly Drive, Suite 250
Atlanta, GA 30324

National Down Syndrome Society
666 Broadway
New York, NY 10012

National Easter Seal Society
230 W. Monroe
Chicago, IL 60606

National Handicapped Sports
451 Hungerford Drive, Suite 100
Rockville, MD 20850

National Head Injury Foundation
1776 Massachusetts Ave., NW
Washington, DC 20036

National Information Center
on Deafness
Gallaudet College
800 Florida Avenue
Washington, DC 20002

National Information Center for
Children and Youth with Disabilities
P.O. Box 1492
Washington, DC 20013

National Mental Health Association
1021 Prince Street
Alexandria, VA 22314

National Multiple Sclerosis Society
733 Third Avenue
New York, NY 10017

National Rehabilitation Association
633 S. Washington Street
Alexandria, VA 22314

National Rehabilitation Info. Center
8455 Colesville Road, Suite 935
Silver Spring, MD 20910

National Society to Prevent Blindness
500 E. Remington Road
Schaumburg, IL 60173

National Spinal Cord Injury
Association
600 W. Cummings Park, Suite 2000
Woburn, MA 01801

Orton Dyslexia Society
Chester Building, Suite 382
8600 LaSalle Road
Baltimore, MD 21286

Spina Bifida Association of America
4590 MacArthur Blvd. N.W., # 250
Washington, DC 20007

Special Recreation, Inc.
362 Koser Avenue
Iowa City, IA 52246

The Association for Persons with
Severe Handicaps (TASH)
11201 Greenwood Avenue N.
Seattle, WA 98133

United Cerebral Palsy Associations
1522 K Street NW
Washington, DC 20005

Very Special Arts
Education Office
John F. Kennedy Center for
the Performing Arts
Washington, DC 20566

Vision Foundation
818 Mt. Auburn Street
Watertown, MA 02172

Appendix A

TYPES OF FEDERAL ASSISTANCE

A. Formula Grants—Allocations of money to states or their subdivisions in accordance with a distribution formula prescribed by law or administrative regulation, for activities of a continuing nature not confined to a specific project.

B. Project Grants—The funding, for fixed or known periods, of specific projects or the delivery of specific services or products without liability for damages for failure to perform. Project grants include fellowships, scholarships, research grants, training grants, traineeships, experimental and demonstration grants, evaluation grants, planning grants, technical assistance grants, survey grants, construction grants, and unsolicited contractual agreements.

C. Direct Payments for Specified Use—Financial assistance from the Federal government provided directly to individuals, private firms, and other private institutions to encourage or subsidize a particular activity by conditioning the receipt of the assistance on a particular performance by the recipient. This does not include solicited contracts for the procurement of goods and services for the Federal government.

D. Direct Payments with Unrestricted Use—Financial assistance from the Federal government provided directly to beneficiaries who satisfy Federal eligibility requirements with no restrictions being imposed on the recipient as to how the money is spent. Included are payments under retirement, pension, and compensation programs.

E. Direct Loans—Financial assistance provided through the lending of Federal monies for a specific period of time, with a reasonable expectation of repayment. Such loans may or may not require the payment of interest.

F. Guaranteed/Insured Loans—Programs in which the Federal government makes an arrangement to indemnify a lender against part or all of any defaults by those responsible for repayment of loans.

G. Insurance—Financial assistance provided to assure reimbursement for losses sustained under specified conditions. Coverage may be provided directly by the Federal government or through private carriers and may or may not involve the payment of premiums.

H. Sale, Exchange, or Donation of Property and Goods—Programs which provide for the sale, exchange, or donation of Federal real property, personal property, commodities, and other goods including land, buildings, equipment, food and drugs. This does not include the loan of, use of, or access to Federal facilities or property.

I. Use of Property, Facilities, and Equipment—Programs which provide for the loan of, use of, or access to Federal facilities or property wherein the federally-owned facilities or property do not remain in the possession of the recipient of the assistance.

J. Provision of Specialized Services—Programs which provide Federal personnel to directly perform certain tasks for the benefit of communities or individuals. These services may be performed in conjunction with nonfederal personnel, but they involve more than consultation, advice, or counseling.

K. Advisory Services and Counseling—Programs which provide Federal specialists to consult, advise, or counsel communities or individuals, to include conferences, workshops, or personal contacts. This may involve the use of published information, but only in a secondary capacity.

L. Dissemination of Technical Information—Programs which provide for the publication and distribution of information or data of a specialized technical nature frequently through clearinghouses or libraries. This does not include conventional public information services designed for general public consumption.

M. Training—Programs which provide instructional activities conducted directly by a Federal agency for individuals not employed by the Federal government.

N. Investigation of Complaints—Federal administrative agency activities that are initiated in response to requests, either formal or informal, to examine or investigate claims of violations of Federal statutes, policy, or procedure. The origination of such claims must come from outside the Federal government.

O. Federal Employment—Programs which reflect the government-wide responsibilities of the Office of Personnel Management in the recruitment and hiring of Federal civilian agency personnel.

Appendix B
The Foundation Center

The Foundation Center is an independent national service organization established by foundations to provide an authoritative source of information on private philanthropic giving. In fulfilling its mission, The Foundation Center disseminates information on private giving through public service programs, publications and through a national network of library reference collections for free public use. The New York, Washington, DC, Atlanta, Cleveland and San Francisco reference collections operated by The Foundation Center offer a wide variety of services and comprehensive collections of information on foundations and grants. The Cooperating Collections are libraries, community foundations and other nonprofit agencies that provide a core collection of Foundation Center publications and a variety of supplementary materials and services in subject areas useful to grantseekers.

Many of the network members make available sets of private foundation information returns (IRS Form 990-PF) for their state and/or neighboring states which are available for public use. A complete set of U.S. foundation returns can be found at the New York and Washington, DC, offices of the Foundation Center. The Atlanta, Cleveland, and San Francisco offices contain IRS Form 990-PF returns for the southeastern, midwestern, and western states, respectively.

Those collections marked with a bullet (•) have sets of private foundation returns (IRS Form 990-PF) for their states or regions, available for public reference.

Because the collections vary in their hours, materials and services, IT IS RECOMMENDED THAT YOU CALL EACH COLLECTION IN ADVANCE.

To check on new locations or current information, call toll-free 1-800-424-9836.

Reference Collections
• The Foundation Center
79 Fifth Ave., 8th Fl.
New York, NY 10003
(212) 620-4230
• The Foundation Center
312 Sutter St., Suite 312
San Francisco, CA 94108
(415) 397-0902
• The Foundation Center
1001 Connecticut Ave., N.W.
Washington, DC 20036
(202) 331-1400
• The Foundation Center
Kent H. Smith Library
1422 Euclid, Suite 1356
Cleveland, OH 44115
(216) 861-1933
• The Foundation Center
Suite 150, Grand Lobby
Hurt Building, 50 Hurt Plaza
Atlanta, GA 30303
(404) 880-0094

COOPERATING COLLECTIONS
Alabama
• Birmingham Public Library
Government Documents
2100 Park Place
Birmingham, AL 35203
(205) 226-3600

Huntsville Public Library
915 Monroe Street
Huntsville, AL 35801
(205) 532-5940
• University of South Alabama
Library Building
Mobile, AL 36688
(205) 460-7025
• Auburn University at
Montgomery Library
7300 University Drive
Montgomery, AL 36117
(205) 244-3653
Alaska
• University of Alaska at
Anchorage, Library
3211 Providence Drive
Anchorage, AK 99508
(907) 786-1848
Juneau Public Library
292 Marine Way
Juneau, AK 99801
(907) 586-5267
Arizona
• Phoenix Public Library
Business and Sciences Unit
12 E. McDowell Road
Phoenix, AZ 85004
(602) 262-4636

• Tucson Pima Library
101 N. Stone Avenue
Tucson, AZ 85701
(602) 791-4010
Arkansas
• Westark Community College
Borham Library
5210 Grand Avenue
Fort Smith, AR 72913
(501) 785-7133
• Central Arkansas Library Sys.
700 Louisiana Street
Little Rock, AR 72201
(501) 370-5952
Pine Bluff-Jefferson County
Library System
200 East Eighth
Pine Bluff, AR 71601
(501) 534-2159
California
• Ventura Co. Comm. Foundation
Funding and Information
Resource Center
1355 Del Norte Road
Camarillo, CA 93010
(805) 988-0196
• California Community Foundation
Funding Information Center
606 S. Olive Street, Suite 2400
Los Angeles, CA 90014
(213) 413-4042

Community Foundation for
Monterey County
177 Van Buren
Monterey, CA 93940
(408) 375-9712
Grant and Resource Center of
Northern California
Building C, Suite A
2280 Benton Drive
Redding, CA 96003
(916) 244-1219
Riverside City and County
Public Library
3581 7th Street
Riverside, CA 92502
(714) 782-5201
Nonprofit Resource Center
Sacramento Public Library
828 I Street, 2nd Floor
Sacramento, CA 95812
(916) 552-8817
• San Diego Community Foundation
Funding Information Center
101 W. Broadway, Suite 1120
San Diego, CA 92101
(619) 239-8815
• Nonprofit Development
Center Library
1922 The Alameda, Suite 210
San Jose, CA 95126
(408) 248-9505
• Peninsula Community Foundation
Funding Information Library
1700 S. El Camino Real, R301
San Mateo, CA 94402
(415) 358-9392
• Volunteer Center of Greater
Orange County
Nonprofit Management Assistance Ctr
1000 E. Santa Ana Blvd., Suite 200
Santa Ana, CA 92701
(714) 953-1655
• Santa Barbara Public Library
40 East Anapamu
Santa Barbara, CA 93101
(805) 962-7653
Santa Monica Public Library
1343 Sixth Street
Santa Monica, CA 90401
(310) 458-8600
Sonoma County Library
3rd & E Streets
Santa Rosa, CA 95404
(707) 545-0831

Colorado
Pikes Peak Library District
20 North Cascade Avenue
Colorado Springs, CO 80901
(719) 531-6333
• Denver Public Library
Social Sciences and Genealogy
1357 Broadway
Denver, CO 80203
(303) 640-8870
Connecticut
Danbury Public Library
170 Main Street
Danbury, CT 06810
(203) 797-4527
• Hartford Public Library
500 Main Street
Hartford, CT 06103
(203) 293-6000
D.A.T.A.
70 Audubon Street
New Haven, CT 06510
(203) 772-1345
Delaware
• University of Delaware
Hugh Morris Library
Newark, DE 19717
(302) 831-2432
District of Columbia
• The Foundation Center
1001 Connecticut Avenue, NW
Washington, DC 20036
(202) 331-1400
Florida
Volusia County Library Center
City Island
Daytona Beach, FL 32014
(904) 255-3765
• Nova University
Einstein Library
3301 College Avenue
Ft. Lauderdale, FL 33314
(305) 475-7050
Indian River Comm. College
Charles S. Miley Learning
Resource Center
3209 Virginia Avenue
Ft. Pierce, FL 34981
(407) 468-4757
• Jacksonville Public Library
Grants Resource Center
122 North Ocean Street
Jacksonville, FL 32202
(904) 630-2665

• Miami-Dade Public Library
Humanities/Social Science
101 W. Flagler Street
Miami, FL 33130
(305) 375-5015
• Orlando Public Library
Social Sciences Department
101 E. Central Blvd.
Orlando, FL 32801
(407) 425-4694
Selby Public Library
1001 Boulevard of the Arts
Sarasota, FL 34236
(813) 951-5501
• Tampa-Hillsborough County
Public Library
900 N. Ashley Drive
Tampa, FL 33602
(813) 273-3628
Community Foundation for
Palm Beach and Martin Counties
324 Datura Street, Suite 340
West Palm Beach, FL 33401
(407) 659-6800
Georgia
• Atlanta-Fulton Public Library
Foundation Collection
Ivan Allen Department
1 Margaret Mitchell Square
Atlanta, GA 30303
(404) 730-1900
• The Foundation Center
Suite 150, Grand Lobby
Hurt Building, 50 Hurt Plaza
Atlanta, GA 30303
(404) 880-0094
Dalton Regional Library
310 Cappes Street
Dalton, GA 30720
(706) 278-4507
Hawaii
• University of Hawaii
Hamilton Library
2550 The Mall
Honolulu, HI 96822
(808) 956-7214
Hawaii Community Foundation
Hawaii Resource Center
222 Merchant Street, 2nd Floor
Honolulu, HI 96813
(808) 537-6333
Idaho
• Boise Public Library
715 S. Capitol Blvd.
Boise, ID 83702
(208) 384-4024

• Caldwell Public Library
1010 Dearborn Street
Caldwell, ID 83605
(208) 459-3242

Illinois
• Donors Forum of Chicago
53 W. Jackson Blvd., #430
Chicago, IL 60604
(312) 431-0265
• Evanston Public Library
1703 Orrington Avenue
Evanston, IL 60201
(708) 866-0305
Rock Island Public Library
401 19th Street
Rock Island, IL 61201
(309) 788-7627
• Sangamon State University
Library
Shepherd Road
Springfield, IL 62794
(217) 786-6633

Indiana
• Allen County Public Library
900 Webster Street
Fort Wayne, IN 46802
(219) 424-0544
Indiana University
Northwest Library
3400 Broadway
Gary, IN 46408
(219) 980-6582
• Indianapolis-Marion County
Public Library
Social Sciences
40 E. St. Clair Street
Indianapolis, IN 46206
(317) 269-1733

Iowa
• Cedar Rapids Public Library
Funding Center Collection
500 First Street, SE
Cedar Rapids, IA 52401
(319) 398-5123
• Southwestern Community
College
Learning Resource Center
1501 W. Townline Road
Creston, IA 50801
(515) 782-7081
• Public Library of Des Moines
100 Locust Street
Des Moines, IA 50309
(515) 283-4152

Kansas
• Topeka and Shawnee County
Public Library
1515 W. Tenth Avenue
Topeka, KS 66604
(913) 233-2040
• Wichita Public Library
223 South Main Street
Wichita, KS 67202
(316) 262-0611

Kentucky
Western Kentucky University
Helm-Cravens Library
Bowling Green, KY 42101
(502) 745-6125
• Louisville Free Public Library
301 York Street
Louisville, KY 40203
(502) 574-1611

Louisiana
• East Baton Rouge Parish Library
Centroplex Branch Grants Collection
120 St. Louis Street
Baton Rouge, LA 70802
(504) 389-4960
Beauregard Parish Library
205 S. Washington Avenue
De Ridder, LA 70634
(318) 463-6217
• New Orleans Public Library
Business and Science Division
219 Loyola Avenue
New Orleans, LA 70140
(504) 596-2580
• Shreve Memorial Library
424 Texas Street
Shreveport, LA 71120
(318) 226-5894

Maine
• University of Southern Maine
Office of Sponsored Research
246 Deering Avenue, Room 628
Portland, ME 04103
(207) 780-4871

Maryland
• Enoch Pratt Free Library
Social Science and History Dept.
400 Cathedral Street
Baltimore, MD 21201
(301) 396-5430

Massachusetts
• Associated Grantmakers
of Massachusetts
Suite 840
294 Washington Street
Boston, MA 02108
(617) 426-2606
• Boston Public Library
Social Science Reference
666 Boylston Street
Boston, MA 02117
(617) 536-5400
Western Mass. Funding
Resource Center
65 Elliot Street
Springfield, MA 01101
(413) 732-3175
• Worcester Public Library
Grants Resource Center
Salem Square
Worcester, MA 01608
(508) 799-1655

Michigan
• Alpena County Library
211 N. First Street
Alpena, MI 49707
(517) 356-6188
• University of Michigan
Graduate Library
Reference & Research Services Dept.
Ann Arbor, MI 48109
(313) 664-9373
• Battle Creek Community Foundation
Southwest Michigan Funding
Resource Center
2 Riverwalk Centre
34 W. Jackson Street
Battle Creek, MI 49017
(616) 962-2181
• Henry Ford Centennial Library
Adult Services
16301 Michigan Avenue
Dearborn, MI 48126
(313) 943-2330
• Wayne State University
Purdy-Kresge Library
5265 Cass Avenue
Detroit, MI 48202
(313) 577-6424
• Michigan State University Libraries
Social Sciences/Humanities
Main Library
East Lansing, MI 48824
(517) 353-8818

• Farmington Comm. Library
32737 W. 12 Mile Road
Farmington Hills, MI 48018
(313) 553-0300
• University of Michigan
Flint Library
Flint, MI 48502
(313) 762-3408
• Grand Rapids Public Library
Business Department, 3rd Floor
60 Library Plaza NE
Grand Rapids, MI 49503
(616) 456-3600
• Michigan Technological University
Van Pelt Library
1400 Townsend Drive
Houghton, MI 49931
(906) 487-2507
Sault Ste. Marie Area
Public Schools
Office of Compensatory Education
460 W. Spruce Street
Sault Ste. Marie, MI 49783
(906) 635-6619
• Northwestern Michigan College
Mark & Helen Osterin Library
1701 E. Front Street
Traverse City, MI 49684
(616) 922-1060
Minnesota
• Duluth Public Library
520 W. Superior Street
Duluth, MN 55802
(218) 723-3802
Southwest State University
University Library
Marshall, MN 56258
(507) 537-6176
• Minneapolis Public Library
Sociology Department
300 Nicollet Mall
Minneapolis, MN 55401
(612) 372-6555
Rochester Public Library
11 First Street, SE
Rochester, MN 55904
(507) 285-8002
Saint Paul Public Library
90 W. Fourth Street
Saint Paul, MN 55102
(612) 292-6307
Mississippi
• Jackson/Hinds Library System
300 N. State Street
Jackson, MS 39201
(601) 968-5803

Missouri
• Clearinghouse for Midcontinent
Foundations
University of Missouri
5315 Rockhill Road
Kansas City, MO 64110
(816) 235-1176
• Kansas City Public Library
311 E. 12th Street
Kansas City, MO 64106
(816) 235-9650
• Metropolitan Association for
Philanthropy, Inc.
5615 Pershing Avenue, Suite 20
St. Louis, MO 63112
(314) 361-3900
• Springfield-Greene Co. Library
397 E. Central Street
Springfield, MO 65802
(417) 869-9400
Montana
• Eastern Montana College Library
Special Collections-Grants
1500 N. 30th Street
Billings, MT 59101
(406) 657-1662
Bozeman Public Library
220 E. Lamme
Bozeman, MT 59715
(406) 586-4787
• Montana State Library
Library Services
1515 E. 6th Avenue
Helena, MT 59620
(406) 444-3004
Nebraska
• University of Nebraska
Love Library
14th and R Streets
Lincoln, NE 68588
(402) 472-2848
• W. Dale Clark Library
Social Sciences Department
215 S. 15th Street
Omaha, NE 68102
(402) 444-4826
Nevada
• Las Vegas-Clark County
Library District
833 Las Vegas Blvd. North
Las Vegas, NV 89101
(702) 382-5280
• Washoe County Library
301 S. Center Street
Reno, NV 89501
(702) 785-4010

New Hampshire
• New Hampshire Charitable Fdn.
37 Pleasant Street
Concord, NH 03301
(603) 225-6641
• Plymouth State College
Herbert H. Lamson Library
Plymouth, NH 03264
(603) 535-2258
New Jersey
Cumberland County Library
New Jersey Room
800 E. Commerce Street
Bridgeton, NJ 08302
(609) 453-2210
• Free Public Library of Elizabeth
11 S. Broad Street
Elizabeth, NJ 07202
(908) 354-6060
County College of Morris
Learning Resource Center
214 Center Grove Road
Randolph, NJ 07869
(201) 328-5296
• New Jersey State Library
Governmental Reference Services
185 W. State Street
Trenton, NJ 08625
(609) 292-6220
New Mexico
Albuquerque Community Foundation
3301 Menual N.E., Suite 16
Albuquerque, NM 87176
(505) 883-6240
• New Mexico State Library
Information Services
325 Don Gaspar
Santa Fe, NM 87503
(505) 827-3824
New York
• New York State Library
Humanities Reference
Cultural Education Center
Empire State Plaza
Albany, NY 12230
(518) 474-5355
Suffolk Coop Library System
627 N. Sunrise Service Road
Bellport, NY 11713
(516) 286-1600
New York Public Library
Fordham Branch
2556 Bainbridge Avenue
Bronx, NY 10458
(212) 220-6575

Brooklyn-In-Touch Information Ctr.
Room 2504
One Hanson Place
Brooklyn, NY 11243
(718) 230-3200
• Buffalo and Erie County
Public Library
History Department
Lafayette Square
Buffalo, NY 14203
(716) 858-7103
Huntington Public Library
338 Main Street
Huntington, NY 11743
(516) 427-5165
Queens Borough Public Library
Social Sciences Division
89-11 Merrick Blvd.
Jamaica, NY 11432
(718) 990-0700
• Levittown Public Library
One Bluegrass Lane
Levittown, NY 11756
(516) 731-5728
New York Public Library
Countee Cullen Branch Library
104 West 136th Street
New York, NY 10030
(212) 491-2070
• The Foundation Center
79 Fifth Avenue
New York, NY 10003
(212) 620-4230
Adriance Memorial Library
Special Services Department
93 Market Street
Poughkeepsie, NY 12601
(914) 485-3445
• Rochester Public Library
Business, Economics and Law
115 South Avenue
Rochester, NY 14604
(716) 428-7328
Onondaga Co. Public Library
447 S. Salina Street
Syracuse, NY 13202
(315) 448-4700
Utica Public Library
303 Genesee Street
Utica, NY 13501
(315) 735-2279

• White Plains Public Library
100 Martine Avenue
White Plains, NY 10601
(914) 442-1480
North Carolina
• Asheville-Buncombe Technical
Community College
Learning Resources Center
14 College Street
P.O. Box 1888
Asheville, NC 28801
(704) 254-4960
• The Duke Endowment
100 N. Tryon Street, Suite 3500
Charlotte, NC 28202
(704) 376-0291
Durham County Public Library
301 N. Roxboro Street
Durham, NC 27702
(919) 560-0110
• State Library of North Carolina
Government and Business Services
Archives Building
109 E. Jones Street
Raleigh, NC 27601
(919) 733-3270
• The Winston-Salem Foundation
310 W. 4th Street, Suite 229
Winston-Salem, NC 27101
(919) 725-2382
North Dakota
• North Dakota State University
The Library
Fargo, ND 58105
(701) 237-8886
Ohio
Stark County District Library
Humanities
715 Market Avenue North
Canton, OH 44702
(216) 452-0665
• Public Library of Cincinnati
and Hamilton County
Grants Resource Center
800 Vine Street-Library Square
Cincinnati, OH 45202
(513) 369-6940
• The Foundation Center
Kent H. Smith Library
1442 Euclid Building, Suite 1356
Cleveland, OH 44115
(216) 861-1933

Columbus Metro. Library
Business and Technology
96 S. Grant Ave.
Columbus, OH 43215
(614) 645-2590
• Dayton and Montgomery County
Public Library
215 E. Third Street
Dayton, OH 45402
(513) 227-9500 ext. 211
• Toledo-Lucas County
Public Library
Social Science Department
325 Michigan Street
Toledo, OH 43624
(419) 259-5245
Youngstown & Mahoning
County Library
305 Wick Avenue
Youngstown, OH 44503
(216) 744-8636
Muskinghum County Library
220 N. 5th Street
Zanesville, OH 43701
(614) 453-0391
Oklahoma
• Oklahoma City University
Dulaney Browne Library
2501 N. Blackwelder
Oklahoma City, OK 73106
(405) 521-5072
• Tulsa City-Co. Library System
400 Civic Center
Tulsa, OK 74103
(918) 596-7944
Oregon
Oregon Inst. of Technology Library
3201 Campus Drive
Klamath Falls, OR 97601
(503) 885-1773
Pacific Non-Profit Network
Grantsmanship Resource Library
33 N. Central, Suite 211
Medford, OR 97501
(503) 779-6044
• Multnomah County Library
Government Documents
801 S.W. Tenth Avenue
Portland, OR 97205
(503) 248-5123
Oregon State Library
State Library Building
Salem, OR 97310
(503) 378-4277

Pennsylvania

Northampton Community College
Learning Resources Center
3835 Green Pond Road
Bethlehem, PA 18017
(215) 861-5360
Erie County Library System
27 S. Park Row
Erie, PA 16501
(814) 451-6927
Dauphin County Library System
Central Library
101 Walnut Street
Harrisburg, PA 17101
(717) 234-4961
Lancaster County Public Library
125 N. Duke Street
Lancaster, PA 17602
(717) 394-2651
• Free Library of Philadelphia
Regional Foundation Center
Logan Square
Philadelphia, PA 19103
(215) 686-5423
• Carnegie Library of Pittsburgh
Foundation Collection
4400 Forbes Avenue
Pittsburgh, PA 15213
(412) 622-1917
Pocono Northeast Development Fund
James Pettinger Memorial Library
1151 Oak Street
Pittston, PA 18640
(717) 655-5581
Reading Public Library
100 S. Fifth Street
Reading, PA 19602
(215) 655-6355
Martin Library
159 Market Street
York, PA 17401
(717) 846-5300

Rhode Island

• Providence Public Library
150 Empire Street
Providence, RI 02906
(401) 521-7722

South Carolina

• Charleston County Library
404 King Street
Charleston, SC 29403
(803) 723-1645
• South Carolina State Library
1500 Senate Street
Columbia, SC 29211
(803) 734-8666

South Dakota

Nonprofit Grants Assistance Center
Business and Education Institute
Washington Street, East Hall
Dakota State University
Madison, SD 57042
(605) 256-5555
• South Dakota State Library
800 Governors Drive
Pierre, SD 57501
(605) 773-5070
(800) 592-1841 (SD residents)
Sioux Falls Area Foundation
141 N. Main Ave., Suite 310
Sioux Falls, SD 57102
(605) 336-7055

Tennessee

• Knox County Public Library
500 W. Church Avenue
Knoxville, TN 37902
(615) 544-5700
• Memphis & Shelby County
Public Library
1850 Peabody Avenue
Memphis, TN 38104
(901) 725-8877
• Nashville Public Library
Business Information Division
225 Polk Avenue
Nashville, TN 37203
(615) 862-5843

Texas

Community Foundation of Abilene
Funding Information Library
500 N. Chestnut, Suite 1509
Abilene, TX 79604
(915) 676-3883
• Amarillo Area Foundation
700 First National Place
801 S. Fillmore
Amarillo, TX 79101
(806) 376-4521
• Hogg Foundation for
Mental Health
Will C. Hogg Building, Suite 301
Inner Campus Drive
University of Texas
Austin, TX 78713
(512) 471-5041
Texas A & M University
Library-Reference Dept.
6300 Ocean Drive
Corpus Christi, TX 78412
(512) 994-2608

• Dallas Public Library
Urban Information
1515 Young Street
Dallas, TX 75201
(214) 670-1487
El Paso Community Foundation
1616 Texas Commerce Building
El Paso, TX 79901
(915) 533-4020
• Funding Information Center
Texas Christian University Library
2800 S. University Drive
Ft. Worth, TX 76129
(817) 921-7664
• Houston Public Library
Bibliographic Information Center
500 McKinney Avenue
Houston, TX 77002
(713) 236-1313
• Longview Public Library
222 W. Cotton Street
Longview, TX 75601
(903) 237-1352
Lubbock Area Foundation
502 Texas Commerce Bank Bldg.
Lubbock, TX 79401
(806) 762-8061
• Funding Information Center
530 McCullough, Suite 600
San Antonio, TX 78212
(210) 227-4333
North Texas Center for
Nonprofit Management
624 Indiana, Suite 307
Wichita Falls, TX 76301
(817) 322-4961

Utah

• Salt Lake City Public Library
209 E. 500 South
Salt Lake City, UT 84111
(801) 524-8200

Vermont

• Vermont Department of Libraries
Reference & Law Info. Services
109 State Street
Montpelier, VT 05609
(802) 828-3268

Virginia

• Hampton Public Library
4207 Victoria Blvd.
Hampton, VA 23669
(804) 727-1312

• Richmond Public Library
Business, Science & Technology
Department
101 E. Franklin Street
Richmond, VA 23219
(804) 780-8223
• Roanoke City Public
Library System
Central Library
706 S. Jefferson Street
Roanoke, VA 24016
(703) 981-2477
Washington
• Mid-Columbia Library
405 S. Dayton
Kennewick, WA 99336
(509) 586-3156
• Seattle Public Library
Science, Social Science
1000 Fourth Avenue
Seattle, WA 98104
(206) 386-4620
• Spokane Public Library
Funding Information Center
West 811 Main Avenue
Spokane, WA 99201
(509) 838-3364
• United Way of Pierce County
Center for Nonprofit Development
734 Broadway
P.O. Box 2215
Tacoma, WA 98401
(206) 597-6686
Greater Wenatchee Community
Foundation at the Wenatchee
Public Library
310 Douglas Street
Wenatchee, WA 98807
(509) 662-5021
West Virginia
• Kanawha County Public Library
123 Capital Street
Charleston, WV 25301
(304) 343-4646
Wisconsin
• University of Wisconsin
Memorial Library
728 State Street
Madison, WI 53706
(608) 262-3242
• Marquette University
Memorial Library
Funding Information Center
1415 W. Wisconsin Avenue
Milwaukee, WI 53233
(414) 288-1515

Wyoming
• Natrona County Public Library
307 East 2nd Street
Casper, WY 82601
(307) 237-4935
• Laramie Co. Community College
Instructional Resource Center
1400 E. College Drive
Cheyenne, WY 82007
(307) 778-1206
• Campbell County Public Library
2101 4-J Road
Gillette, WY 82716
(307) 682-3223
• Teton County Library
320 South King Street
Jackson, WY 83001
(307) 733-2164
Rock Springs Library
400 C Street
Rock Springs, WY 82901
(307) 362-6212

Puerto Rico
University of Puerto Rico
Ponce Technological College
Library
Box 7186
Ponce, PR 00732
(809) 844-8181
Universidad Del Sagrado
Corazon
M.M.T. Guevara Library
Santurce, PR 00914
(809) 728-1515 ext. 357

Appendix C

The Grantsmanship Center

The Grantsmanship Center is the world's oldest and largest training organization for the nonprofit sector. Since it was founded in 1972, the Center has trained more than 60,000 staff members of public and private agencies in grantsmanship, program management and fundraising.

The five-day Grantsmanship Training Program, first offered in 1972 and continuously updated, began a new era in training seminars and workshops for nonprofit agencies. Over 30,000 nonprofit agency staff members have attended this demanding, week-long workshop, the single most widely attended training program in the history of the nonprofit sector. It covers all aspects of researching for grants, writing grant proposals, and negotiating with funding sources.

The Grant Proposal Writing Workshop, an intensive three-day laboratory, teaches you how to write a good proposal and plan better programs at the same time, using the Grantsmanship Center's program planning and proposal writing format.

The Center also produces publications on grantsmanship, planning, fundraising, management, and personnel issues for nonprofit agencies. Its Program Planning and Proposal Writing booklet is now a classic in the field and has been used by hundreds of thousands of successful grant seekers.

For detailed information about The Grantsmanship Center's training programs, publications, and other services to the nonprofit sector, write to The Grantsmanship Center, Dept. DD, P.O. Box 17220, Los Angeles, CA 90017 and ask for a free copy of *The Grantsmanship Center Magazine*.

Index to Foundations

(Alphabetical)

Citations are by entry number

Bloom (Charles) Foundation, Inc., 44

Blount Foundation, Inc., 3

Blowitz-Ridgeway Foundation, 295

Blum-Kovler Foundation, 296

Bodman Foundation, 593

Boettcher Foundation, 136

Boh Foundation, 389

Bonfils-Stanton Foundation, 137

Borden (Mary Owen) Memorial Foundation, 564

Borkee-Hagley Foundation, Inc., 179

Boston Foundation, Inc., 425

Bothin Foundation, 45

Bovaird (Mervin) Foundation, 686

Boynton (John W.) Fund, 426

Brach (Helen) Foundation, 297

Bradley (Lynde and Harry) Foundation, Inc., 825

Bradley (Thomas W.) Foundation, Inc., 404

Bradley-Turner Foundation, 256

Bremer (Otto) Foundation, 497

Bristol-Myers Squibb Foundation, Inc., 594

Broadhurst Foundation, 687

Brooks (Gladys) Foundation, 595

Brooks (Harold) Foundation, 427

Brotz (Frank G.) Family Foundation, Inc., 826

Broward Community Foundation, Inc., 216

Brown (Alex) and Sons Charitable Fdn., 405

Brown (James Graham) Foundation, Inc., 380

Bruening (Eva L. and Joseph M.) Foundation, 654

Bryan (Kathleen Price and Joseph M.) Family Foundation, 641

Buffalo Foundation, 596

Buhl Foundation, 705

Bullitt Foundation, Inc., 804

Burnand (Alphonse A.) Medical and Educational Foundation, 46

Burns (Fritz B.) Foundation, 47

Bush (Edyth) Charitable Foundation, Inc., 217

Bush Foundation, 498

Butler (Patrick and Aimee) Family Foundation, 499

Byrd (Isaac W.) Family Foundation, Inc., 218

C

Cafritz (Morris and Gwendolyn) Foundation, 190

Cain (Effie & Wofford) Foundation, 750

California Community Foundation, 48

Callaway Foundation, Inc., 257

Callaway (Fuller E.) Foundation, 258

Callison Foundation, 49

Cameron (Harry S. and Isabel C.) Foundation, 751

Campbell (Bushrod H.) and Adah F. Hall Charity Fund, 428

Campbell Foundation, Inc., 406

Capital Fund Foundation, 50

Carey (Charles E.) Foundation, Inc., 368

Carolyn Foundation, 500

Carter (Amon G.) Foundation, 752

Carver (Roy J.) Charitable Trust, 357

Casey (Eugene B.) Foundation, 407

Castle (Harold K.L.) Foundation, 277

Castle (Samuel N. and Mary) Foundation, 278

Castle Foundation, 789

Caterpillar Foundation, 298

Central Carolina Community Foundation, 735

Central New York Community Foundation, Inc., 597

Cessna Foundation, Inc., 369

Chamberlain Foundation, 138

Chamberlin (Clarence and Grace) Foundation, 458

Chatlos Foundation, Inc., 219

Cheney (Ben B.) Foundation, Inc., 805

Chicago Community Trust, 299

Childs (Roberta M.) Charitable Foundation, 429

Clapp (Anne L. and George H.) Charitable and Educational Trust, 706

Clark-Winchcole Foundation, 408

Cleveland Foundation, 655

Clipper Ship Foundation, Inc., 430

Clorox Company Foundation, 51

Close Foundation, Inc., 736

Clowes Fund, Inc., 341

Cockrell Foundation, 753

Cole (Olive B.) Foundation, Inc., 342

Coleman Foundation, Inc., 300

Collier, Jr. (Barron) Foundation, 220

Collins Foundation, 139

Collins Foundation, 698

Columbia Foundation, 409

Columbus Foundation, 656

Community Foundation, Inc., 527

Community Foundation of Abilene, 754

Community Foundation for the Capital Region, N.Y., 598

Community Foundation of Collier County, 221

Community Foundation of the Eastern Shore, 410

Community Foundation of the Elmira-Corning Area, 599

Community Foundation for the Fox Valley Region, Inc., 827

Jerome Foundation, 85

Johnson (Helen K. and Arthur E.) Foundation, 148

Johnson (Robert Wood) Foundation, 570

Johnson's Wax Fund, Inc., 832

Joslyn (Carl W. and Carrie Mae) Charitable Trust, 149

Journal Gazette Foundation, Inc., 351

Joyce Foundation, 311

Julia R. and Estelle L. Foundation, Inc., 613

K

Kalamazoo Foundation, 472

Kaplan (Mayer and Morris) Family Foundation, 312

Kavanagh (T. James) Foundation, 710

Keck (W.M.) Foundation, 86

Kellwood Foundation, 534

Kelly (Donald P. and Byrd M.) Foundation, 313

Kempner (Harris and Eliza) Fund, 773

Kenduskeag Foundation, 398

Kennedy, Jr. (Joseph P.) Foundation, 199

Kieckhefer (J.W.) Foundation, 22

Killough (Walter H. D.) Trust, 614

Kilworth (Florence B.) Charitable Foundation, 810

Kinney-Lindstrom Foundation, Inc., 360

Kiplinger Foundation, 200

Kirby (F.M.) Foundation, Inc., 571

Kirchgessner (Karl) Foundation, 87

Kline (Josiah W. and Bessie H.) Foundation, 711

Knight (John S. and James L.) Foundation, 240

Knistrom (Fanny & Svante) Foundation, 572

Knott (Marion I. and Henry J.) Foundation, 415

Knudsen (Tom and Valley) Foundation, 88

Koch (David H.) Charitable Foundation, 375

Komes Foundation, 89

Koopman Fund, Inc., 172

Koret Foundation, 90

Kramer (Charles G. and Rheta) Foundation, 314

Kramer (Louise) Foundation, 668

Krause (Henry) Charitable Foundation, 376

Kresge Foundation, 473

Kulas Foundation, 669

L

L and L Foundation, 615

La Crosse Community Foundation, 833

Laffey-McHugh Foundation, 184

Laird, Norton Foundation, 811

Lattner (Forrest C.) Foundation, Inc., 241

Laurie (Blanche and Irving) Foundation, 573

Leavey (Thomas and Dorothy) Foundation, 91

Lee (Ray M. and Mary Elizabeth) Foundation, 265

Lehmann (Otto W.) Foundation, 315

Leidy (John J.) Foundation, 416

Leslie Fund, Inc., 316

Levi Strauss Foundation, 92

Lilly (Eli) and Company Foundation, 352

Lincoln Foundation, Inc., 550

Lindsay (Agnes M.) Trust, 561

Longwood Foundation, Inc., 185

Louisville Community Foundation, Inc., 383

Loussac (Z.J.) Trust, 15

Love (John Allan) Charitable Foundation, 535

Lovett Foundation, Inc., 186

Lowe (Joe and Emily) Foundation, Inc., 242

Lowe Foundation, 150

Lubrizol Foundation, 670

Lucas-Spindletop (Anthony Francis) Fdn., 201

Lynn (Elizabeth A.) Foundation, 812

Lyon (General and Mrs. William) Family Fdn., 93

Lytel (Bertha Ross) Foundation, 94

M

Mabee (J.E. and L.E.) Foundation, Inc., 689

Macht (Morton and Sophia) Foundation, 417

Maddox (J.F.) Foundation, 586

Madison Community Foundation, 834

Magale Foundation, Inc., 394

MAHADH Foundation, 510

Margoes Foundation, 95

Marin Community Foundation, 96

Marley Fund, 377

Marshall (George Preston) Foundation, 418

Martin Foundation, Inc., 353

Mascoma Savings Bank Foundation, 562

Massachusetts Charitable Mechanic Association, 443

Massey Foundation, 797

Mattel Foundation, 97

Maytag (Fred) Family Foundation, 361

McBeath (Faye) Foundation, 835

McCasland Foundation, 690

McConnell Foundation, 98

McCormick (Robert R.) Tribune Foundation, 317

McCune Foundation, 712

McCune (John R.) Charitable Trust, 713

Index to Foundations

(Subject Index)

Citations are by entry number

ACCESSIBILITY PROJECTS—35, 39, 98, 140, 144, 145, 169, 185, 227, 234, 240, 281, 288, 342, 350, 355, 415, 420, 431, 459, 497, 502, 504, 517, 566, 569, 596, 597, 624, 642, 663, 671, 674, 677, 700, 710, 712, 715, 730, 740, 771, 809, 822, 845

BLIND/VISUALLY IMPAIRED—3, 4, 5, 7, 8, 9, 10, 12, 13, 15, 18, 22, 23, 26, 27, 28, 30, 31, 32, 36, 37, 38, 39, 40, 43, 44, 45, 46, 47, 48, 49, 50, 56, 58, 61, 63, 64, 65, 67, 68, 70, 72, 73, 74, 75, 76, 77, 78, 80, 82, 83, 84, 85, 86, 87, 88, 89, 90, 91, 98, 99, 100, 101, 103, 104, 105, 107, 109, 111, 112, 113, 115, 116, 117, 118, 119, 120, 121, 125, 126, 128, 129, 130, 132, 133, 134, 135, 136, 137, 140, 141, 142, 143, 145, 147, 148, 149, 151, 153, 155, 158, 159, 161, 163, 166, 171, 172, 173, 174, 178, 184, 186, 188, 189, 190, 191, 192, 194, 196, 197, 200, 202, 203, 207, 208, 209, 212, 215, 216, 219, 222, 223, 224, 227, 228, 229, 230, 232, 233, 235, 236, 237, 238, 239, 240, 242, 243, 245, 246, 249, 251, 253, 254, 255, 257, 260, 262, 263, 264, 265, 274, 288, 292, 293, 296, 299, 304, 305, 308, 309, 312, 315, 316, 317, 318, 319, 321, 323, 324, 325, 326, 327, 328, 333, 334, 336, 337, 341, 342, 344, 345, 347, 348, 354, 357, 358, 359, 361, 367, 371, 372, 373, 377, 378, 380, 381, 382, 383, 384, 386, 388, 389, 391, 394, 395, 396, 406, 407, 408, 411, 414, 416, 417, 418, 420, 422, 425, 426, 428, 429, 430, 432, 433, 435, 438, 439, 440, 443, 445, 447, 448, 449, 450, 451, 458, 460, 461, 463, 465, 468, 469, 470, 473, 474, 478, 479, 480, 482, 484, 486, 487, 488, 489, 494, 495, 496, 502, 505, 509, 515, 516, 518, 519, 520, 523, 525, 526, 527, 528, 531, 533, 534, 536, 538, 545, 549, 550, 556, 557, 560, 563, 565, 566, 569, 571, 574, 576, 577, 580, 581, 588, 589, 590, 591, 592, 598, 601, 602, 604, 605, 606, 609, 611, 612, 614, 615, 616, 617, 618, 619, 620, 622, 623, 625, 626, 630, 631, 634, 635, 641, 642, 645, 647, 650, 651, 652, 653, 656, 659, 660, 662, 663, 665, 666, 667, 677, 678, 679, 682, 686, 687, 688, 690, 694, 701, 703, 704, 705, 706, 709, 712, 714, 715, 716, 717, 718, 719, 720, 721, 722, 724, 725, 726, 727, 729, 733, 734, 736, 738, 742, 743, 744, 746, 749, 752, 755, 758, 759, 760, 762, 763, 766, 767, 768, 769, 770, 771, 772, 773, 776, 778, 779, 781, 782, 783, 789, 790, 791, 792, 793, 794, 798, 800, 802, 806, 808, 811, 813, 814, 815, 816, 821, 825, 826, 828, 829, 830, 831, 834, 835, 836, 838, 839, 842, 845

CULTURAL PROGRAMS—16, 25, 39, 59, 62, 86, 142, 157, 168, 172, 190, 211, 288, 324, 339, 340, 349, 350, 351, 360, 425, 435, 441, 444, 453, 500, 511, 517, 554, 583, 591, 611, 618, 622, 632, 657, 669, 679, 730, 732, 779, 809, 832, 835, 836

DEAF/HARD-OF-HEARING—3, 7, 8, 13, 18, 26, 30, 49, 58, 62, 64, 65, 69, 70, 77, 78, 80, 81, 89, 108, 111, 112, 113, 116, 118, 134, 142, 143, 149, 157, 158, 159, 160, 171, 173, 196, 201, 203, 204, 206, 207, 208, 221, 223, 228, 230, 235, 238, 239, 241, 248, 250, 257, 271, 274, 290, 292, 308, 314, 319, 324, 325, 326, 336, 337, 375, 380, 381, 382, 383, 384, 386, 388, 396, 399, 407, 422, 428, 429, 435, 438, 440, 449, 452, 453, 456, 460, 465, 467, 471, 473, 492, 494, 501, 502, 504, 509, 524, 531, 532, 534, 540, 545, 547, 549, 553, 560, 568, 590, 594, 596, 607, 610, 611, 613, 619, 620, 621, 622, 623, 626, 632, 637, 639, 653, 654, 659, 669, 670, 679, 680, 685, 689, 694, 700, 701, 704, 705, 713, 715, 720, 721, 733, 736, 739, 744, 746, 747, 751, 769, 772, 776, 783, 786, 797, 806, 807, 809, 810, 812, 815, 816, 817, 818, 829, 831, 835, 836

PHYSICALLY DISABLED—1, 2, 3, 4, 5, 6, 7, 9, 12, 14, 15, 16, 17, 18, 19, 20, 21, 22, 24, 25, 26, 28, 29, 30, 34, 36, 37, 40, 41, 42, 43, 45, 47, 48, 49, 50, 51, 52, 53, 54, 55, 56, 57, 60, 63, 65, 66, 68, 69, 70, 71, 73, 74, 75, 76, 78, 79, 81, 85, 89, 90, 92, 94, 96, 97, 98, 99, 100, 101, 102, 105, 107, 110, 111, 112, 113, 114, 115, 117, 118, 119, 121, 122, 123, 124, 125, 126, 128, 130, 131, 133, 134, 135, 136, 137, 139, 140, 142, 143, 144, 145, 147, 148, 149, 150, 151, 153, 154, 157, 158, 159, 161, 162, 163, 164, 165, 167, 168, 169, 170, 171, 174, 175, 176, 177, 180, 181, 182, 184, 185, 186, 188, 189, 190, 192, 194, 195, 197, 199, 200, 203, 205, 206, 207, 209, 210, 211, 212, 213, 214, 215, 216, 217, 218, 220, 221, 222, 223, 224, 225, 226, 227, 228, 229, 230, 231, 232, 233, 234, 235, 236, 239, 241, 242, 243, 244, 245, 246, 247, 248, 249, 251, 252, 256, 257, 258, 259, 261, 263, 265, 266, 270, 272, 273, 274, 275, 276, 277, 278, 279, 280, 281, 282, 283, 284, 285, 288, 291, 292, 294, 296, 297, 298, 301, 302, 303, 306, 307, 310, 311, 314, 315, 317, 318, 319, 320, 321, 322, 323, 324, 325, 326, 328, 329, 330, 332, 333, 334, 335, 336, 337, 338, 343, 344, 346, 349, 350, 353, 354, 358, 359, 360, 361, 362, 363, 364, 365, 366, 367, 369, 370, 371, 372, 373, 374, 375, 376, 377, 378, 379, 380, 382, 386, 387, 390, 392, 393, 395, 398, 400, 402, 403, 404, 407, 408, 409, 410, 411, 412, 413, 414, 415, 416, 417, 418, 420, 421, 423, 424, 427, 428, 429, 430, 432, 433, 434, 435, 436, 437, 439, 440, 442, 443, 444, 448, 449, 451, 453, 454, 457, 461, 462, 463, 464, 467, 468, 470, 473, 477, 479, 480, 481, 483, 485, 486, 487, 490, 491, 494, 497, 498, 500, 501, 502, 505, 506, 507, 508, 509, 510, 511, 512, 513, 514, 515, 516, 517, 518, 520, 522, 523, 525, 526, 527, 528, 529, 530, 531, 532, 533, 534, 535, 536, 537, 538, 539, 541, 542, 543, 544, 545, 546, 547, 548, 551, 553, 554, 555, 557, 558, 559, 561, 563, 564, 565, 567, 569, 570, 571, 572, 573, 575, 577, 579, 581, 583, 584, 585, 586, 587, 588, 589, 590, 591, 593, 594, 596, 597, 598, 599, 600, 601, 603, 604, 606, 607, 608, 610, 611, 612, 613, 615, 616, 618, 620, 627, 628, 629, 630, 631, 633, 634, 635, 636, 640, 641, 642, 643, 646, 647, 648, 650, 651, 654, 657, 658, 659, 661, 662, 663, 664, 665, 668, 669, 671, 672, 674, 675, 676, 677, 678, 682, 683, 685, 686, 689, 691, 692, 694, 695, 696, 697, 698, 699, 700, 701, 702, 703, 705, 706, 707, 708, 710, 712, 713, 714, 715, 716, 718, 719, 720, 721, 722, 723, 724, 725, 727, 728, 729, 730, 731, 732, 733, 734, 735, 739, 741, 742, 743, 744, 745, 746, 748, 749, 750, 751, 752, 753, 755, 756, 757, 758, 759, 761, 763, 764, 765, 766, 767, 768, 769, 770, 771, 773, 775, 776, 777, 780, 781, 782, 783, 784, 785, 787, 788, 789, 790, 791, 792, 793, 795, 797, 799, 800, 801, 803, 804, 805, 807, 809, 811, 812, 813, 814, 815, 816, 817, 818, 819, 820, 821, 822, 823, 824, 825, 826, 827, 828, 831, 833, 835, 836, 837, 838, 839, 840, 841, 843, 845, 846

RECREATION—1, 17, 20, 21, 26, 37, 39, 49, 50, 54, 56, 57, 58, 61, 68, 69, 70, 75, 76, 92, 99, 100, 101, 103, 105, 113, 117, 134, 136, 139, 140, 144, 145, 146, 148, 152, 154, 158, 161, 170, 171, 179, 181, 184, 194, 197, 203, 213, 216, 221, 223, 239, 240, 241, 243, 247, 257, 264, 265, 272, 273, 277, 278, 285, 287, 288, 289, 292, 295, 302, 308, 317, 318, 320, 324, 326, 331, 336, 337, 338, 339, 349, 352, 357, 359, 364, 367, 370, 371, 374, 376, 379, 386, 389, 392, 394, 397, 404, 405, 408, 411, 415, 416, 421, 422, 423, 444, 448, 449, 451, 453, 462, 469, 475, 476, 483, 484, 488, 490, 496, 497, 501, 502, 507, 513, 518, 527, 529, 531, 534, 545, 548, 549, 554, 556, 558, 559, 594, 598, 603, 604, 642, 643, 644, 645, 650, 652, 654, 659, 671, 672, 674, 675, 677, 680, 690, 691, 693, 695, 696, 705, 708, 711, 717, 730, 732, 735, 738, 740, 742, 744, 748, 764, 780, 783, 787, 791, 792, 793, 798, 801, 802, 803, 807, 811, 813, 815, 816, 817, 822, 824, 826, 827, 828

REHABILITATION—54, 95, 128, 159, 162, 163, 175, 177, 193, 224, 226, 235, 267, 284, 287, 299, 300, 308, 317, 336, 344, 354, 356, 430, 453, 454, 458, 590, 594, 630, 697, 714, 717, 781, 787, 788

RESEARCH—5, 28, 69, 77, 87, 108, 118, 121, 134, 178, 199, 210, 219, 236, 251, 253, 257, 308, 367, 369, 375, 378, 395, 407, 408, 465, 492, 503, 535, 565, 568, 571, 589, 601, 611, 619, 626, 630, 645, 665, 687, 694, 704, 746, 769, 772, 781

SPEECH IMPAIRED—26, 58, 80, 81, 113, 116, 123, 141, 157, 169, 207, 230, 238, 260, 261, 268, 308, 324, 385, 390, 448, 460, 467, 471, 503, 523, 524, 531, 558, 565, 567, 571, 577, 578, 580, 596, 627, 633, 639, 652, 653, 654, 670, 685, 701, 739, 747, 751, 803, 814, 816, 836

VOCATIONAL TRAINING/EMPLOYMENT PROJECTS—34, 39, 43, 48, 55, 71, 86, 92, 95, 102, 105, 109, 120, 125, 137, 139, 142, 144, 148, 149, 153, 154, 162, 168, 190, 193, 198, 200, 203, 212, 213, 220, 222, 232, 238, 239, 240, 250, 255, 265, 272, 284, 291, 292, 299, 306, 317, 326, 331, 335, 336, 341, 348, 350, 356, 364, 366, 367, 369, 371, 374, 376, 378, 392, 400, 401, 403, 408, 416, 425, 446, 457, 460, 480, 481, 484, 496, 498, 501, 509, 511, 513, 514, 515, 533, 538, 540, 551, 553, 563, 571, 577, 591, 593, 600, 601, 607, 610, 612, 613, 619, 622, 639, 644, 648, 650, 653, 655, 656, 657, 663, 664, 666, 668, 670, 676, 686, 687, 688, 689, 698, 699, 701, 704, 707, 714, 717, 728, 733, 745, 747, 754, 769, 770, 776, 781, 783, 786, 787, 795, 799, 806, 808, 810, 816, 819, 823, 824, 825, 832, 835, 836, 840, 841

YOUTH PROGRAMS—2, 12, 18, 23, 24, 26, 30, 33, 37, 39, 40, 41, 42, 43, 47, 49, 55, 58, 59, 60, 62, 66, 68, 69, 70, 74, 75, 83, 85, 86, 87, 89, 96, 97, 101, 102, 105, 106, 109, 111, 113, 116, 121, 122, 130, 133, 136, 145, 148, 150, 157, 161, 169, 170, 173, 176, 185, 190, 202, 203, 204, 205, 207, 211, 213, 215, 223, 228, 230, 235, 239, 240, 244, 253, 257, 258, 279, 281, 290, 292, 299, 306, 314, 315, 317, 319, 324, 326, 334, 349, 359, 364, 372, 374, 377, 379, 393, 397, 402, 404, 408, 425, 427, 428, 429, 433, 435, 441, 448, 449, 455, 458, 459, 462, 463, 465, 477, 479, 481, 484, 487, 490, 501, 505, 509, 526, 527, 531, 532, 533, 534, 536, 537, 540, 541, 542, 545, 546, 547, 548, 551, 558, 561, 566, 570, 571, 577, 586, 587, 590, 591, 593, 604, 609, 611, 612, 615, 620, 627, 636, 638, 642, 648, 649, 656, 659, 664, 667, 671, 674, 681, 689, 695, 700, 705, 706, 709, 712, 716, 719, 720, 721, 723, 724, 725, 727, 728, 730, 731, 740, 741, 753, 755, 756, 764, 769, 772, 776, 786, 787, 790, 797, 798, 805, 807, 809, 815, 817, 818, 822, 827, 828, 831, 835, 836, 840, 846

Index to Federal Programs

(By Agency)